*The Revolutionary War
Lives and Letters
of Lucy and Henry Knox*

THE REVOLUTIONARY WAR
LIVES AND LETTERS
OF LUCY AND HENRY KNOX

Phillip Hamilton

Johns Hopkins University Press

Baltimore

© 2017 Johns Hopkins University Press
All rights reserved. Published 2017
Printed in the United States of America on acid-free paper

2 4 6 8 9 7 5 3 1

Johns Hopkins University Press
2715 North Charles Street
Baltimore, Maryland 21218-4363
www.press.jhu.edu

Library of Congress Cataloging-in-Publication Data

Names: Knox, Henry, 1750–1806. | Hamilton, Phillip, 1961–, editor.
Title: The Revolutionary War lives and letters of Lucy and Henry Knox /
Phillip Hamilton.
Description: Baltimore : Johns Hopkins University Press, 2017. | Includes
bibliographical references and index.
Identifiers: LCCN 2017004266| ISBN 9781421423456 (pbk. : alk. paper) | ISBN
9781421423463 (electronic) | ISBN 1421423456 (pbk. : alk. paper) | ISBN
1421423463 (electronic)
Subjects: LCSH: Knox, Henry, 1750–1806—Correspondence. | Knox, Lucy
Flucker, 1760–1824—Correspondence. | United States—History—Revolution,
1775–1783—Personal narratives. | United States—History—Revolution,
1775–1783—Sources. | Generals—United States—Correspondence. | Military
spouses—United States—Correspondence. | Married people—United
States—Correspondence.
Classification: LCC E207.K74 A4 2017 | DDC 973.3092—dc23
LC record available at https://lccn.loc.gov/2017004266

A catalog record for this book is available from the British Library.

*Special discounts are available for bulk purchases of this book. For more
information, please contact Special Sales at 410-516-6936 or
specialsales@press.jhu.edu.*

Johns Hopkins University Press uses environmentally friendly book materials,
including recycled text paper that is composed of at least 30 percent post-
consumer waste, whenever possible.

In memory of my parents,
Jake and Nancy Hamilton

CONTENTS

I have accumulated a long list of debts in the preparation of this book. I'd first like to thank the staff of the Gilder Lehrman Institute of American History for their invaluable assistance. Sandra Trenholm, director of the Gilder Lehrman Collection (where the Henry Knox Papers are deposited), particularly helped my ideas for this book become a reality. Sandy always made time, space, and resources available to me during trips to New York City. Moreover, she provided helpful comments on early drafts of the manuscript and shared with me her own keen understanding of the Knoxes' relationship. Sandy also oversaw and supervised the initial transcriptions of the couple's original letters. This effort allowed me to master Henry Knox's rather unique handwriting style and accelerated the volume's completion. Other members of the collection's staff who provided me with assistance include Alinda Borell, Beth Huffer, and Tom Mullusky. I would also like to thank James Basker, president of the Gilder Lehrman Institute, for his unwavering support for this project, as well as for the larger biography of General Knox that I am currently writing. I also wish to express my deep gratitude to Lewis E. Lehrman. Many years ago, he encouraged me to look at the Knox Papers. He knew I would be intrigued, and he was correct.

Several colleagues have read all or part of this book at various stages in its production, and their feedback has both strengthened its arguments and saved me from many errors. Above all, I'd like to thank Woody Holton, who read the entire manuscript and offered many incisive comments and suggestions. Ellen Pawelczak and Daniel Preston each gave me important insights on how to improve the points I made. My editor at Johns Hopkins University Press, Elizabeth Demers, has been a pleasure to work with. She supported my book's publication from the start and skillfully ushered it through the review process. I would also like to thank the anonymous reader for the Press who offered additional valuable criticisms that made this a better piece of scholarship.

The project has also been generously supported. I received a Gilder Lehrman Research Fellowship, which funded several visits to New York City. Christopher Newport University provided me with a Faculty Development Grant and a sabbatical leave, and the History Department underwrote the expenses associated with the book's map and several of its images. Our department's administrative assistant, Nancy Wilson, helped me navigate the intricacies of Word, as well as assisted with many other details involving the manuscript's production. My faculty colleagues at Christopher Newport have also contributed to this book by creating a wonderful environment in which to teach, write, and share ideas.

My family remains my most important buttress. Working on a book about marriage and family has made me especially thankful for their perpetual encouragement. My wife, Chris, not only read the entire manuscript, but she always understands the time book projects take away from loved ones. Charles Hamilton, my brother, and Anita Samuelsen, my mother-in-law, have continually encouraged me in my work, and the latter graciously opened her house in Maine to me during a research trip to New England. Tommy and Jake, my two children, have provided much-appreciated support throughout their lives, including enduring many trips to historic sites (such as to the Henry Knox House in Montpellier, Maine) and allowing me to name our newest family member, a golden retriever puppy, "Lucy." This book is dedicated to the memory of my parents, who taught me to treasure both history and family.

The Revolutionary War
Lives and Letters
of Lucy and Henry Knox

Introduction

Henry Knox and his wife, Lucy Flucker, experienced the American Revolution at its very center. Married in Boston in 1774, the couple left the city soon after the war's opening battles at Lexington and Concord, whereupon Knox joined the Continental army and served until the revolution's end in 1783. Throughout the conflict, he and Lucy struggled against the British, lived and traveled with the army, and coped with the war's many upheavals and uncertainties. The conflict also frequently separated the pair, and, as a result, they wrote scores of letters to each other. In them, they expressed their love, discussed the war, and debated its impact on their marriage and family. Although very few near-complete sets of correspondence between revolutionary-era spouses exist, scholars have largely overlooked the Knoxes' wartime letters. John and Abigail Adams, however, are beloved by historians, and with good reason. Witty, erudite, and always near the center of action themselves, 'their 500-plus letters open a window into the important events and ideas that reshaped late eighteenth-century America.¹ Hence the Adamses' correspondence has been published in many venues and continues to be read by large numbers of history students today.

The lack of scholarly attention to the Knoxes' relationship is puzzling, though, because a close reading of their letters reveals a wealth of information about the American Revolution and how the conflict transformed the lives of individuals and families. Indeed, like the Adamses, Lucy and Henry wrote about their decisions and actions, as well as about the many people they met and interacted with. The couple also shared their hopes and fears about the war with each other throughout its entire length. But the Knoxes provide other perspectives on the American Revolution. In contrast to John and Abigail Adams, for instance, Henry and Lucy allow us to peer into the workings of the Continental army, with correspondence about its leaders, daily operations, and key battles. Lucy Flucker Knox, moreover, belonged to an important Loyalist family. Soon after the war commenced, her father, mother, and sisters left for England, whereupon they cut off all contact with Lucy. Consequently, she endured not only an absent husband who was often in harm's way, but also what she viewed as abandonment by her family.

The Knoxes' letters, above all, permit us to see two young individuals maturing amid a momentous war, while also learning to understand and work with a partner whom they deeply loved. Only 24 and 18 years old, respectively, at the time of Lexington and Concord, they had been married less than a year, had no children, and, as yet, had little direction in their future life together.[2] Throughout the war, they each faced considerable challenges and dangers, which forced them to leave their youth behind and enter mature adulthood. Therefore, when the war ended, Henry and Lucy were significantly changed, both as individuals and as a married couple.

In general, scholars of the American Revolution only dimly understand the broader social transformations that confronted spouses during the conflict and fundamentally altered their lives. Part of the problem is that they have access to few collections of letters between couples that span the crucial years of 1775–1783. Although we have learned much over the past two generations about women and their contributions to the Revolutionary War, there is as yet little understanding (perhaps with the exception of the Adamses) about how revolutionary-era spouses worked together and coped with the multiple challenges they faced throughout the entirety of the conflict. How did couples understand and debate the issues that gave rise to the American Revolution? How did they preserve their emotional relationship amid long physical separations and the uncertainties of war? How did spouses raise children and keep households going in such a turbulent environment? Lastly, how did men and women change as individuals as the revolution unfolded and a new nation emerged?

This volume of wartime letters from the Henry Knox Papers in the Gilder Lehrman Collection attempts to answer some of these questions and illuminate the complex world the Knoxes occupied. Over the course of their 32-year marriage, they wrote hundreds of letters to each other, many of which have survived. Although not as polished as the Adamses' letters, the Knox correspondence is vivid in its details and comprehensive in the range of issues discussed. Both partners, moreover, wrote in a straightforward and accessible manner. Like all couples separated by circumstances, they corresponded for many reasons. First and foremost, they wished to express their love and friendship for one another and to share their daily activities. They penned letters to discuss the course of the war and give voice to their concerns for each other's safety. They sometimes wrote to articulate their loyalty to the new nation and express their hopes for its future. Lastly, the Knoxes used letters to impose order on the seemingly chaotic day-to-day events then occurring around them and sympathize with their respective plights. Hence their correspondence explores many facets of life during the American Revolution, and readers will gain important insights into the many transformations that reshaped late eighteenth-century America, as well as have a better grasp of the dynamic interplay between the public and private spheres of wartime life.

Henry Knox (1750–1806) is certainly familiar to historians of the American Revolution. He is best known as the Massachusetts bookseller who joined the Continental army at the war's outset and, in the winter of 1775/76, heroically transported 59 captured British cannon from Fort Ticonderoga to American forces near Boston. Knox's guns eventually compelled the King's troops to leave the city and gave George Washington his first major military victory. Gaining the commander-in-chief's trust and respect, Knox took charge of the army's artillery brigade and, by the war's end, had risen to the rank of major general. When Washington assumed the presidency in 1789, he asked his old comrade to join the administration as secretary of war, a post Knox had occupied under the Confederation Congress and in which he continued under the new president until 1795. Afterwards, the former artilleryman retired to New England's northern frontier, settling with his wife and children in Maine, where he engaged in land speculation and other business ventures until his death in 1806, at the age of 56.

Less well known to historians are the details of Knox's private life. Born in Boston on 25 July 1750 to William and Mary Campbell Knox, as a boy he lived on Sea Street, in the town's South End. His father was a shipmaster and small wharf owner who struggled financially as Henry grew up. In 1759, William sailed to the West Indies to try and recoup his fortunes. He died in 1762, without ever returning to Massachusetts.[3] William and Mary Knox had 10 sons together (Henry was the seventh), but only 4 survived to adulthood. The couple's two eldest boys, John and Benjamin, became mariners, and both apparently died at sea. Thus Henry grew to manhood with neither his father nor older siblings around him. He attended the Boston Latin Grammar School for two years, but the family's strained finances forced him to leave, in order to help support his mother and youngest brother, William (1756–1795). Young Henry soon found employment in a bookstore owned by Nicholas Bowes and John Wharton. The job proved to be propitious for a number of reasons: it gave Knox a chance to earn money, to learn the bookselling trade, and to demonstrate his innate intelligence and reliability to influential employers. Even more importantly, the position gave Knox access to thousands of books. A voracious yet thoughtful reader, he soon learned French (and he occasionally used French words and expressions in his later letters), classical history, and some political science. He especially read books on military science and artillery. Perhaps as a result of these gleanings, Knox joined Boston's Ancient and Honorable Artillery Company in 1768, where he began to learn the rudiments of military training and discipline.[4]

On his twenty-first birthday in 1771, Knox opened his own shop, which he named the "London Book-Store." According to an announcement in the *Boston Gazette* on 25 July 1771, the store possessed "a large and very elegant assortment of the most modern Books in all branches of Literature, Arts and Sciences."[5] Knox's store thrived under his direction, largely due to his energy and personality. By 1771, he had grown into a physically large young man who radiated a cheerful bonhomie. Knowledgeable about literature, history, and politics, he loved engaging in conversations and easily struck up friendships. When his lifelong acquaintance Henry Jackson took a trip to Canada in 1774, Knox wrote that he longed "to converse" with his absent friend "in our social and heart[ily] interesting manner."[6] Ambitious, eager to rise above the hardships of his youth, and supremely confident in himself, Knox always engaged his customers in similar discussions. He also understood that a genteel deportment and appearance mattered in the eighteenth century. Therefore, he always dressed in the most elegant suits he could afford, and he remained fastidious about his appearance throughout his life. For instance, after a hunting accident in 1773 on nearby Noodle Island cost him two fingers on his left hand, Knox consistently made sure to wrap the disfigured limb within a fine silk handkerchief. The store also prospered, because of Knox's ability to master its commercial and financial details. Indeed, both his surviving wastebook (a financial ledger in which Knox wrote down many of his daily transactions) and correspondence with customers reveal the care with which he managed the overall operation.

The bookshop's location, near the center of Boston, further contributed to its success. Before 1771, the city already supported 15 book and print shops, due to the fact that its 16,000 residents were mostly literate, because of the Congregationalists' belief that all people should read the Bible for themselves. The city, moreover, was ground zero for the protest movement against British imperialism that followed the French and Indian War. Therefore, many Bostonians sought out both political magazines and books on history and constitutional theory, in order to better understand and respond to the crisis.[7] A seafaring community through and through, the city's streets teemed with shipowners, masters, sailors, fishermen, lobstermen, and scores of artisans who made their living from the Atlantic Ocean, all of whom Knox rubbed elbows with on a daily basis. While Knox focused his energies in a landward direction, he nonetheless fully understood Boston's maritime character and its fundamental importance to the city's commerce and culture. Although Boston had suffered economic stagnation since the mid-eighteenth century and appeared generally hostile to outsiders, it possessed deep economic, social, and intellectual connections to the wider British Empire and its imperial capital, London. Indeed, ties to that great metropolis gave Knox regular access to thousands of recently published books and magazines, as well as to the latest news regarding literary trends, social fads, and political intelligence. Recognizing the desire of his fellow Bostonians to feel connected to this larger empire and its celebrated city, Knox had purposefully named his shop the "*London* Book-Store." The prominent Bostonian Harrison Gray Otis later characterized the store as "one of great display and attraction for young and old, and a fashionable morning lounge."[8]

Situated in Boston's Cornhill section, the shop stood less than one block south of the Massachusetts Town House, later called the "Old State House." In 1771, this structure served as the headquarters for the colony's royal government. Therefore, not only Whigs and members of the Sons of Liberty frequented the bookstore, but Crown officials, American Tories, and British officers also stopped by on a daily basis. Henry Burbeck, Knox's future comrade in the Continental artillery, remembered the shop as "a great resort for the British officers and Tory ladies" of the town.[9] Given its close proximity to his place of work, Lucy's father undoubtedly entered the store at some point during its first year of operation. Henry Knox would have instantly recognized Thomas Flucker Sr. Not only was he one of Boston's wealthiest merchants, but he was also the colony's royal secretary, making him the third-ranking Crown official in Massachusetts. Flucker's family connections were equally exalted. In 1750, he had married Hannah Waldo, daughter of

Brigadier General Samuel Waldo (1698–1759). Waldo, a prosperous merchant and land speculator in his own right, had helped lead New England troops in the capture of Louisbourg in 1745, during King George's War. He had also gained proprietorship of the "Muscongus Patent" (later known as the "Waldo Patent"), a 30-square-mile tract of land north of Falmouth, Maine, situated along the Penobscot River and Bay. When the general died in 1759, his daughter and son-in-law inherited three-fifths of this enormous grant.[10]

Lucy Waldo Flucker (1756–1824), Thomas and Hannah Flucker's middle daughter, probably entered Knox's establishment for the first time in 1772. Though only 16 years old, she already possessed a formidable personality. Her correspondence reveals that, even as a teenager, she had a quick mind, strong opinions, and deeply felt emotions, which she rarely hesitated to share with others. Before the Revolutionary War, she was remarkably close to her family, especially her brother, Thomas Jr., a captain in the British army, as well as her two sisters, Hannah and Sally. Above all, though, Lucy was devoted to her father. Born on 2 August 1756, Lucy came of age during the imperial crisis, where challenges to established authority, including to her father's post as colonial royal secretary, were growing with each passing day. At several points during the 1760s and 1770s, she witnessed Boston's Patriot women publicly protesting against Parliamentary authority and defending the rights of colonial Americans. To a strong-willed girl entering adulthood, such female assertiveness must have seemed attractive. Perhaps, as a result, she developed an exceptionally strong streak of independence.[11] The historical record is silent regarding Lucy's education, but it was clearly substantial. Trained to write in the italianate hand, she learned to express her thoughts and sentiments with precision and vigor. Like her future husband, she developed a love of reading and particularly enjoyed conversations about literature and other social topics. Many Bostonians remembered Lucy in her youth as a "distinguished . . . young lady of high intellectual endowments."[12] Moreover, having been raised in wealth and luxury, Lucy Flucker expected that such comforts and security would be hers throughout her life. The day she entered Henry Knox's bookstore, however, her future—and his—began to move in a very different direction.

⁓

The 104 letters collected and reproduced in this volume (75 by Henry and 29 by Lucy) are all from the Gilder Lehrman Collection. The couple exchanged

(*Opposite*) Relevant Revolutionary War locales, ca. 1780s. Map by Robert Cronan.

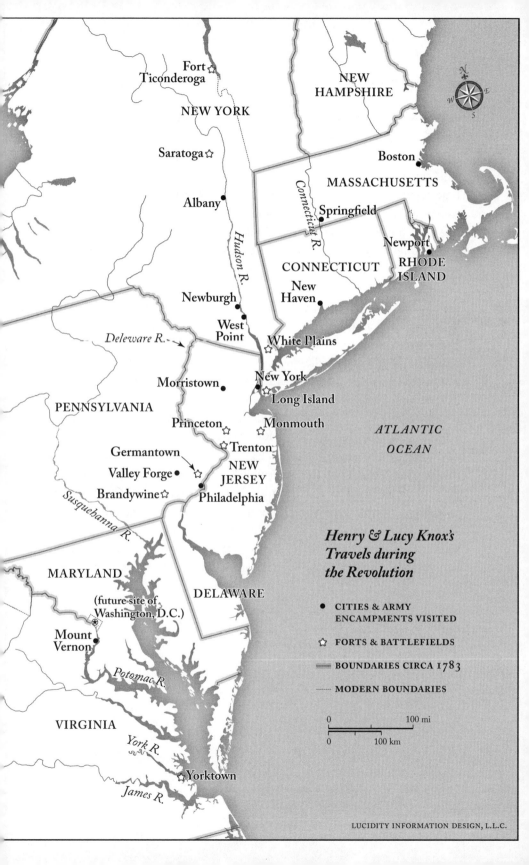

Fort Ticonderoga ☆

NEW YORK

NEW HAMPSHIRE

Saratoga ☆

• Albany

Hudson R.

MASSACHUSETTS

Boston •

Connecticut R.

Springfield •

Newport •

CONNECTICUT

RHODE ISLAND

• Newburgh

West Point

New Haven

White Plains ☆

Deleware R. →

PENNSYLVANIA

Morristown •

New York •

Long Island ☆

ATLANTIC OCEAN

Princeton ☆

Monmouth ☆

Germantown →

☆ Trenton

Valley Forge •

☆

NEW JERSEY

Brandywine ☆

• Philadelphia

Susquehanna R.

Henry & Lucy Knox's Travels during the Revolution

MARYLAND

DELAWARE

(future site of Washington, D.C.) ✹

Mount Vernon •

Potomac R.

• CITIES & ARMY ENCAMPMENTS VISITED

☆ FORTS & BATTLEFIELDS

── BOUNDARIES CIRCA 1783

···· MODERN BOUNDARIES

0   100 mi

0   100 km

VIRGINIA

York R.

Yorktown ☆

James R.

LUCIDITY INFORMATION DESIGN, L.L.C.

well over 200 epistles during the Revolutionary War, and approximately 150 have survived.[13] Not surprisingly, many of their letters were lost, due to the confusions and upheavals of the war itself. This is particularly the case regarding Lucy's correspondence. Because Knox generally received his wife's letters while in the field, a number of them were misplaced or disappeared amid the bustle and dangers of active campaigning. All of her surviving wartime correspondence is included in this book. Henry's letters in the volume were selected not only because of the important issues they raise, but also due to their direct engagement with Lucy's experiences and feelings.

These letters collectively illuminate several general themes. First, they shed light on Henry Knox's military rise in the Continental army, as well as the army's evolution over the course of a long and difficult war. Second, the letters illustrate how the Knoxes themselves changed and matured, both as individuals and as a couple. In particular, they demonstrate that the American Revolution proved to be an accelerant to the process of social change, in terms of more-equal relations between spouses. Lastly, the Knoxes' correspondence will help historians better understand how married couples in general not only endured the Revolutionary War, but also how they took proactive steps to survive the conflict. The Knoxes' letters are largely in their original form. They are annotated, however, in order to provide readers with additional context about the people and events discussed in them. Much of this information is drawn from the published correspondence of the nation's major founders (and available via the National Archives' *Founders Online* database) and from general histories and reference works about the war.[14] In a bow to modern sensibilities, the first letter of many sentences has been silently capitalized. In addition, the spelling of some words and the punctuation of some sentences have been corrected for the sake of clarity.

CHAPTER ONE

Courtship and Marriage (1773–1775)

"The most perfect disinterested love"

Lucy Flucker and Henry Knox experienced a passionate courtship. While it is not known how long the couple knew one another before their romance began, at some point in 1773, they started to exchange furtive glances inside Knox's bookstore and then had flirtatious tête-à-têtes at a nearby coffeehouse. Lucy seems to have been smitten first. A cousin later remembered that, after the pair initially met, Lucy visited Knox's shop many times and gave him "much encouragement" during their conversations. "In fact," her kinsman recalled, she seemed "to have courted him at first."[1] Twenty-three-year-old Henry Knox cut an impressive figure—physically large and fit, an officer in the city's elite militia company, and a witty and knowledgeable conversationalist on most subjects. Thus he seemed to be a dashing and attractive catch. Lucy would hardly have been alone in being drawn to someone with such traits. Like most young couples in the mid-eighteenth century, love and physical attraction were increasingly important—indeed, vital—to a courtship's success. Although very few prewar letters between Lucy and Henry survive (all of them penned by Henry), they point to a relationship already filled with excitement and longing.[2]

Yet Lucy Flucker was also making complicated and high-stakes choices in her pursuit of a mate. As she herself most likely realized, the emotional and material quality of a woman's life was largely determined by the decisions she made during courtships. Therefore, beyond her obvious infatuation, Lucy surely considered Knox's ability to support her and any future children they might have together. Although he came from humbler stock than her wealthy and well-connected family, his commercial success with the London Book-Store signified that she most likely could count on a reasonably secure material future. Furthermore, Lucy had to think about the opinions of her friends and family. Here, however, she met with resistance. Not only did her closest friends oppose the match, but Thomas Flucker Sr. steadfastly refused to give his consent. From his perspective, Knox was an orphaned son of a bankrupt mariner, as well as a tradesman with little formal education. He would bring few visible assets to any marriage and thus hardly seemed to be an appropriate husband for Flucker's favorite daughter. Other issues probably also influenced Flucker's opinion, not only as a father, but also as a Crown official. Although Knox was never thought to be a radical Whig, most Bostonians believed he had sympathies in that direction. In 1774, moreover, the new royal governor, General Thomas Gage, appointed Flucker to be one of the colony's new "Mandamus Councillors" under the terms of Parliament's Massachusetts Government Act. The position not only made Flucker a member of the upper house of the colonial legislature, but it tied him more closely than ever to the ministry in London and its policies. Therefore, he hardly wanted a son-in-law tainted with Patriot affiliations.

Regardless of her father's sentiments, Lucy refused to end her relationship with Henry Knox, especially once she discovered that he was equally smitten with her. Knox undoubtedly enjoyed the excitement of a new romance and found Lucy's personality, knowledge of books and literature, and beauty to be intoxicating. Nor could he help but notice her family's lofty social position and considerable wealth, both of which might be of assistance to him in the future. As a result, the couple decided to marry in early 1774. Henry's second surviving letter to Lucy indicates that he let her take the lead in communicating their plans to Flucker. That March, he asked if she had spoken to her father yet and wondered "what news" she had on "the subject."[3]

Flucker initially refused to countenance any marriage. Soon, however, other family members became reconciled to the match, and some even supported it, including Lucy's sister Hannah and her father's brother-in-law, Isaac Winslow of Roxbury. Winslow had married General Waldo's eldest daughter Lucy in 1747 and was strongly attached to his wife's namesake. Winslow also seems to have admired young Knox for his energy and intelligence. Isaac therefore went to his niece's father and urged Thomas to approve the match. Flucker finally relented, and the wedding took place on 23 June 1774, at Henry's house in Cornhill. Lucy's parents, though, refused to attend. Nevertheless, both her sister Hannah and "Aunt Waldo," probably Sarah Erving Waldo, were present. Isaac Winslow traveled to Boston in order to give his niece away during the ceremony. Knox wrote to his friend Henry Jackson that these few family members, plus several additional guests, made up "our little happy party." Despite his in-laws' absence, Knox refused to be bitter. He told Jackson that "my dearest Lucy" was "everything I can wish." He was, therefore, "the happiest of mortals." But tensions remained. In the weeks following the marriage, Lucy's parents had "several times manifested an inclination of being reconcil'd to it, but have never yet made it out" to visit the newlyweds in their lodgings in Cornhill.[4]

Henry and Lucy Knox fell in love in a land rapidly descending into revolution and war. Henry, although politically circumspect, had witnessed a great deal in the years preceding his marriage. He was present at the Boston Massacre in March 1770, and he had personally told British captain Thomas Preston that evening that Preston would be responsible to the law if his men fired on the crowd gathered in front of the Customs House. Knox, moreover, later testified for the prosecution at that officer's trial. As a bookstore owner, Henry read a great deal and conversed with numerous shop patrons about the crisis. By the time of his marriage, he had become convinced that the ministry in London was bent on tyranny. Unburdening himself to Jackson two months after his wedding, Knox wrote, "Public affairs wear a most disagreeable aspect—Mr. Gage and his Co-adjustors must recede or we shall all be thrown into confusion." Pointing to the possibility of conflict, he added, "There never was any thing like the flame the last 2 Acts produced in the Country—only erect a standard and . . . [I] believe in a fortnight there would be ten thous'd Country people flock to it and abide by the consequences." While admitting that he could not peer into the future, Knox concluded, "It is impossible to say what wil[l] be the event—but under the present appearance, carnage and bloodshed seem inevitable."[5]

Despite the escalating crisis, the newlywed couple attempted to carry on as normal a domestic life as possible. After their marriage, they set up housekeeping in Knox's rented townhouse in Cornhill, purchasing furniture and a number of other household items, including an expensive "Persian carpet" for £23. Public events, though, soon overwhelmed all efforts at normalcy. On 1 September 1774, General Gage ordered his soldiers to seize Patriot gunpowder stored in Cambridge, Massachusetts, a move that dramatically heightened tensions throughout the colony. Five months later, in February 1775, the British commander attempted to capture Patriot cannon located in the port town of Salem, Massachusetts. This time, however, Whig leaders learned of the raid in advance. Tipped off perhaps by Knox himself, they successfully removed the artillery before the British regulars arrived.[6] As the "carnage and bloodshed" Henry feared approached, he struggled to keep his bookstore open. The last advertisement for a pamphlet he offered for sale appeared in the *Boston Gazette* on 20 March 1775. This was a pro-Whig piece entitled "The Farmer refuted: . . . intended as a further Vindication of the Congress." Its author was, ironically, a recent émigré from the Caribbean and Henry's future comrade-in-arms, Alexander Hamilton.[7]

1773

HENRY KNOX TO LUCY WALDO FLUCKER, BOSTON, MA, CA. 1773

I have been upon the utmost rack of expectation for above two hours past, expecting some message from you.[8] . . . Is there any thing I can say or do that will affect it. If there is command it and [it] shall be done. If my assurance of the most perfect disinterested love that ever filled the breast of an youth, if the most sacred promises of the continuation of that love with interest, as time increases upon it will tend to raise your Spirits you have them, and God Almighty is witness that if all the riches of the world were in my possession they should back my asseverations. My tooth by the help of two or three jerks of the Doctor's is past giving me pain.

To the Coffee house tomorrow evening? Do you ask me? Or is it only like the banter affixed at the head of your letter? N- N- N- No. . . . Let me hear from or see you. I could write a volume to you, but I write so much in a hurry as your woman is waiting, that you could not read. God have you in his kind protection is the desire of your Harry Knox.

P.S. I forgot. I send the Gentle Shepherd.[9]

———

1774

HENRY KNOX TO LUCY WALDO FLUCKER, BOSTON, MA,
MONDAY, 7 MARCH 1774

Were I writing to a lady who was indifferent to me, and to whom I thought myself indifferent, possibly imagination might expand herself and endevor at a feeble sparkle. Prompted by ambition and an expectation of approbations every reservoir of the brain would be put to the most exquisite torture to produce one seeming brilliant thought. But how opposite to this, my dearest Speria, when I am writing to thee![10] Every particle of heat seems to be eradicated from the head, or else entirely absorbed in the widely raging fire emitted from the heart. . . . How much I long to hear from you I might with difficulty say; but to tell you how much I long to see you would be impossible. So my good girl, let me hear from you some way or other.

I wish the medium of our correspondence settled, in order to which I must endevor to see you when we will settle it.

What news? Have you spoken to your father, or he to you upon the subject? What appearance has this [text loss] grand affair at your house at present? Do you go to the ball tomorrow evening? I am in a state of anxiety heretofore unknown. My only consolation is in you, and in order it should be well grounded permit me to beg two things of you with the greatest ardency. Never distrust my affection for you without the most rational and convincing proof. If you do not hear from me in a reasonable time do not lay it to my want of love, but want of opportunity; and do not, in consequence of such distrust, omit writing to me as often as possible.

My love is, as it were, in its infancy. It will increase to youth, it will arrive at the most perfect manhood, it will grow with such a steady brightness that if the youth of both sexes do not esteem it their chiefest glory to come and light their tapers at it, want of discernment must be the reason. Pho! Pho! profound nonsense. No, no; Speria no. But if it is thank yourself; but don't distrust the sincerity of your Fidelio.

Monday evening March 7 74

CHAPTER TWO

The Excitement of War
(April 1775–June 1776)

"Citizens of the world"

The American Revolution began on 19 April 1775, when British regulars clashed with Massachusetts militiamen at Lexington and Concord. In the days following the engagement, thousands of musket-wielding New Englanders converged on Boston and trapped the British garrison inside the city. With circumstances unalterably changed, Lucy and Henry decided to flee, and the pair slipped out, most likely in early to mid-May. After settling Lucy 40 miles to the west, in Worcester, Massachusetts, Henry rode back and volunteered his services to the gathering militia army.[1]

The American Revolution's first 15 months proved to be a heady and even thrilling time for the Knoxes. Although occasionally separated from one another, they both saw the colonies' struggle against the British ministry and Parliament as something akin to a great shared adventure—exciting, heroic, and not too costly yet in terms of sacrifice and bloodshed—and their correspondence reflects their youthful enthusiasm for a rebellion that they expected to soon end in triumph. Like many Americans at this stage in the war, Henry believed that colonial pluck and determination would eventually defeat the king's troops. Lucy Knox, likewise, faithfully supported her husband in the American cause. She did not challenge Henry's service in the ranks or question the propriety of a war against the mother country, one in which her parents and siblings had taken the opposite side.

General Artemas Ward, the colonial army's first commander, quickly recognized that Henry Knox had a good deal to offer to Ward's irregular and undisciplined troops. In addition to having read many books about artillery, military science, and engineering, Knox brought practical experience to the army, gained primarily through his service with Boston's Ancient and Honorable Artillery

Company. Furthermore, in 1772, he had helped establish an elite militia unit in the city, known as the Boston Grenadier Corps. As its second-in-command, Knox had continued to learn the fundamentals of military drill and discipline.[2] Given the young man's knowledge and background, Ward soon found work for the 24-year-old.[3] Knox probably helped to construct the army's fortifications on Breed's Hill and assisted in positioning the troops' artillery on the night of 16 June 1775 (although there is no evidence that he participated in the famous battle, named for nearly Bunker Hill, the next day).[4]

Knox continued to work on the Continental army's fortifications following that battle. His talents and energy soon came to the attention of the new commander-in-chief, George Washington. On 5 July, Knox fortuitously met the general, who had arrived from Philadelphia only three days before. Washington spent his first several days in camp, inspecting the men and fortifications surrounding Boston. On the morning of the 5th, Knox had just finished working on defenses near Roxbury, southwest of the city, and was riding northward toward army headquarters in Cambridge to report. On the road, he came upon the commander, along with General Charles Lee and an entourage of officers. After meeting Knox, Washington said that he wished to inspect the young man's work, and the party all rode to Roxbury. Knox wrote to Lucy on the following day that Washington "express'd the greatest pleasure and surprise" after examining the defenses, impressed both by their strength and by the bookseller's obvious talent for engineering.[5] Although Washington left no record of this meeting, he probably recognized Knox's abilities there and then and perhaps saw the young man's intense ambition. Washington, a shrewd judge of character and always willing to promote the careers of talented subordinates, marked out Knox for greater responsibilities as a result of this chance encounter. Knox's rising stature in the Continental army could also be measured in the several months that followed, through the increasing number of visits he made to army headquarters, where he occasionally dined at Washington's table.[6]

On 16 November 1775, the general gave Knox a task of the greatest weight and responsibility. He ordered the bookseller to transport several dozen British cannon and mortars, captured the previous May at Fort Ticonderoga (in northern New York State), to Boston. Knox set off immediately and, over the next two months, brilliantly performed his mission. Reaching the fort in early December, Knox and the men under his command constructed 42 enormous sleds for the heavy armaments and carried them first across the Hudson River and then through the snow-covered Berkshire Mountains in western Massachusetts. As Knox wrote to Lucy, the journey was arduous, and he suffered considerably from the cold. But fulfilling this mission not only demonstrated Henry's ability to command men under difficult and challenging circumstances, but also proved to Washington that the self-taught Knox could get things done. When the guns at last arrived in the American encampment in mid-January 1776, they fundamentally altered the military situation. Positioned atop Dorchester Heights (in South Boston) in early March, they put the Continental army in a position to rain shot and shell down on the city, thus forcing the British army's new commander, General William Howe, to order its evacuation. As a result of his abilities and accomplishments, Knox received a colonel's commission and command of the army's artillery branch.[7]

Lucy Knox, compared with Henry, experienced a very different revolution in 1775. Unfortunately, none of her letters from this year have survived. Therefore, her exact thoughts and activities are difficult to reconstruct. It is not hard, however, to imagine some of challenges she faced. Lucy was 18 years old when she fled Boston, and she found herself living nearly alone, in a strange town, with a husband engaged in a dangerous war. Nevertheless, Lucy seems to have accepted her situation. Henry never noted any complaints from her throughout this period, though he did make sure he saw and wrote to her as often as possible. During his Ticonderoga trek, for instance, he repeatedly wrote to pledge his love to his "dearest Companion" and kept her informed of his health and progress. He also penned letters with news about the people and places he was seeing for the first time, including New York City, where "the houses are better than at Boston." Above all, though, he let Lucy know how much he wanted to be with her. He once even wrote that he wished he could fly through the air to her, but, poking fun at his physique, joked that if he did, he would "look like a tennis ball" in flight.[8]

Knox's Fort Ticonderoga mission helped bring the Continental army's siege of Boston to a triumphant close. The victory, though, ironically resulted in more separations for the couple and more changes in their extended family. In particular, Lucy's mother and two sisters, along with the British fleet, evacuated the city in late March, and the trio eventually joined Thomas Flucker Sr. who, as the Massachusetts colony's royal secretary, had already left for London the previous autumn. None would ever see Lucy, Boston, or America again.[9] The siege's conclusion also shifted the war's focus to New York City, due to its central strategic location and large natural harbor. Expecting the British to soon attack that city, Washington at once ordered the Continental army to move south. Knox received orders in early April and left Boston in the middle of the month. Confronting an uncertain but exciting future, he cheerfully told Lucy that they were now "Citizens of the world" and "any place will be our home." But, for the time being, their days would have to be spent apart.[10]

General Henry Knox. Miniature by Charles Willson
Peale, 1778. The Metropolitan Museum of Art, www
.metmuseum.org.

As Henry traveled south, he left behind not only his wife, but also a three-month-old daughter, whom the couple had also named Lucy. Mother and daughter soon returned to their house in Cornhill, where Lucy attempted to put the couple's property and bookshop back into some order. With Henry gone, her parents and siblings heading across the Atlantic Ocean, and a newborn child to care for by herself, Lucy at last began to feel the strains of war. Because the British army was nowhere in sight after leaving Boston, she wrote that she wished to go to New York City to be with her husband. Imagining him "surrounded with gaiety and scenes of high life" in the army's new encampment, she also wanted Henry to know how unhappy their separation made her. Other Continental army officers had called their wives to the city, she claimed, but no letters from him had asked her to come.[11] Always wishing to please Lucy and genuinely feeling her absence himself, Henry wrote a letter in early May, telling her to come south. By the end of that month, the Knoxes were reunited. The couple and their daughter lodged on the second floor of the great Kennedy mansion, at No. 1 Broadway, at the tip of Manhattan Island.[12]

Lucy Knox in silhouette, ca. 1790s, after the American Revolution. Collection of the Massachusetts Historical Society.

Henry and Lucy spent a blissful month together throughout June 1776. Although military duties consumed most of Knox's time, and Lucy was sometimes ill, he spent as many hours as he could with his little family. The couple undoubtedly discussed their future and the many events that had occurred since their flight from Boston 13 months earlier. Confident in the American cause and the colonies' ultimate victory, Henry probably sketched out his plans for what the family would do once the fighting ended. Despite these halcyon days, Knox had "certain information" from headquarters that a British fleet was approaching New York City. Knowing that a clash of arms would eventually occur, and being concerned for his family's safety, Knox explained to his brother William that he had purchased a carriage and pair of horses, so Lucy and their daughter could escape the city at the first "appearance of danger."[13] It was a wise and sensible precaution, for the initial and most exciting phase of the Revolutionary War was about to end.

1775

HENRY KNOX TO LUCY FLUCKER KNOX, ROXBURY, MA,
THURSDAY, 6 JULY 1775

Roxbury Leml. Childs, Thursday morng 6 oClock

My dear Lucy,

I wrote to you Yesterday by Mr. Langdon and as I am determin'd to write by every opportunity . . . and shall go presently to Cambridge on the express purpose of carrying the Letter. . . .

Yesterday, as I was going to Cambridge, I met the General,[14] who beg'd me to return to Roxbury again which I did. When they had view'd the works they express'd the greatest pleasure & surprize at their situation and apparent utility to say nothing of the plan which did not escape their praise. You may remember Genl. Lee's Letter[15] which Doctor Church[16] was to have sent into Boston to Genl. Burgoyne.[17] Yesterday Mr. Webb[18] took it to the Lines at Bunkers Hill where Major Bruce of the 38th[19] came out to him. . . . Mr. W. said "Sir here is a Letter from Genl. Lee to Genl. Burgoyne will you be pleas'd to give it to him [text loss] as some part of it requires an immediate answer, I sho[uld] be glad you would do it directly and also here is another Letter to a sister of mine in Boston, Mrs. Simpson, to whom I should be Glad you would Deliver it." The Major gave him every assurance that would deliver the Letter to Mrs. Simpson himself & to Genl. Burgoyne, but could not do it immediately as the Genl. was on the other Lines meaning Boston Neck. Genl. Lee, good God Sir, is Genl. Lee the one I served two years with . . . in Portugal. Tell him, Sir, that I am extremely sorry that my profession obliges me to be his opposite in this unhappy affair. Can't it be made up, let me beg of you to use your influence and endevor to Heal this unatural breach.[20] Mr. Webb told him that it was not the work of one side only. . . . Genl. Lee . . . inclos'd a List of our kill'd and wounded in Bunker hill & begg'd to have an exact List of theirs. The reason was that some person who came out of Boston brought on with him a damn'd infamous acco[un]tt printed in Boston by Genl. Gage[21] in which he says that Genl. Howe[22] went out with "about" 2000 men & that the Rebels had thrice that number, that the Kings troops after surmounting almost incredible difficulties carried our

almost impenetrable works with the Loss of 170 Kill'd on their part besides a great [number] wounded. Major Bruce told Mr. Webb that Colo.
Abercrombie[23] was dead of a fever. The trumpeter says that Major Peter-
son [w]ith a great number of officers were kill'd. Upon the whole, their
[losses] from the best accotts must have been above a thousand kill'd and
wounded. . . . Their inaction since proves it to me beyond a d[oubt].
Mr. Sherburn will go for Worcester to morrow by whom I shall write
again.

> I am my dear Lucy
> Your ever affectionate
> HKnox

HENRY KNOX TO LUCY FLUCKER KNOX, WATERTOWN, MA,
MONDAY, 10 JULY 1775

Watertown July 11 Monday 75[24]

My dear Lucy,

I most heartily thank you for your two kind Letters of last Tuesday &
Wednesday which I rec'd on Saturday.[25] I have written to the dear Idol
of my heart everyday that I have been from her except yesterday when
no opportunity offered. Indeed I write at present without having any
carriage for it in view.

I go to Roxbury & Cambridge in the morning and return here every
evening for the sake of Mr. Jackson's company.[26] We are here in a very
decent private house, Mr. Cookes near the bridge. I shall endever to
set off for my dear girl to morrow in the afternoon if possible. If not,
on Wednesday afternoon and reach home on Thursday. Believe me,
my dear, nothing in the world should detain me from you but absolute
necessity. Did I not think I was doing my oppress'd Country an essential
service, I should have come home to my lovely girl before this. General
Lee Yesterday had a trumpeter come out of Boston to him with a Letter
from Genl. Burgoine and among other things desiring an interview with
him. General will not grant that except the Congress should order him
& then not without witnesses. You heard I suppose by our neighbor
Curtis that our people burnt Brown's House on Boston Neck, except
the stone.[27] It was a brave action & well perform'd. The regulars were in
such a trepidation in Boston & on the lines that I perfectly believe 750

men would at that time [have] taken the full possession of the town. The new Generals are of infinite service in the army. They have to reduce [the men to] order almost from a perfect Chaos & think they are in a fair way of doing it. Our troops still "affect to hold the army besieged" & will effectively continue to do so. . . . Keep up your spirits my dearest girl & take care of your health for the sake of him who loves you much dearer than life. That the God of Grace may keep you in his special protection is the earnest prayer of your

    Harry Knox

HENRY KNOX TO LUCY FLUCKER KNOX, WATERTOWN, MA,
THURSDAY, 10[?] AUGUST 1775

Watertown Thursday Morng. Aug 9 75[28]

My dear Lucy,

I wrote to you who is the animating object of My Life yesterday but had no opportunity of sending it. Therefore, to make my promise good and agreable to my own inclinations, I attempt[ed] to talk to my Lucy this morning, but alas forty miles [away], she can't hear me. What did I say. I shall attempt to talk to her this morning. I am allways talking inwardly to her. I think of rarely any thing else. Indeed, my dear Girl, I love you too well to be seperated from you at all.

I was yesterday at Cambridge. General[s] Washington & Lee inquired after you. I din'd at General W. While I was there, the navy prisoners, who I wrote to you about yesterday, came there on horses. There were seven, vizs [i.e., namely] one Lieut., one Doctor, one master, & four midshipmen. All handsome Genteel looking men, and Mr. Ichabod. The officers were dispos'd of Genteely for the present and are soon to be sent into the Country. Mr. Jones will I presume be sent to Goal.[29] To counterballance this, the regulars have lately made a fine prize at Fishers Island off Connecticut of 2000 very lean sheep & one hundred & fifty head of Cattle. All the fat Cattle & sheep they took from the Island last Thursday & Fryday, and left the lean ones supposing no body would Touch them, but they were mistaken. People who are starving don't stand for delicacy whether their meat is fat or Lean. Those sheep will make very good broth.[30]

I think, my dear, I shall be home on next Monday. I am with the most perfect attachment that ever posses'd the human heart your sincerly

Affectionate husband

Harry Knox

HENRY KNOX TO LUCY FLUCKER KNOX, CAMBRIDGE, MA, FRIDAY, 16 NOVEMBER 1775

Cambridge November 16, 1775

After the most tender inquiries concerning my dear Girl's Health Inform her that My horse tired before I got to Marlbro where I got Mr. Gilbt Speakman[31] who was so polite as to offer Him with the utmost freedom. I lodg'd at Barkers and arriv'd here Yesterday in the most violent N. East Storm that I almost ever knew. Keep up your Spirits, my dear Girl, I shall be with you to morrow night & don't be alarm'd when I tell you that the General has order'd me to go to the West Ward as far as Ticonderoga, about a three Weeks Journey. Don't be afraid, there is no fighting in the Case. I am going upon buisness [*sic*] only.[32] My only regret will be to leave my love who will I am sure be as easy as possible under such circumstances. Mr. Jackson[33] will, I believe, go up with me. If he does not, he will go up on friday or saturday & will bring you down to Mr. Pelhams.

I am My dearest

Yours most Affectionately

Harry Knox

HENRY KNOX TO LUCY FLUCKER KNOX, FORT GEORGE, NY, SUNDAY, 17 DECEMBER 1775

Fort George Dec 17. 1775—

My dearest Companion,

It is now twelve days since I've had the least opportunity of writing to her who I value more than life itself. How does my charmer? Is she in health & in spirits? I trust in God she is. My last Letter mention'd that I was just going of Lake George about 36 miles in length. We had a tedious time of it altho the passage was fine, in coming back it was exceedingly disagreable. But all danger and the principal difficulty is now past &, by next Thursday, I hope we shall be able to set out from hence on our way home with our very valuable & precious Convoy. If we have the good fortune to have snow, I hope to have the pleasure to see my dearest in three weeks from this date. Don't grieve my dear at its length. I wish to heaven it was [in my] power to shorten the time, a time already elaps'd far beyond the bearance of an eager expectation to see you. We shall cut no small figure in going thro' the county with our Cannon, Mortars &c drawn by eighty Yoke Oxen.

I have not had an Unwell hour since I left you. My brother Wm[34] is also exceedingly well & has been of the utmost service to me. I most fervently wish that my dear dear Lucy might have been equally happy with respect to her health. Had I the power to transport myself to you, how eagerly rapid would be my flight. It makes me smile to think how I should look, like a tennis ball bow'ld down. . . . Give my love to my friend Harry.[35] I certainly should have written to him, but every minute of my time is taken up in forwarding the important Business I'm up[on]. . . . I have had the pleasure of seeing a considerable number of our enemies prisoners to the Bravery of America, Enemies who would not before this allow the Americans a spark of military virtue. Their note is now chang'd. Some are to be much pitied, others are not so much. All in a degree. Their infatuation is surprising, but trust will have its end. May he who holds the hearts of all flesh in his hands incline America[ns] to put their sole confidence in him & then he will still continue to be their Leader & may he condescend to take particular care & give special directions to your Guardian Angell Concerning You

>Adieu My only Love
>for the present Adieu
>H Knox

1776

HENRY KNOX TO LUCY FLUCKER KNOX, ALBANY, NY,
FRIDAY, 5 JANUARY 1776

Albany Jany 5 1776—

My lovely & dearest friend,

Those people who love, as you & I do, never ought to part. It is with the greatest anxiety that I am forc'd to date my letter at this distance from my love at a time too when I thought to have been happily in [your] Arms. I feel for you my Lucy, I feel for myself, but as the seeing her without whom life is a blank must in the course of Events be protracted for a week or two longer, I am resolv'd to write her a long letter. A man whom General Washington has sent Express to General Schuyler[36] has promis'd me to deliver it with his own hands to you, for which you will give [him] something. With what raptures should I receive a Letter from my angels hands, I should think it one of the best forms of heaven. I would kiss [it,] I would put it in my bosom & wear it there 'till no part remain'd. Yet though it would be the last token of her love, it would not be the freshest in my memory, my Lucy is perpetually in my mind constantly in my heart. I wish my Interest was as sure in heaven as I am it is in my Lucy. I would pray without ceasing for her happiness. May that Being who blesses the universe with the rays of his benign Providence, bless you with a happy new Year, give You every joy & every wish necessary to your felicity. I am exceedingly concern'd for fear my love should repine at my not being able to come at the time expected, do not, I beseech you, consider & keep in mind the happy, very happy meeting we shall have after two months of very painful absence.[37] . . . This is only the fourth letter that I have had an opportunity to write to you, one of them a very little sneaking one indeed, which was owing to its being written before day in the most pressing hurry as General Schuyler had just then arriv'd from Ticonderoga over Lake George and was going to set out immediately for Albany. Often since, when I reflected upon its shortness, I would almost wish I had sent none. In my last I inform'd you, which was Decr 17, that I hop'd to be with you in three weeks. There was little or no snow then. On Christmas Eve, there was a plentiful Fall with some exceeding cold weather after it as I ever knew. The weather for three or four days past has been intolerably warm considering my wishes. The Thaw has been so great that I've trembl'd for the Consequences, for without Snow my very important charge cannot get along.[38] I came from lake George some days ago in the severely cold weather & suffer'd by it considerably, excepting which, altho' I cannot say much for the pleasantry of the Journey, yet it has been tolerable. My brother is now at lake George Busily employ'd in loading the sleds as they come up. There are a considerable number employ'd in getting them down to this place where, if the weather should come cold which I hope for, they will all be on next Tuesday or Wednesday, & the next Tuesday at Springfield & four

or five days after at Cambridge. After I see them all set off from Springfield, I shall leave them & push on, on the wings of expectation & Love.
A little about my travels—New York is a place where I think in General
the houses are better than at Boston. They are Generally of Brick, and
three Stories high with the largest kind of windows. Their Churches
are Grand, their Colleges & workhouse & hospitals Most excellently
situated & also exceedingly commodious. Their principal streets much
wider than ours. The people—why, the people are magnificent in their
equipages which are numerous, in their house furniture which is fine. In
their pride & conceit which are inimitable, in their profaneness which is
intolerable, in their want of principle which is prevalent. In their Tory-
ism which is Unsufferable & for which they must repent in dust & ashes.
The Country from New York [City] to this City is not very populous; not
the fifth part so much so as in New England & with much greater marks
of poverty than there. The people of this City, of which there are about
5000 to 6000, are I believe honest enough & many of them sensible people, much more so than in any other part of the Government which I've
Seen. There are few very good Buildings for public Worship, with a State
House, the remains of Capital Barracks, Hospital, & Fort, which must
in their day have been very clever. It is situated on the side of a Hill, the
foot of which I reach'd by Hudsons River, which is Navigable for Vessells
of 70 or 80 tons as far as this. Albany from its Situation, commanding the
trade of the Lakes, & the immense territories westward must one day be,
if not the Capital yet nearly to it of America, and there are a number of
Gentlemens' very elegant seats in view from that part of the river before
the Town, among them I think General Schuylers claims the preference,
it is very large & with a most commanding situation, the Owner of which
is Sensible & polite & I think behaved with vast propriety to the British
officers who by the course of War have fallen into our hands. If there was
such a thing as discrimination, they must see the infinite difference with
which they are treated to [that] which our officers are who are so unfortunate as to fall in to their hands. Seventeen of them set out from this
for Pensylvania Yesterday, among whom was General Presscott[39] who
has by all accounts behav'd excessively ill in putting Colo. Allen of ours,
who was taken at Montreal. General Schuyler favor'd me with the Sight
of a Letter which General Washington sent to General Howe in Boston &
Mr. Howe's answer. It respects [i.e., in respect to] Genl. Presscott, Genl.
W. tells Genl. Howe as soon as he gets authenticated facts of Presscott's

treatment of Allen, that Presscott shall be serv'd in the same manner. I think Mr. Presscott [will be] in a disagreeable situation. . . . The Women & children suffer Amazingly at this advanced Season of the Year in being transported in so frozen a Climate. It is now past twelve o Clock, therefore My blessing I wish for a good nights Repose & will mention you in my prayers

Adieu for to Night Adieu

My paper is so full & I'm so hurri'd that I've no opportunity writing any more. Give my Love to Harry.[40]

HENRY KNOX TO LUCY FLUCKER KNOX, MA, CA. 5–17 MARCH 1776

My only Love,

I rec'd your letter by my brother which gave me the most sensible pleasure. You tenderly ask what is become of me. "No evil has happen'd" but an excessive hurry of business has prevented my paying my Lucy that tribute of affection which is so justly her due. The ladies you say told you of strange movements indeed. I know not how to clearly account for them. Certain it is they (the enemy) are packing up & going off bag & baggage.[41] How far or where is yet uncertain. If to New York, my Dear Lucy must prepare to follow them as we are Citizens of the World, any place will be our home & equally cheap. I most earnestly wish to see you, but believe [I] shall not have ye pleasure 'till I've been in to Boston, which I fully expect in the course of two or three days, whether as at present or reduced to a heap of rubbish is uncertain. God preserve You my Greatest earthly blessing

HKnox—

Kiss your heavenly babe

& bless it for me—[42]

HENRY KNOX TO LUCY FLUCKER KNOX, NEW LONDON, CT,
WEDNESDAY, 24 APRIL 1776

New London April 24 1776

My tender dear friend,

I write to you with all that Love & affection with which our hearts are united, I maledict the man who first brought on this war only because it separates me from my Love. I have received General Washingtons directions to inspect this Harbour in order to its being fortified [at] the Continental expense as a rendezvous & safe retreat for our Ships or the American Navy. I have been on board Admiral Hopkins,[43] and I've been in Company with his Gallant son who was wounded in the engagement with the Glasgow.[44] The admiral is an antiquated figure, he brought to my mind Van Tromp the famous Dutch admiral.[45] Tho' antiquated in figure, he is shrew'd & sensible. I, who you think am not a little enthusiastic, should have taken him for an Angell only he swore now & then which to be sure is not angelic. His Son, Capt. John Hopkins, is a sensible genteel man about 30 Years old and who will one day (if he don't get kill'd) make a most formidable figure in American History. How does my babe. I most devoutly long to see you & may our kind heavenly parent preserve you both. When I get to New York, which I expect will be about the 2d or third of May, I shall be able to judge of the propriety of sending for my Lucy. She can't possibly be more anxious to see me than I am to see her. Give my love to Your Aunt Waldo[46] & children. My brother Billey & Harry Jackson, I should have written to them & a much longer Letter than this Scrawl to you, but a perpetual Hurry forbids.

    Adieu my Love Adieu

    Harry Knox

LUCY FLUCKER KNOX TO HENRY KNOX, BOSTON, MA,
MONDAY OR TUESDAY, 29 OR 30 APRIL 1776

I should long before this have indulged myself in the pleasure of writing to him who is allways in my thoughts, whose image is deeply imprinted on my heart and whom I love too much for my peace, but the fear that the language of a tender wife might appear ridiculous to an impartial reader (should it miscarry) has restrain'd me.

Is my Harry well. Is he happy. No, that cannot be when he reflects how wretched he has left me. I doubt not, but the plea of his little girl, as he used fondly to call me, must sometimes draw a thought from him tho surrounded with gaiety and scenes of high life. The remembrance of his tender infant must also greatly affect him when he considers it at so great a distance from its Father, its natural guardian in a place exposed to an enraged enemy and almost defenceless.

Your three kind letters from Newport, Norwich & New London came
safe to hand. I thank you for your attention in writing so often, but impatiently expect the letter from New York for which place Mrs. Greene[47]
and Mrs. Morgan[48] sett out on Sunday next. They fully expected me
to have gone with them. What is the reason I am not as happy as they
since[?] I love as well and am as well beloved. As I shall write again this
week, I will only add that our babe was christened last Sunday at Trinity
Church and that Mr. Inman, Mrs. Rowe, Mrs. Jarvis were the sponsors.[49]
Pray for us both, my dear Harry. Be assured that whether present or absent, you are and ever will be dear to your faithful and affectionate Wife
    Lucy Knox

We have been greatly alarmed today by the enemy taking possession
of Georges Island where they have erected a fort or battery.[50] What will
become of me & my child should they come to the town. . . .

———

HENRY KNOX TO LUCY FLUCKER KNOX, NEW YORK, NY,
THURSDAY, 2 MAY 1776

New York May 2d 1776

My dearest friend,

I arriv'd here on the 30th of April after a Journey not very pleasant
owing to a number of complex circumstances. Affairs here have an
aspect very formidable, the works are strong & well constructed, so that
this place will be much more secure from the attacks of shipping than almost any harbour I know. The situation of the City being nearly centrical
to the other Colonies will be of the utmost importance to America & will
of course be first in such a state of Defence that an injunction with the
army that must be station'd here may bid defiance to a very large Army. I
sigh for my love. I think of her night & day & I wish her here, but dread
the fatigues of the Journey. I am extremely chagrin'd that I received no
letters from her by the last post. What can be the reason? But my love
did not know I am being at New York, she must have thought me on the
road.

You will prepare for your Journey with as much haste as convenient.
I think you had better come in Coates coach with four horses. Make the
bargain so that he shall maintain the horses on the road. This method

has its fault for if you come without a carriage, it will be rather inconvenient when you are here. You will want one. If you could purchase a Phaeton for about 100 dollars also & your Betty[51] and babe and all come in that, it could remedy that affair, but [if] that cannot be, sell Romeo.[52] He never will be of any service to you. I really feell for the difficulties you will have to surmount, Billey must come with you as a Guard. I need not even hint to you to be as much an economist as possible for my love thinks much more of that matter than I do. I know not what we shall do for house furniture. As for houses, there are plenty & good ones too. Write me immediately on the receipt of this Letter, particularly when you set out & how. Don't forget to bring a proper proportion of house Linens with you, Spoons &c.

> I am my dearest love Your
> unalterably Harry Knox

———————

CHAPTER THREE

The Perils of War I

THE NEW YORK–NEW JERSEY CAMPAIGN OF 1776

"The horrid Scenes of War"

"The appearance of Danger" came on the morning of 1 July 1776, just after Henry and Lucy sat down to breakfast in front of a large, second-floor window overlooking New York City's harbor. As they ate and chatted about the coming day, they suddenly saw scores of British men-of-war and transport ships, "with a fair wind and rapid tide" behind them, advancing through the New York Narrows toward Manhattan's shoreline. The enemy's armada of over 100 vessels and tens of thousands of men had arrived. As the couple stared, transfixed, at the scene below them, the city exploded in an uproar. In the streets below, alarm guns popped, drums beat, and troops rushed to their fortifications. Confusion reigned inside the Knoxes' lodgings, as well. Angry, perhaps with himself for allowing his wife and child to have remained so long by his side, Henry instead raged at Lucy. "I scolded like a fury at her for not having gone before," he wrote to his brother William several days later. But now she must be off. Needing to get to his men and guns, Knox added, "I [am] not at liberty to attend her as my countrys calls were loudest."[1] With Nathanael Greene's wife, Catharine, at her side, a distraught Lucy fled the city with her baby, in the carriage Henry had purchased. Thus opened the pivotal month of July 1776, ushering in the second and most perilous phase both of the Revolutionary War and for the Knoxes.

The stunning size of the British force unquestionably gave both the Knoxes pause that morning. The reality of coming to grips with such an overwhelming host instantly dashed all hopes for a quick victory and made the American Revolution a more dangerous and uncertain affair. As Henry and Lucy would soon learn, their perils would only multiply in the months ahead. From mid-1776 to early 1778, the Continental army suffered repeated battlefield defeats, and the American cause often seemed lost. Amid these hazards, the Knoxes endured long and painful separations from one another. But these harrowing days also forced the couple to grow and mature, as they came to comprehend the full gravity of the war and determined how best to respond to its transformations. Henry, for instance, skillfully expanded and improved the army's artillery branch, as well as honed his own capacity for command. As a result, his responsibilities in the Continental army continued to grow, and his position within its leadership rose accordingly. From 1776 to 1778, Lucy Knox learned to work arduously (and largely on her own) to raise their daughter and preserve the family's remaining properties in Boston and other parts of Massachusetts.

Although the war's escalation compelled the Knoxes to operate largely in separate spheres, they remained deeply committed to one another, with words of love and tenderness filling many letters. Writing under near-constant stress, the couple also periodically exchanged words of frustration and anger, all the while acknowledging their mutual dependence on the other to sustain their relationship and family. Lucy generally recognized that she needed to work hard, in order to support her husband in the field and her child at home. Henry grasped his responsibility to preserve his life and health in the ranks, so he could ultimately return home to care for his wife and child. This growing interdependence eventually altered the dynamics of their marriage. For example, Lucy started to forcefully insist that her opinions, whether about the American cause, the family, or their finances, be listened to and acted on. In periods of acute tension, she even demanded that Henry think more about his family, rather than focus on the army. Knox, on the other hand, greatly depended on his wife's emotional support, as well as her efforts to obtain essential supplies for him and his military staff. Thus, even though the Revolutionary War required the Knoxes to make difficult sacrifices and live largely apart, it led them to forge a new and more equitable relationship.

⌀

As Lucy's carriage rumbled northward, away from New York City, the Knoxes' future together seemed unclear and uncertain. Troubled and worried at the war's sudden escalation, after the couple parted, they almost immediately began to quarrel about what they should do next. In particular, they argued about how far away Lucy and their daughter should go from the theater of war. Because the British had not assaulted the city on the morning of 1 July, but instead had established a base camp on Staten Island, Lucy wished to return to Manhattan as soon as possible. She had initially gone only to Stamford, Connecticut—a mere 40 miles from the American encampment—and refused to go any farther. She was, moreover, still fuming at Henry for his admonishments and angry words when she left New York City. Henry himself lost his temper at this, as well as at her supposed female stubbornness and anxieties. Telling her that he expected his wife to overcome the typical frailties of her sex, he ordered her to go straight on to New Haven, Connecticut, 40 miles farther up the state's coastline. As the family's sacrifices steadily mounted, Henry also felt compelled to explain to Lucy why he needed to serve in the ranks and be away from her. He and his comrades were fighting, he stressed, not simply for the present generation, but for the unborn millions who also deserved to enjoy the fruits of liberty.[2] By summer's end, Lucy had sullenly bowed to her husband's demands, and she and her daughter moved to New Haven, along with the wives of several other Continental army officers, where they rented a small house together.

The summer's close, however, also marked the beginning of active military operations outside New York City, and events straightaway took a disastrous turn. On 27 August, the British commander, General William Howe, attacked and overwhelmed 8,000 Continental soldiers on the western edge of Long Island, near the village of Brooklyn, killing and wounding over 300 Americans and capturing another 1,000. Knox did not take part in the battle. Instead, he remained with his batteries on lower Manhattan Island, in order to watch British warships just off the island's tip, in case they should launch an amphibious assault. Knowing that Lucy would be "alarm'd" at news of the rout, he wrote to her the next evening. Because time was short and his tasks many, he could only assure her of his own safety and that he loved her.[3]

During the campaign's remaining months, letters between the Knoxes traveled back and forth across the mid-Atlantic war zone of New York, New Jersey, and Pennsylvania. With the American forces suffering one defeat after another and in almost constant retreat, Henry penned letters whenever he could. He informed Lucy of the army's movements and difficulties, assured her of his love, and called on her to maintain her strength in such traumatic times. Henry persevered before such challenges and generally maintained his natural optimism, probably a key factor in his success as a military commander. After the American defeat at the battle of White Plains in late October, for instance, he confessed what must have seemed painfully obvious to Lucy, "This Campaign I think may be term'd a loosing Campaign." But with a cheerfulness that was a fundamental part of his character, Knox refused to admit that the British had achieved significant advantages over the Americans. Rather, he concluded, "It has been a Tragic Comedy of errors on both sides."[4]

Throughout that fall, Lucy also wrote to Henry as often as she could. Her letters from the latter months of 1776 have not survived, however, probably lost amid the bustle of an active campaign. Surviving epistles that she penned to her brother-in-law, William Knox, though, reveal that she acutely felt the strains of war. After settling in New Haven, for example, she heard rumors that the British had taken Henry prisoner on Manhattan Island. Although the reports proved to be false, she later received news that the Continental army desperately needed clothes. Thus she worried about Henry's health, especially with the approach of colder weather. She admitted to William that amid the conflicting news of battles and retreats, "my brain is confused," but she wanted to join her husband, regardless of the dangers. Indeed, as the Continental army withdrew from Manhattan, she wrote to her brother-in-law that she would soon head to the New York area—or wherever the army was—in order to be with her husband.[5] She sent similar missives to Henry.[6]

Lucy grew even more despondent as that autumn progressed and the military situation deteriorated even further. The nadir came in mid-November, following the American defeat at Fort Washington and the surrender of 3,000 Continentals. This debacle set off another fiery exchange of letters between the couple. With the conflict's end nowhere in sight and Howe's next move uncertain, Henry ordered Lucy and the baby to leave New Haven for the comparative safety of Boston. Lucy responded with a deeply pessimistic letter of her own, which reached her husband on 21 November. Although this missive is no longer extant, Henry characterized it "as full as it can hold of the melancholies." Afraid that their present separation would stretch on forever, Lucy not only refused to return to New England, but even made Henry feel like an "unprincipl'd villian [sic]" for wanting to send her farther away. Deeply burdened with the stress of command amid an unraveling military situation, Knox exploded in anger and demanded that she put aside such doubts. Instead, she must rouse her "native dignity of sentiment" and know positively that they would be together again.[7]

The six weeks that followed proved to be the most crucial of the American Revolution, culminating with the near-miraculous victories at Trenton and Princeton in New Jersey. With the army in constant motion, the Knoxes wrote and sent letters whenever possible. In addition to conveying news about the events in which they took part, the pair continued to express their fears and hopes for each other, their family, and the future. Knox, for example, wrote to Lucy during the Continental army's desperate retreat across New Jersey and into Pennsylvania. Mortified by such reverses, he apologized on 15 December for the terrible anxiety she must feel at the dismal news of the army's plight. Only his "sacred attachment" to his country, he pleaded, kept him from his family. But, he finished, they must trust in God, as His benevolence would soon set all things right.[8]

After receiving her husband's mid-December letter, Lucy heard nothing for nearly two weeks. Most likely desperate with worry, she finally received a euphoric, five-page missive dated 28 December, describing the battle at Trenton that had concluded only 36 hours before. Henry began with his usual pledges of love and then launched into an extended description of the army's crossing of the Delaware River and Washington's surprise attack. As if surprised himself at the American triumph, Knox confessed that the battle against the Hessians was "a scene of war of which I had often Conceived but never saw before." Indeed, the panic and disorder in the enemy's ranks throughout the action was something Knox would never forget. His soldiers, he further pointed out, had behaved "like men contending for everything," and their victory would give joy to every true patriot believing in American rights.[9] In the weeks following the battle, Henry wrote additional letters, including one penned four days after a second American triumph at nearby Princeton. He joked that the town's occupying garrison of British soldiers had seemed shocked when they saw Continental forces arrayed against them, as "if our Army had drop'd perpendicularly upon them." Observing that the enemy had now been cleared from western New Jersey, Henry hoped all of America would soon be completely rid of the hated British.[10]

If Lucy rejoiced at these American victories, and at Knox's promotion to brigadier general that December, she refused to admit it in letters to him. By early 1777, she had finally left New Haven and returned to Boston. But she remained deeply depressed at her ongoing separation from her husband, as well as at the news of additional battles. Even triumphs meant that Henry remained exposed—and in danger. That January, she wrote a short, heartsick letter that pointedly expressed her loneliness and emotional anguish. Having endured "almost every distress" thus far in the war, she reminded Henry that she had sided with him and the American cause over her own parents and siblings. Yet he still remained with the army, despite her many pleas for them to be together. Therefore, she concluded, "You forsake me." Feeling alone and abandoned, she shut herself up in her room and sank deep into gloom.[11]

Henry responded with heartfelt letters of his own. As soon as the army marched into its winter encampment at Morristown, New Jersey, he wrote to her. Characterizing the American Revolution as a "Contest of Virtue with vice," he again said that he had a "sacred" need to be with the army. As if giving his wife a primer on the reasons for the war, he explained that "my Country demands my poor pittance" to save it from British cruelty, viciousness, and tyranny. Most importantly, he served not simply because of the present danger to America, but also to guarantee a better future for his wife and their little family.[12]

Soon after sending off that letter, Knox received orders to travel to Massachusetts. With the New Jersey campaign finally over, he needed to recruit additional soldiers to replace those who had permanently left the army for home. Furthermore, Knox wanted to inspect a new artillery foundry that had been established in the state, at Springfield. The trip northward at last permitted him to reunite with Lucy and their daughter in Boston. The four weeks the couple spent together allowed them to begin recovering from the emotional traumas of the past six months. Indeed, despite their recent quarrels, they both realized how much they still loved and needed one another. Soon after Henry left Boston, in early March, to return to the Morristown, New Jersey, encampment, he confessed, "I knew not untill now . . . how dear you were to me and how necessary to my happiness." Lucy responded in kind, writing that it was the most difficult parting from another person she had ever experienced.[13]

The Knoxes' reunion late that winter proved to be vital to their relationship in other ways. In the course of their time together, they undoubtedly discussed American independence and the current state of the war. Grasping that a long conflict stretched before them, they realized that additional sacrifices would probably be necessary. Confronting both new realities and hard choices, Lucy and Henry crafted a three-pronged domestic survival strategy to cope with the difficulties another year of fighting might bring. They first decided that Lucy should legally transfer ownership of her parents' home on Boston's Summer Street to Henry. That winter, the state government had discussed seizing Loyalist property as a means of funding the war effort, and the Knoxes wanted to avoid the loss of all of Thomas Flucker Sr.'s assets. On 3 April, Lucy met with Boston attorney Benjamin Hichborn to arrange the details and sign the necessary paperwork. The transfer required the couple to pay "the modest Sum" of £5,050 (in cash or in-kind), most likely to the state treasury. Hichborn further told Lucy that she and Henry might be able to assume control of Flucker's "Georges estate" (i.e., his three-fifths ownership of the Waldo Patent) in the near future. Lucy wrote afterwards that "this affair gives me pain," but she believed that her father would agree with their actions once he fully understood the situation. She feared, however, that the transaction would lead others (particularly her Tory kinsmen) to condemn Knox as a fortune hunter, who was only after the Fluckers' wealth.[14]

The couple's next move involved attempting to reestablish direct contact with Lucy's parents and siblings, despite the war and their political differences. During the siege of Boston, Lucy had sent a number of letters across military lines to individual family members. Much to her distress, none responded. Her pain at their rebuffs, as well as her ignorance of their whereabouts, health, and well-being, only added to her emotional anguish during the previous year. In March or April 1777, however, she heard a rumor that her eldest sister, Hannah, might be in Halifax, Nova Scotia. Lucy therefore decided to write to her, in hopes that the letter would reach her sister and rekindle some familial bonds of affection. Desperate for news, Lucy began her missive with questions about their mother, father, brother, youngest sister, and Hannah's son. Turning to the American Revolution, she characterized the struggle not as a "Contest of virtue with vice," but as a "horrid" war, pitting "Brother against Brother—and the parent against the child." Thus she prayed for a speedy peace and a joyous reunion with her loved ones. Still, as Lucy continued on with her letter, the emotional damage caused by the conflict and the pain of her family's long silence bubbled to the surface. Toward the epistle's end, she pledged her "love and most Dutiful affection" to her parents. Yet, as she reflected on how they had treated Henry, as well as ignored her for over two years, she struck out the word "love" and merely pledged her "most Dutiful affection." Though a small gesture, it points to the Revolutionary War's costs in terms of shattered families and relationships.[15]

A week after her meeting with Hichborn, and probably after she had sent her letter off to Hannah, the Knoxes took a third important step to prepare for the coming year of war. Lucy and her 14-month-old daughter both underwent smallpox inoculations. Lucy had considered an inoculation in the spring of 1776, but, still expecting a short conflict and fearful of the procedure, she had decided against it. By 1777, however, with a long war now all but inevitable, Lucy accepted the hazards. Given "the present state of things," she had explained to her sister, she wanted to be able to travel anywhere in America without dread of contracting the disease.[16] An army doctor administered the inoculations in mid-April. Small rashes quickly appeared, and, much to everyone's relief, nonlethal cases of the disease soon developed in the two females. Quarantined inside a military hospital in Brookline, Massachusetts, Lucy happily told Henry that only twenty spots had appeared on her face as the virus ran its course. Her relief at the procedure's success soon vanished, however, when a soldier (who had received his inoculation the same day she did) took a turn for the worse and died. This young man, with a wife about to give birth, left behind a family that now was without any means of support. His sudden death and the hardships that awaited his new widow reawakened in Lucy all her own fears about Henry's safety and her family's well-being. Realizing that another dangerous campaign beckoned, she plaintively wrote, "Indeed my Henry, I am serious I cannot live at this distance from you." A week later, on the morning of 8 May, Lucy's mood had darkened even further. Little Lucy's case of smallpox, apparently contracted the "natural way" shortly before her inoculation, had turned extremely serious. Covered with smallpox sores, the child had listlessly lain in bed for two days. News had arrived, furthermore, that General

John Burgoyne's British army in Canada was likely to invade New England, with Boston as its ultimate objective. Lastly, Lucy had just learned that Isaac Winslow, her beloved uncle who, three years previously, had given her away at her wedding, had died in London. While little Lucy's condition had suddenly improved later that same day, her mother nevertheless remained depressed and pleaded with Henry that they must all be together, despite the army, the war, and the American Revolution itself.[17]

1776

HENRY KNOX TO LUCY FLUCKER KNOX, NEW YORK, NY, THURSDAY, 4 JULY 1776

New York, July 4, 1776

My dearest Love,

I regret & feel the keenest pain and anxiety on the account of the precipitation with which you and the Ladies were oblig'd to decamp. Your Harry scolding, the enemy approaching, all in Confusion. That was the moment I most dreaded of any thing, your being here and obliging me to feel the highest pangs. I most earnestly long to hear how you are and [that] you keep your spirits. The enemy fairly baulk'd us then and came too off Staten Island full in view about 5 miles distance. They have landed there, and are received with a hearty welcome by its rascally Tory inhabitants.[18] The Jersey people a[re] getting their militia together and will I hope prevent there [*sic*] making incursions into the Jersies. We are in good preparation for a Battle and I think with the blessing of that tremendously great Being who governs heaven and earth, we shall make them repent their attempts to subjugate the people of America. It makes me smile [that] their ships keep aloof. They don't like the looks of our Batteries. I sent all my money away the other day so that I am in considerable distress for the same. I wish you to send my trunk back with the papers that are in it & paper money, taking out what you want and the two account books mark[ed] Waste and Ledger. I want your direction where you are and there to send your cloaths. I wish to write you more, but business presses me hard. Kiss my dear dear little babe for me & bless it. Pray to heaven for a blessing on her & her Father and his dear Lucy. My affection for you my dear Lucy is unbounded

HKnox

This shall go by the post to Fairfield, Mrs. Smith is going away and I shall send another by her to you.[19]

New York July 8. 6 oClock in the Morng.

My dear Lucy

I received yours of last Saturday[20] by Mr. Belford. Mrs. Greene's Return was a vast surprize to us as to Miss Airey. I conjecture her whimsical mother sent these Gentlemen up after her. My Lucy acted herself and acted right in not returning to this place. It is a happiness and the greatest happiness for me to be with you, but to be under a continued uneasiness on account of your safety is what You would not wish. As to Mrs. G.'s husband being happy to see her in all times and in all places, I must [be] mistaken if it would not have Di[s]abled him from the service [or] whether he had not have rather lost his arm than have seen her here at this time. He was over here at this time she arriv'd and would not believe she was coming untill he saw her. Genl. Putnam ask'd her if she had ever read Betsey Thoutghtely [sic].[21] Other people may view the light in a different manner from me. But we must stand and fall by our own opinion and not by theirs. The peace of this Town and the safety of the Ladies is upon the most precarious tenor imaginable. The enemy at farthist [is] not more than three quarters of an hours sail from us, and if they should come of a dark night [it would] not [be] more possibly than ten minutes before we must be in action. Think my dear Lucy of ten minutes to get your carriage tack'd [i.e., harnessed up], to get on and dress yourself, and get out of Town in a dark night not knowing whither to go, not knowing the road, the Carriage as likely as not oversetting & my dear Girl fright'd to death. Add her heavenly Gift the sweet babe to it & the very view would be insupportable, the reality would kill me. You say the enemy are landed on Staten Island waiting a reinforcement, what security have we of this? By the best accounts they are 10,000, and the reinforcement may be in to day. The eyes of all America are upon us. The matters [on] which we are to act are of infinitely high importance. As we play our part, posterity will bless or curse us, and, my dear, it will be no common blessing or cursing. It will be in the most divine gratitude or the keenest execrations of the heart. As to what you mention of leaving our dear little pledge at Fairfield, I am very certain you could not be serious. I know not what you will do for a servant. I think it must be difficult where you are. If possible, I will send you one by the return of Mrs. Greene which I think cannot be long. The Ladies tell dismal stories of your Living. You did not go where you were told to, but there were some of you who think you know more than you surely do. Advice when it comes from disinterested parties ought to be followed. I am really afraid of one thing. Palfrey[22] tells me he has wrote for his Wife & she is at Fairfield. Take not her advice in the present circumstances of things. It must be certain she wants to see her husband and he wants to see her because she is a Woman. I don't mean to say that is solely the reason, besides Mr. Palfrey is in [a] very different department from me. . . . [If] he must fly & shall as [also] Mrs. Palfrey, they are at a distance from where the action must commence. We are at [an] advanc'd post, he is two miles in the rear. A piece of News—a party of Artillery with 2 12 pounders last Thursday morning shatter'd one of his majestys sloops or tenders so much that the people quitted her. She mounted 14 Guns, mostly six pounders. It is reported the enemy have since burnt her. We kill'd a few and wounded some more. The enemy were so supriz'd they [illegible] very little spirit. We also have had another shooting match at the ships as they come [text loss] narrows. We like[ly] . . . have killed a Capt. of one of [text loss] shot away his bed from under him and kill'd a number of his people. Write me my love as often as lays in your power and believe me to have no other earthly love but you.

    Harry Knox

Kiss and bless your babe for me. Remember me to Mrs. Pollard.[23] I live at the house [but] I don't like Mrs. A. I have turn'd Packard away.[24] I think he must have cheated you in his market accounts most egregiously

---

LUCY FLUCKER KNOX TO HENRY KNOX, STAMFORD, CT, MONDAY, [8?] JULY 1776

My only friend,

    I will go to N[ew] Haven, indeed I will; but first must beg your patience to read this, which I think will shew that I am not deserving of the

severe censure that I have received. When I left N[ew] York, you may remember, I left my Harry in a state of mind that prevented me [from hav-
ing] an opportunity of saying a word to him of the tender kind, of which
I had many in my heart. This induced me to stay a little time as near as
possible in hopes, by some smile of providence, I might be favor'd with a
more affectionate parting, which would have afforded me some consolation upon reflection. But when these hopes vanished and the melancholy
pleasure I promised myself was denied me, I determined to go immediately to Fairfield, but was prevented by a message from Mr. Burr,[25] letting
me know he had rec'd a letter from you desiring him to procure me a
place there, which he could not effect except an empty house without a
garden which was absolutely necessary. Nor could he gett us an article of
furniture. This I thought sufficient to end that place.

You are pleased frequently in your letters to remind me of my inca-
pacity of judging for myself. I now assure you that I have a deep sense of
my own weakness and ignorance and a very high opinion of the abilities
of him in whose eyes mine are so contemptable. I am affraid you do not
bestow the time to read my scrawls with any degree of attention. If you
did, you would have noticed that request which regarded your Daughter. I now beg you to apply to some phisician for proper medecines for
a child subject to a violent cholic, also some volatile drops which Mrs.
Pollard will bring me. She is going to see her husband. Mrs. Greene has
had ten days with hers. Poor Lucy. But a truce to complaints, they are an
old story and of course disregarded. I am told you keep [an] open house.
I hope you have things to your mind but be asured, however agreable
they may be, they are not provided by a person more solicitous to please
[you] than your unhappy girl. You should have told me you had rec'd
your money by Mr. Bedford and have given me orders relating to your
Box of papers. I shall remain here till Mrs. Pollards return. Pray tell me
when I am to see Mr. Smith and send me a servant or I cannot move.
Mrs. Greene is discontented and I have no fondness for such an obligation. When you send my cloaths be so kind to remember the stockings.
Some loose letters which I left in my chamber I beg may be put into the
trunk and pray give to Mrs. Pollard a red leather trunk locked which
contains that correspondance which passed in those days when no evil
was sufficient to part us. With an aching heart and eyes drown'd with
tears, I bid you Farwell. May the God of heaven bless you. Oh do not ne-

glect to pray to him for your dear self, your poor innocent babe, and your distress'd

> Wife Lucy Knox
> Stamford Monday evening 11 oclock

You did not write by the last post. Pray do not grieve me so again. Tis hard to deny me any thing which will cost you so little trouble. I do not mean to persecute you in this manner. Indeed, I will not write too often if you should favor me with the materials for so doings

---

HENRY KNOX TO LUCY KNOX, NEW YORK, NY, THURSDAY, 11 JULY 1776

New York, 10 oClock Thursday morning, July 11th

My dear Lucy,

I am griev'd and distress'd from the receipt of your Letter. Your pain and inconvenience must in a great measure arise from the stupid advice of some bad fool who advis'd you not to go at Fairfield at first, where I am credibly inform'd your company was wish'd for by Mrs. Burr who would have provided you with Comfortable and decent Lodgings, and the Miss Van Hornes who most earnestly long'd for you. I gave you my reasons in my last . . . more fully than I can at present why I wish'd you not to come here until something decisive had taken place. As to Mrs. Greene, the Genl. told her & told me that he never was sorry to see her before, but that he now was most heartily. She would have set off back immediately if he could have got a carriage. She has gone this day to Newark after [the] Genl.'s Brother who is [to] go . . . with her back either to Fairfield or Providence, which[ever] she pleases. Mrs. Pollard may do as she pleases, but if she comes here I am sure she must nearly distract he[r] husband. My whole conduct towards you has been of the most disinterested friendship cemented by the tenderest love. That Great being who searchest the hearts of the children of men knows I value you above every blessing, and for that Reason I wish you to be at such a distance from the horrid Scenes of War. We are fighting for our Country for posterity perhaps on the success of this Campaign the happiness or misery of Million[s] may depend.

Go to Fairfield & try it awhile. I am sure you will like it better. I wrote to Mr. Burr two days after you went from this place, he will stand [as]

your friend. The small pox is spreading in Boston by Inoculation. God
bless You and give you happiness, God bless your babe

    Amen amen

    HKnox

I ever wished my Lucy to soar above the Generality of her Sex many
of whom to be sure are trifling insignificant animals, dreading what
never will come to pass.

I have stole this time when the people are gazing at some men of wars
boats who have come near the Town appearing to be ascending. They
are since gone off.

HENRY KNOX TO LUCY FLUCKER KNOX, NEW YORK, NY,
MONDAY, 15 JULY 1776

    New York July 15. 1776.

My dear Lucy

I received your tender expostulating Letter by the post. Indeed, my
Lucy, I am both griev'd and angry that you should subject yourself to
so many inconveniences when you have it in your power instantly to
remedy them. Every body that comes from Stamford or Norwalk . . . tells
me of the very rascally manner in which you live. They likewise bring
messages from you to me by way of complaint, as if I was the cause of
it. There is not one Town between us that is so good as the one where
you are, & that is so very bad that I wish from the bottom of my heart
you would push off from it immediately. I'm sure you put your own
good sense to pain when you follow any person's advice to stay there.
I am your friend, I am your Lover, I am blessed be God your Husband,
blending all these together and putting my whole behaviour to you in
support of these Relations. Can it be suppos'd I would wish you to be in
an unhapy situation? Beware my dear of the person or persons who gives
you contrary advice to mine. They injure you, they injure me more than
possibly you are aware of. Reject any more foolish advice & any more
foolish practice by staying at that infamous Town with disdain. Exert
your own good sense and see that there can be no essential difference,
as you have a carriages and Horses, betwen coming from New Haven or
Fairfield than from Stanford [sic]. . . . You may very easily come here in
two days, and it must take you more than one to come from Norwalk.

Mr. Burr, to whom I wrote to get you a place at Fairfield, says they are so full there that there is no getting a place, and they have no fresh provisions. At New Haven they have good accommodations, good Company & good provisions. Colo. Sears[26] & Colo. Broome[27] & Capt. Smith will all wish you to go there. From sundry matters which have turn'd up, this Country for many miles round here must in the course of events be an exceedingly disagreable place for a Woman separated from her husband. The anxiety that I must have for you would be so exceeding great that I had rather not be at all than to live under such circumstances. New Haven from every circumstance is the place I wish you to go, and as you value my love, as you value my peace of mind, I beg you to set off instantly for that place. Let no advice, my dearest Life, interfere with mine, and if you refuse to follow, you must make me most miserable. I am sure you cannot refuse, I am sure you will not. You have heard & before this, I hope, received the Letter I wrote you by Mr. Eliot who carried Mrs. Palfrey off from this [place]. Poor woman, I pitied her, but how much I underwent in the separation from my Lucy. By every thing that is good, it was like the eternal separation of the Spirit from the body when the mind should be in the fullest Vigor. Since the Ships past [*sic*] us, we have had nothing new. On that occasion my men behaved with that Spirit which promises solid advantages to their Country, [but] a little too fiery. It is reported we damaged the Ships exceedingly. How that may be I know not. This I know, it rain'd balls round them and proves to me beyond a doubt that their Ships cannot lay before our Batteries. This summer will be the most important that America ever saw.[28]

Lord Howe, who arriv'd last Friday about 2 Hours after the ships past the Town, yesterday sent a flag of truce up to the city.[29] They came within about 4 miles of the city and were met by some of Colo. Tupper's people[30] who detain'd them until his Excellency's pleasure should be known accordingly. Colo. Read[31] & myself went down in the barge to receive the message when we came to them. The Officer, who was I believe Captn of the Eagle man of war, rose up and bow'd. Keeping his hat off [he said], "I have a Letter Sir from Lord Howe to Mr. Washington." "Sir," says Collo. Read, "we have no person in our army with that address." "Sir," says the officer, "will you look at the address." "Yes Sir." He then took out of his pocket which was this—

George Washington Esqr
New York

———————

Howe

"No Sir," says Colo. Read, "I cannot Receive that Letter." "I am very sorry," says the officer, "& so will be Lord Howe that any error in the superscription should prevent the Letter being received by General Washington." "Why sir," says Colo. Read, "I must obey orders." "O Yes Sir You must obey orders to be sure." Then after giving him a Letter from Colo. Campbell[32] to General Howe and some other Letters from prisoners to their friends, we went off after having saluted & bowed to each other. After we had got a little way, the officer put about his barge and stood for us and ask'd by what particular title he chose to be addressed. Colo. Read said, "you are sensible Sir of the rank General Washington bears in our army." "Yes Sir, we are. I am sure my Lord Howe will lament exceedingly this affair as the Letter is quite of a civil nature and not of a military one. He laments exceedingly that he was not here a little sooner," which we suppos'd to allude to the Declaration of Independence, upon which we bow'd and parted in the most genteel terms imaginable.

My brother writes me from Boston that the smallpox is become general, that your Sister Hannah sail'd with the fleet for New York in hopes to meet Urqhuart,[33] that your Mother and sister Sally liv'd in one single Room at Halifax, that your papa had wrote to her that if she was [of] a mind to come to England she might, altho he did not invite her. This was our supposition, she was in Boston. I shall send your things to New Haven the first opportunity & I pray God you hesitate no longer to go there. Kiss my sweet babe and I'll return them ten fold.

Adieu My Only Love

H Knox—

Mrs. Green is at the Jersies at present waiting for her brother to set out for home. Every body is to go off the Island that does not belong. . . .[34]

LUCY FLUCKER KNOX TO HENRY KNOX, STAMFORD, CT,
THURSDAY, 18 JULY 1776

Stamford July 18th 1776—

I have just received my dear Harry's letter of yesterday. It gives me great pleasure that amidst the hurry of public business he steals so much time for me. If I wanted proof of his affection this wou'd be sufficient, but thank heaven, that is not the case. I believe I have missed of but one letter which was that by last Thursdays post. It must be gone to N[ew] Haven where I hope to be on Monday next. I wou'd sett out this afternoon if I possibly could. [I] shall rise early tomorrow and go to Fairfield, there spend the sabbath, and on Monday finish my journeying for the present.

Our dear babe bears fatigue surprisingly [well]. She grows more engaging every day, has learned a little language which wou'd please you vastly. Oh, that you may soon hear it. Lett us, my only love, offer up our prayers with fervency to him that made us, and we shall not be rejected. Remember, my Harry, that the prayer of faith shall save life and sure I am that you wish to live to make me happy, and to protect your innocent child.

I have a long epistle from our Brother Wm which I have answered by today's post.[35] He gives me a sad account of the state of my poor Mother. My heart aches for her as I fear she is in great want of ready money. I wish if there are any more flags [of truce] you would inquire if Urquhart is with the enemy. If he is not, write a line to Hannah and invite her to come to me. This, I am sure, you will readily do as she is perhaps distressed. You know what some people are capable of. I will take the best care of your Books.[36]

Pray what has become of the boy that was mustered out of the regiment. If he is to be had, I wish you to send him to me as the Negro is too heavy for the Horse. The boy I have is a soldier [and] is anxious to go back to the army. There is an honest fellow in a house that Mrs. Durvane[?] lived in who would hire himself for a servant. Ask Pollard about him.[37] The lady you speak of has some good qualities, tho no strength of mind. [I] am sorry to hear from Mr. Webb that my Harry was a little rough with her. Pray write me what Mrs. Airey has done to offend you! She had two pair of my sheets when I came away. If they are not return'd, I would ask for them. There was a bed bolster & pillows of hers at our house, also a small cotton counterpain [i.e., counterpane, or bedspread], 1 p[ai]r blankets, and a course cloth in making [an ex]change. I owed her 10 shillings, but sent her daughter three dollars. Here she promised me a receipt which I did not get. Mr. Webb thinks you were afraid of finding me there the evening you saw Mrs. P[ollard]. It mortifies me that you think me possessed of so little spirits as to run the risk of a cold look from you. No, my love, my reason entirely approves of your conduct and it grieves me that I have ever professed what has given you pain, but I am sure you will forget and forgive when you reflect that my affection for my dear Harry led me into the error. I wrote to Aunt Waldo by today's post which you will approve. I have a letter from Mrs. Jarvis.[38] There are from twelve to fourteen thousand in the small pox. Shall I go take it. I am very sorry that I removed [to] here, as I missed of Mrs. Smith. . . . [I] have been well accommodated since I have been here with two clean rooms in the house of a Widow. The complaints that you have heard were few of them mine.

I want to know what has become of Capt. Bauman's family.[39] I am to have a visit this afternoon, from the priest & priestes[s?] and their Daughter. The Squires family have been [here] already. The Lady is forty six and has twin sons of the age of my Lucy.

Farwell my dear, I am going far from you. Don't forget Me and when you think of Me, lett the bright side present itself or you will imperceptibly cease to love Me. May I live to see you and to convince you with what sincerity I am yours—

Lucy Knox

Romeo is very nigh as fat as the first one who has not lost under my care.[40] I have kept them well but find it two [*sic*] expensive. [I] intend to get pasture for them at New Haven

---

HENRY KNOX TO LUCY FLUCKER KNOX, NEW YORK, NY, MONDAY, 22 JULY 1776

New York July 22 1776—

My lovely love,

I wrote you yesterday under the persuasion that I should send it by Mr. Gerry, one of the members of Congress,[41] who went out too early yesterday morning for to be able receiv'd my Letter, but I sent it unfinish'd as it was [sent] by some other Gentleman whose names I do not know. . . . I have got a fine likely boy for your servant. I've purchas'd three years of his time. I will send you his Indentures, his name is Thomas Eliot. After he has learn'd to drive, which I would get some experienc'd person to teach him, he will be of great service to you. I am cloathing him and shall send him tomorrow under the care of Mr. Enoch Brown on the little Horse, which you will send back by Mrs. Greene's servant. Capt.

Bauman's family are gone into the Jersies. Why do you enquire? With respect to the matters you enquire about of Mrs. Aireys and yours, I will take proper notice of [them]. I sincerely feel for you[r] poor mother, it's very odd that the friendship of her friends did not extend to carry her to England. I will ask about Hannah and, if she is in the enemy's fleet and [has] no prospect of Urquhart's coming, will make the proposal you desire, but wish she may not reject it. On Saturday I wrote you we had a capital flag of Truce [with] no less than the adjutant general of General Howes army. He had an Interview with General Washington at our House.[42] The purport of his Message was in very elegant polite strains to endever to persuade General W. to receive a letter directed to "George Washington Eqr &c &c." In the course of his talk, every other word was we may please your Excellency [and] if your Excellency &c pleases. In short, no person could pay more respect than the said Adj. Genl. whose name is Colo. Patterson, a person we do not know.[43] He said the &c &c implied every thing. It does so says the General and any thing. He said Lord & General Howe lamented exceedingly that any error in the direction should interrupt that frequent intercourse between both armies, which might be necessary in the course of the Service, [and] that Lord Howe had come out with great power. The General said he had heard that Lord Howe had come out with very great powers to pardon, but he had come to the wrong place. The Americans had not offended, therefore they needed no pardon. This confus'd him [and] after a considerable deal of talk about the good disposition of Lord & General Howe, he ask'd, has your Excellency no particular demands with which you would please to honor me with the Lord & General Howe. Nothing sir, but my particular compliments to both. A good answer. General W. was very handsomely dress'd and made a most elegant appearance. Colo. Patterson appear'd awe struck as if he was before something supernatural. Indeed, I don't wonder at it. He was before a very great man indeed. We had a cold collation provided in which I lamented most exceedingly the absence of my Lucy. The General's servants did it tolerably well, tho' Mr. Adj. Genl. disapointed us. As it grew late, he even excus'd himself from drinking one glass of wine. He said Lord Howe & General Howe and his suite would wait for him as they were to dine on board the Engl[ish] Man of War. He took [h]is leave and went off, since which we have not herd of him. I wrote you by yesterday of the glorious success of General Lee to the southward at Charlestown S. Carolina. The enemy

made a most furious attack on Sullivan's Island with 6 frigates and 2
Capital Ships, each 50 guns. After cannonading for 12 hours, they retreated being exceedingly shattered, many port holes beat into one, their
masts shattered, . . . their rigging cut away, and the Active frigate of 28
guns burnt.[44] They, at the same time of the ships firing, attempted to land
and were beat off with considerable slaughter. The enemy lost 172 kill'd
and wounded. This must give a coup de main to their pretensions to
the southward.[45] I wish to Heaven our success was equal to [i.e., in] the
northward. My love asks me whether she shall go to Boston & with her
babe take the small pox? I wish you had that forsaken from your mind
and wish if it is perfectly agreable, that you with your sweet child would
go to Boston and take [it], but this matter I do not urge or even wish
it, without [i.e., unless] it is agreeable to you. The species seem kind.[46]
Business calls me from conversing with my better half. That god may
preserve & keep you both is the earnest prayer of your

tender affectionate
Husband
HKnox

HENRY KNOX TO LUCY FLUCKER KNOX, NEW YORK, NY,
MONDAY, 29 JULY 1776

N[ew] York Monday morng July 29 1776

My dear Lucy,

I received yours by a Mr. Hart which to be sure was the finest scrap
you ever gave me by Saml and Mr. Tracy for all which I wish I had it in
my power fully to express my love and thanks. I am very glad you have
found Lodgings to your liking. You have had a deal of trouble in your
little Journey. I pray you may never be oblig'd to travel so far again without having your earthly protector with you. The happiness I feel when
I take a pen to write You I should find difficult to describe. Indeed my
dear I love you exceedingly. You mention you are much offended with
Mrs. G[reene]. I don't know your reason, beware of busy bodies, they are
the greatest pests of society. I have a great respect and friendship for her
husband. It is impossible it should mature if you and she are at variance.
Therefore, for the sake of me, smother any little matter which you may
think an Injury. I have no opinion of your informer. I hope the boy[47] will

suit, and I hope he will take good care of your Horses. As to your flattering yourself we shall have no battle I know not how well grounded that may be. I have deferred writing so long that the post is going. I long to see you and my lovely daughter.

Adeiu my dearest

Henry Knox

———————

HENRY KNOX TO LUCY FLUCKER KNOX, NEW YORK, NY,
THURSDAY, 1 AUGUST 1776

N[ew] York Aug 1 1776—

I receiv'd your Letter by Mrs. Halsey and also the one by the post. I know you read my Letters with an exceeding great avidity, I know your affection for me rises to a very great height, but neither of them can be greater or higher than mine. I love you my dearest blessing of heaven with a love, which it is impossible to communicate or describe. You wrote me a Letter concerning the small pox.[48] To be sure I wish my dear Girl and her babe to be eas'd of that dread, which must forever lay on her and my mind[s] until she has a full testimony of not being liable to its attacks for the Future. I will write to William on the Subject of your Letter and Mr. Tracy is to go from here in a few days. If you can persuade him to go the upper Road instead of the lower Road I should be vastly happy in your taking advantage of his protection and I could wish too for the look of the thing that Mrs. Pollard could go with you but this is by the bye.[49] You wish to know how I spend my time. I generally rise with or a little before the Sun, & immediately, with part of the Regiment, attend prayers, sing a Psalm, and read a Chapter in the Grand Battery. General Putnam constantly attends. I dispatch a considerable deal of business before breakfast. From Breakfast to Dinner I am broiling in a Sun hot enough to roast an egg. Indeed, my dear Lucy, I never suffer'd so much from Fatigue in my life. I, like you, am in a high distress, my arms being much broken out. Drink tamarinds and water, a quantity of them I send you by Colo. Sears, who sets out this day for N[ew] Haven by Water. Doctor Eustis[50] advises you to drink it and also sends his Compliments. My dear Lucy makes me smile to demand a written permission from me for her to return. After she has had the small pox, I am almost afraid to tell you how much I long to see you now and how much more shall I then.

Indeed, my dear, you shall return at any time you see proper and it shall be thought prudent so to do.

The affair of the small pox I look upon as a very serious concern of life. No person has recently had it bad at Boston. The Species are very kind. However, if there should be any hesitation in my Lucy's mind, I do not press it. It is left entirely at your option and yet I have given you so much of my mind as to know its desire. Above, I was telling you that I had a blister; I was bled for that and the headach about an half hour ago. Don't be frightened, [it is] only the extreme hot weather and rather too much business. But I don't intend to go much in the sun today. Sometimes I dine at home with not much more than my rations. At others, I dine out at General Washingtons, Lord & Lady Putnams &c &c &c. But I am mortified that I have not had them to dine with me in return. However that cannot be. The Dutch Girl you left behaves well if there is any truth in flint. I find my Cloaths clean and in pretty good order. The other Girl went away a day or two ago. If Henly and she had any correspondence, they kept it entirely from my knowledge. Does Harry Jackson or Bill[51] write you. I have not had a Letter from Bill for two posts. I would have sent you the wine you desire, but there is none in this city but at a Dollar or 5/ Sterl[ing] per Bottle. If You tell me you shall not go to Boston, I will send you a dozen instantly. . . . Lord Howe and [ ][52] had a curious conversation of one hour. I should have been very happy to have gone and it was intended, but [illegible] business prevented. He will tell you when he sees you. However, he will get his friends exchang'd. I am, my only Love, yours with the most perfect affection.

    Yours HKnox

Yes, I forgot to tell you I go to bed about nine oClock or before every night. We intend attacking with the Row Galleys soon & I believe Lord Howe intends attacking us. God preserve You. . . .

LUCY FLUCKER KNOX TO HENRY KNOX, NEW HAVEN, CT,
SUNDAY, 4 AUGUST 1776

This is indeed hard. My Harry is sick and I cannot see him. Lett me beg and intreat of you, as you value my peace, to take care of your precious health. Do not expose yourself in this manner. If you do, you will soon make an end of your life & mine, for I trust our affection is too deep riveted to admit the life of one after the other is gone. God grant us to live to meet again. I am told these dreaded troops are at length arrived.[53] Pray for your little girl. My Harry, she is half distrac[t]ed. I have more fortitude that I thought I had, but there are times when every other consideration gives way to the Soul racking idea of my friend, my husband, my all, exposed to a dangerous enemy. I have wrote you but once for some days for want of opportunity, for believe me, I have no pleasure equal to writing to you, except that of receiving letters from you. I thank you for your kind expressions of love, they are very pleasing to me, tho I do not need them to convince me of its truth. Your baby is as well as the very hott weather and my surfeit will permit. I have not received the tamarinds, which I suppose is owing to Capt. Sears not coming as he intend'd. Write me, I pray, all the particulars of the movements of our enemies. I like to know all that you are at liberty to communicate and you, I know, are ever fond to oblige me. I went the other day to see the [gun]powder mills in this town. A sample of the powder I send you made of American salt petre. I have received no letter from Mr. Jackson and but two from Billey. I will think of the matter of small pox when I know whether I am permitted to take it if I go. But I believe the arrival of the foreign troops will prevent my going so far. When I thought of going first I indulged a foolish hope that they wou'd never come. How apt we are to believe what we wish.

I write this between day light and dark, the latter of which now prevails. May every blessing attend you, may guardian angels from above protect you from the horrors of war, and the danger of sickness, and may we soon meet and be happy, are the constant prayers of her who is with unfeign'd affection

     entirely yours

     Lucy Knox

N[ew] Haven August the 4th 1776 Sunday evening. Don't say I don't date my letters—

HENRY KNOX TO LUCY FLUCKER KNOX, NEW YORK, NY,
THURSDAY, 15 AUGUST 1776

Thursday Morning 15 Augt 1776—

My dearest tenderest friend,

I received your highly valuable, and very welcome Letter by the post last evening—What a great happiness and consolation it is in our present separated situation to be able [to] reciprocally hear from and communicate our undisguis'd sentiments to each other. I wish my situation permitted me to employ more time in writing to the dear object of my whole affections. I lament very much when I am oblig'd to break of[f] that, as sometimes I am forc'd to do, and that even at a time that my full determination has been to write an exceeding long Letter. But, my dear Girl, you must excuse long Letters for the present &, by & bye, heaven will reunite us & give us to enjoy a long Life to be spent in the most social joys, in being good and happy ourselves, and endeavoring to make all happy around us. Indeed, my Love, without Goodness or an endever after it here, we shall be miserable, contemptible creatures both in the present and future State. How happy should we be were all our actions free from prejud[ice] and passion, when brighten'd Reason and Godlike Religion should dictate our line of Conduct. Dont think, my dear, that I am trifling, and intoning this as the mere thought of a moment. I wish to Heaven I thought more frequently of that great change which I most certainly shall under[go] and the Great, tremendously great, consequences after this Change. This is a matter that concerns all and for which all ought to be prepared.

Your intelligence concerning the dear pledge of our mutual affection is to me both interesting and pleasing. I believe I shall make a very [good] family man when peace shall again bless this despis'd, injur'd and insulted Country.

Mr. Root, it appears from your Letter, has alarm'd You by saying he had it from General Washington that we had not more the [i.e., than] 20 000 strong. This must have been some time past. We have had since thousands of very fine troops arrived within these few days from the Southward and Connecticut and we hear certainly of considerable numbers more on their march. Their [i.e., the Britons'] whole reinforcement is now arriv'd, and I suppose they soon will make their ground push.

How or in what shape that will be is a little uncertain at present. We yesterday had a deserter from them who appears to be an addled headed fellow and incapable of giving much Information. The Hessians from every Information appear to be a sett of people formidable only by their numbers, which are about 10 or 12,000, otherwise they, a parcel of poor uninterested scoundrels who have, nor of right ought to have, any other Interest in this quarrel but what money influences. Sir Parker's ship, the Bristol, arrived Yesterday. She came in a lame Duck, nothing present but his foremast, the rest Jury masts.[54] I have very little doubt with the blessing of that God to Whom we ought to look for help that we shall be very well able to withstand the force of these troops. Vain Nation, how hast thou despis'd us! How hast thou oppressed and insulted us as if there were none to help us, and now like a desperate Gambler thou art about to venture thy very existence as a people upon an action in which, if thou shalt be beaten, then art totally lost and gone perhaps for ever. Adieu Britain, forever adieu.

Peter's account to you of the letter as you relate it is humorous; he has [illegible] written Me a Letter, for the Composition and Sentiment of which I love him much, but not to your Right or prejudice. He really is a sensible Lad.[55] My Lucy need not be anxious on the account of the health of her friend,[56] he never has been in [better] health than since he took the emetic. The dysentery[?] I have not had, nor do I believe there has any number dyd of it or that it was more than half as bad as it was at Cambridge last Year. I am pleas'd your boy Thomas behaves to your liking, as he by being bound to you, is not liable to be shifted every day. Cant you contrive to get him taught some writing. All our friends advise you not to take the small pox at present as it has thro the hot weather turn'd rather more malignant. What you mention about the babe, I should rather think it had better be wean'd. I don't seem to like it should suckle any body but you. This may be [a] whine in [i.e., by] me, if so don't regard it. Don't let her hurt your precious health, for remember your health is as dear to me as mine is to you. May God bless you and Remember me in your petitions[?] to that throne where they are due Yours entirely—HKnox

I am glad to hear Mrs. Pollard is better Give my Respects to her & tell her Mr. Pollard is in good Spirits & has no notion of being Kill'd

HENRY KNOX TO LUCY FLUCKER KNOX, NEW YORK, NY,
MONDAY, 26 AUGUST 1776

New York Augt 26 1776

My best beloved,

I received your very acceptable Letter duly by the post. Indeed, my Lucy, it was one of the most acceptable presents I ever received from your much belov'd hands. The sentiments, the style, the every thing was truly charming. I lament that my time is not so much my own that I can answer every part of it particularly. It is not that I do not love my Lucy as well as she does me that my Letters are not as long as hers, & I must by that you would not on that account make your Letters shorter. You seem apprehensive of my resenting your Letter [brought] by Major Lockwood. No my love, your Harry never but for a moment resents any thing that you can say to me. I must have been egregiously mistaken when I wrote you about the Ducks and Chikens. I have rec'd thy part of them and the Whole of the Cheese for which, my love, I thank you. Take care, my love, of permitting your disgust to [i.e., of] the Connecticut people to escape your Lips. Indiscreet expressions are handed from Town to Town and a long while remember'd by people not blessed with expanded minds. The want of that refinement which you seem to speak of is or will be the salvation of America for refinement of Manners introduces corruption and venality. I grant you that most people are in a degree corrupt, but then in young states its only about tops and marbles [i.e., childish games]. In old States . . . Estates [are] gain'd thro an ocean of Iniquity and Blood. There's a kind of simplicity in young states as in young children which is quite pleasing to an attentive observer. Indeed, I am so thoroughly Glutted with the base said Wickederry & horrid Crimes of the Enemies, I have rather revert to barbarism of the original nations of this Land, than have any further connection with them. My Lucy asks what are my amusements and how I spend my leisure hours. Leisure Hours I have none and my amusements is my business. I treat none and am treated not much. Mrs. Airey, Miss Airey, Mrs. Foster, Mrs. Putnam and every other Lady is gone from the place, but how by since I dont know. Poor General Greene has been sick nearly unto death. He is now thank God on the recovery but very weak. He is about 2 miles from here on the Island. Mr. Henley is appointed Aid de camp to General Heath.[57] I was in hopes to have gotten Mr. Pollard likewise promoted to an aid de camp, but the new made Generals had too many friends to provide for. I do not permit Mr. Henley who is well acquainted with this Duty to leave me until after the action. The enemy landed last Thursday on the plains of Flat bush on Long Island and march'd to about 5 miles of our works. We suppos'd they were going to attack them and strongly reinforced on that side between our Works and where the enemy are is a very hilly broken ground, thickly planted with woods. If I had plann'd any thing for six months, it would have been to get the enemy in the very spot where they now are. Our advanced parties and theirs have had a considerable[?] number of skirmishes in which our troops did not find these heroes invincible, having beat them back several times.[58] The prince of Hesse in these skirmishes will be a great gainer [as] we kill'd and found the body of one of his subjects for what the prince will receive thirty Crowns banco. Three wounded [men] makes a kill'd man, so I suppose this paltry fellow of a prince will be receiving 100 crowns or 200 crowns banco every day.[59] General Putnam commands on the Island with a number of other Generals. Upon the security of Long Island will depend that of N[ew] York. I think we shall beat the enemy and with the blessing of heaven preserve them both. We have great numbers of men here. Your Harry is well. How does my baby do. I should like to see it, vastly kiss it bless, & pray for it for my sake. I am with all affection & love

Yours forever

HKnox

———————

HENRY KNOX TO LUCY FLUCKER KNOX, NEW YORK, NY,
WEDNESDAY, 28 AUGUST 1776

New York Augt. 28 1776 9 oClock eve[nin]g—

My dearest Lucy,

The post is not come in, so I shall not have the happiness to answer any Letter which I may receive from you. My time is so precarious that I must embrace every opportunity. My Lucy has heard the account of the Action of yesterday, and that I dare say in a way which has alarm'd her.[60] About two oClock in the morning, the enemy attack'd the woods in front of our works on Long Island where our Riflemen lay. They attack'd with a chosen part of the Hessians and all the light Infantry and Grenadiers of the army, and after about 6 or 7 hours smart skirmishing, our people fell back in front of our works. The enemy lost nearly 1000 kill'd among whom was General Grant[61] and Capt. Neilson of the 52d. We lost about the same number kill'd wounded & taken prisoners, among whom is General Sullivan & Lord Stirling.[62] General Parsons[63] was missing until this morning when he return'd. I wish Lord Stirling and Genl. Sullivan might return too, but I fear they will not. I met with some loss in my Regiment, they behav'd like heroes and are gone to Glory. I was not on the Island myself being obliged to wait on my Lord Howe and the navy Gentry who threatn'd to pay us a visit. Our works on the Island are strong and our forces numerous, so I think with the blessing of heaven that whenever th[ey] chuse to make the appeal, we shall be able to give a good account of them. We took a Lt. Ragg whom I knew at Boston and 25 Grenadiers of the marines, some light Horsemen, some of the 52d Rg. & some Deserters. My friend little Barry of the 52d had the picket last night, [and] we took one of his party. I wish it had been him [as] he should have been well us'd.[64] It is not certain what is become of General Sullivan and Lord Stirling, but it is suppos'd they are kill'd. I have, my dearest friend, in grateful remembrance your kind Letter of last Thursday,[65] and dare say I shall receive no small additional happiness from the perusal of yours of tomorrow. Dear Girl, how much I love you. War will bring peace and bye & bye we will live together, enjoying the felicity & happiness of each other's society 'till time walk us to immortal happiness. Kiss my babe for me &

> Believe me to possess a sincere
> affection for you as it is possible
> for a mortal to do HKnox

HENRY KNOX TO LUCY FLUCKER KNOX, NEW YORK, NY,
MONDAY, 2 SEPTEMBER 1776

New York Sept 2 1776—

My dearest tender friend,

The post is remov'd from here to Kings Bridge so that I have not the pleasure of receiving your Letters which to me are highly pleasing. You must have heard of our evacuating Long Island, a measure necessary wise and prudent. No Retreat under heavens could be better performed. I think it was a master piece. We likewise shall abandon Governors

Island and collect our whole force to one Spot. We are numerous &
collected, the Enemy are divided. I think with the blessing of heaven we
shall make them repent their temerity, we have no intention of aban-
doning this place which we can defend. Our army is divided into three
divisions, one in the middle of the Island, one in the Town and its envi-
rons, and one beyond Kings Bridge, so there is not a possibility of their
surrounding us. I shall write you by every opportunity & am with the
most perfect Love Your most affectionate
    Husband HKnox

HENRY KNOX TO LUCY FLUCKER KNOX, NEW YORK, NY,
THURSDAY, 5 SEPTEMBER 1776

   N[ew] York Sept 5 1776

My dearest hope,

   I received your enchanting Letter with all the raptures of a young
passionate Lover. The sentiments of my Lucy are charming & her Harry
blesses the moment which gave him such a rich Treasure.[66] Yes, my
Love, he is pleased to see You put Events upon so noble a footing as
the dispensation of divine providence. My Lucy has the right kind of
fortitude, dont fail to exercise it. You will see in the course of the this
[*sic*] war cowardice, treachery, Ingratitude with every other vice which
stains the human heart; dont be supriz'd for such there were of old, and
a continuation of human events is nearly a recapitulation of the past. Our
Situation is by no means disagreeable. The enemy must have suffer'd so
much that they are not very much inclin'd to make any desperate pushes.
For my own part, I never was in better Spirits in my Life when separated
from you than at present. I know we [i.e., the Americans] have made false
Steps and I know we must make great exertions to regain what we have
lost. But the British people are on so precarious a footing that one hearty
Drubbing would ruin them entirely. We want great men who when
fortune frowns will not be dismay'd. God will I trust in time give us these
men. The Congress will ruin every thing by their stupid parsimony and
they begin to see it. It is as I always said Misfortune that must rain [i.e.,
rein] us [in]to the Character of a <u>Great people</u>. Two or three smart, tho
not total, defeats would be of great service to us. I now put it upon this
footing that one or two drubbings will be of service to us, and one severe

defeat to the enemy ruin. We must have a standing army, [as] the Militia get sick or think themselves so & run home. This must be check'd with death & wherever they go they spread a panic. I am in raptures with your sentiments & feel every thing that my Dearest Lucy feels for me, but exercize patience. I hope I should be the ease of heaven. This much let the event be as it may I am with the help of God Determin'd to do my Duty. I anticipate the pleasing prospect when War shall cease and I wish my Lucy shall sit down in all the happiness of conjugal happiness. Mr. Livingston gave the pleasing intelligence that our dear babe was better.

> I am my Lucy with
> the most Ardent Affection
> yours entirely
> HKnox

To write by the post will be fruitless as it is remov'd 25 miles from this [place]

———

HENRY KNOX TO LUCY FLUCKER KNOX, NEW YORK, NY, SATURDAY, 7 SEPTEMBER 1776

New York Septr. 7 1776

My dearest love,

The Communication by the post being stop'd by reason of the office being remov'd twenty miles up the River. I shall embrace every opportunity to write to you and most earnestly wish you to do the same. Mr. Robt Temple who came from the enemies fleet yesterday is the bearer of this.[67] Your last letter which I received by Mr. Livingston was so replete with love tenderness & exalted Sentiments that I ever shall have the most grateful remembrance of it. The enemy since our retreat from Long Island have attempted but little. What their next attempt will be is a little uncertain. As I said before, we want men capable of great Ideas & who are acquainted with military matters. The General has such a vast load upon his mind that I wish for some easement to him, but many promotions have been made with very little judgment. Some good men we have, but we all want experience. I am pleased with General Greens getting better and hope in a few days he will be fit for service. It is said

General Lee is expected here any hour. I wish it may be true, his Experience would be of service to us in conquering those Philistines who have come up against us. The Prisoners of ours which are in the enemies hands are treated with great humanity & politeness. I am pleas'd with this Circumstance because it seems to have been in consequence of our kind treatment of their prisoners. I dislike the mode of making war like Savages. War has horrors enough which are inseparable from its nature, [and] we ought [to] try every means in our power to endever to soften its rough visage. We have a considerable number of troops arriv'd from the southward & expect more hourly. This will more than serve to make up for the defection of the militia, who to be sure as danger approaches sicken very fast. With firmness and unanimity joined to the blessing of heaven, I make no doubt we shall make a considerably advantageous Campaign of it. Tho, to be sure, you will say it does not look very like it yet. I hold to my old text that misfortunes will make us rise and, if we possess the spirit of that people whose General Character I admire, the Romans, we shall yet be a happy brave & free people. How this will be, time must prove. The mighty & little Revolutions are in the hands of an infinitely wise and supreme Being "who sees with Equal

> Eye as God of all
> The hero perish as the Sparrow fall"[68]

This much I am certain of—That let the Elements meet in one universal War and all nature go to Wreck, let the great Voice summon the dead from the dreary abode, to appear instantaneously before their awful Judge. That I love you Lucy and all created things [and] I feel for thee my Lucy. I pity your situation, I take in all the Circumstances which surround you, & lift up my heart in a devout supplication that he would support you, and this not from any real danger to which your friend is expos'd, but from the Imaginary one which you fear [text loss]. I know that the pain of a fancied evil is equal to the ev[il] itself, excepting it is infinite. I some time since wrote to Mr. Jackson[69] to get me interested [i.e., a part interest of] 1000 Dollars in a privateer. He wrote me in answer that it was not in his power, but that he had got 1000 Dollars between us. This I hope is agreeable to you my Love. I long to see you & my dear babe and hope heaven will give us that pleasure in due season. Dear little babe, I hope it has gotten better. Mr. Livingston informed me there was a great difference for the better from the time of writing your Letter to the

Time from whence he set out. That heaven who delights in the protection of virtue may bless and preserve you is the earnest prayer of
    Your affectionate Husband HKnox

New Haven, September 20th

Dear Billey,

Before you receive this you will possibly learn that your Brother is a prisoner but dont be frightened, he is not. The story is this—our worthy general, by the advice of his council, having determined to evacuate N[ew]. York had been three days employed on bringing off the army by small detachments, together with the Artillery and other stores which he effected all to one Brigade without the enemy having gained the le[a]st knowledge of the matter. But as soon as they became acquainted with it, they landed a great part of their Army at Harlem. The brigade of course would have been taken had not your brother, who stayed to see the last gun off, ordered them into the fort at Ballards hill, which stratagem had the desired effect, the enemy thought we had made a stand there and, crossing the fields, took another road into the city which our people took the advantage of and joined their main body unhurt. Owing to this delay, Major Putnam,[70] who was of the party but took to his heels, reported in writing that the rest were all prisoners. Judge what I felt until it was contradicted. The Armys are now both upon York Island within half a mile of each other, but it is said ours will retire to kings bridge. In the battle of Monday, we had great success but it was (the battle) not general. About fifteen hundred of ours engaged about an equal number of theirs and drove them two miles wide of their encampment.[71] Our poor creatures want cloaths exceedingly. Those that were last in York left all. What they will do, I know not. I would write you a long letter but my brain is confused. I am going to York or wherever the army are to see your brother, after which I believe I shall come to Boston upon a visit, as I know not what to do with myself. Lucy is well and fat as a doe. My love to Mrs. Jarviss. Tell her I would write her if I could compose myself. Comp[limen]ts to Mr. Jackson, who will be glad to hear my Harry is well. May god bless you.
    Lucy Knox

HENRY KNOX TO LUCY FLUCKER KNOX, NEAR WHITE PLAINS, NY,
FRIDAY, 1 NOVEMBER 1776

Near White plains, Nov.r 1 1776

My dear Lucy,

I am exceedingly afflicted that the medium of Communication is so inter-rupted as it is. We have business in plenty on our hands. Last Monday the enemy hove in sight, [and] with the greatest part of their force, they attack'd a Hill on our right wing, on which were posted without any works about 900 or 1000 of our men under General Mc Dougal and, after a smart engage-ment, they carried it tho' not without some considerable loss.[72] We I believe did not lose many. I think we are on Strong Ground, the Spot where we shall winter. The enemy seem determin'd on something decisive. God grant us the Victory. What think you of wintering in Boston, I think it will be best. If you think so, write to Billey to come for you. Adieu, my dearest dear, that God may keep & preserve you & your sweet babe is the earnest prayer of your

Most Affectionate Husband
HKnox

HENRY KNOX TO LUCY FLUCKER KNOX, CAMP NEAR WHITE PLAINS, NY,
SUNDAY, 10 NOVEMBER 1776

Camp near White Plains Nov.r 10 1776

Dear Lucy,

This makes the 4th Letter which I've written to you within the six days past. Had I time and opportunity I should not let slip one day of writing the sentiments of my heart to her whom my Soul Loves. So sweet is the intercourse & correspondence of tenderly connected friends, and yet I have repeatedly written to you to go farther from me. This is doing the greatest violence to my inclinations but it appears to Me that you will find it both convenient & necessary. The enemy have to be sure maneu-vered us into a scheme of sending part of our Forces to the Jersies under a supposition that they intend if possible to extend their conquests that way. Whether it be their real intentions or only a feint, time must dis-cover. I regret it only as it puts me farther from you, for as to myself, as I am at school endeavoring to learn the great Art of war, it is immaterial to me whether the war be carried on in this place or that, not that I've the least objection to a good warm fire and blanket. This Campaign I think may be term'd a loosing [*sic*] Campaign, not that I think the enemy have gain'd infinite advantages over us. It has been a Tragic Comedy of errors on both sides. The enemy now are encamp'd near to Dobb's Ferry about 4 or 6 miles from this, notwithstanding the fatigue & various hard fares of this Campaign, more, much more, may have been learnt in it than in twenty such as that at Cambridge. General Washington set off this day for the Jersies to take the Command of that part of that army & General Lee Commands here. I shall follow his excellency in a day or two. I shall write to Billey to come for you by this post, and I hope you will think with me that it is best for you to winter in Boston. It will be nearly as easy for me to come to you at Boston as it will to N[ew] Haven. General Carleton[73] dislik'd the attacking Genl. Gates & has retreated back to Canada. I am well pleas'd with it, as I think it will have no small influence on Genl. Howe's operations. Apropos, Mr. Lovell[74] is at last liberated, but has not yet come into this Camp. If he should pass thro' N[ew] Haven, altho it might be a good opportunity for you to go to Boston, yet I had much rather you should wait for my brother to come for you upon the account I think it would be more delicate & accord more with <u>our</u> Ideas of propriety. I have very grateful sensations of Mr. Isaacs' Civilities to you[75] & hope it one day may be in my power to recompense him. Pray tell him I feel anxious for his Recovery. Give my Compliments to Mrs. Isaacs & inform her that Capt. Perrot[?] is well stationed at Fort Washington. Young Hardy Peirce had his head shot off by an accident when fir[ing] at the enemy's ships on 5th Nov.r As soon as Mr. Howe will permit us to go to winter quarters, I shall be obliged to go to Philadelphia on some affairs relative to my department. Wherever I go or whatever I do, my thoughts are upon my Love & my lovely Infant. May that divine Being, who hast & is able to carry us thro vast difficulties, preserve you both. Adieu My Dearest life

    HKnox

HENRY KNOX TO LUCY FLUCKER KNOX, CAMP NEAR WHITE PLAINS, NY, MONDAY, 18 NOVEMBER 1776

Camp near White Plains Nov.r 18 1776—

I am very sorry to inform you of the surrender of Fort Washington on the 16th with 1500 hundred men, a Colo. McGaw[76] of Philadelphia

commanded. I had about one hundred officers and men, among whom
was Capt. Perot[?]. This is the most severe stroke We have received
during the war, as to the number of men I mean, for I can see no other
ill consequences arising. The enemy will triump[h] & we are disgraced.
God grant us a speedy opportunity to retrieve this unhappy affair. I am so
chagrined with this disgraceful affair that I cant write much. I beg your
Love to excuse me.[77] Let me know when Billey comes, but I wish you
not come on before you receive the Leave[?] from me. I am fearful that I
shall be obliged to the southward, however I will write you speedily.

> I am with the utmost tenderness
> Love can inspire Your Very
> Affectionate Husband
> HKnox

———————

HENRY KNOX TO LUCY FLUCKER KNOX, CAMP NEAR WHITE PLAINS, NY,
FRIDAY, 22 NOVEMBER 1776

Camp near White plains Novr 22 1776—

My beloved Wife,

I have received your Letter by Mr. Chew full as it can hold of the
melancholies. Mrs. Rheas[78] certainly affected my Lucy by her fears. To be
seperated from you for years if not for Life, because I wish you to go to
Boston for your own happiness is certainly to doubt my affection for you
& Is making me an unprincipl'd villian indeed. My God, is it possible for
you whom I so tenderly love & for whose happiness I would chearfully
give my Life, To harbour the thought that I would be absent from you for
years.

Awake my dear Lucy to your native dignity of sentiment & encourage
not such Ideas as these as have a tendency to sap that happiness which
we now possess, an unbounded Confidence in each other. I wish you to
go to no place inconsistent with you[r] felicity but by the eternal God
I wish you to shake off any companions that would aid and assist such
sentiments as are in your last letter.

Believe me, my dearest earthly felicity, that your happiness is the first
wish of my heart and that all my efforts shall be to promote it. Indeed
my country have strong claims to the little assistance in my power. This
claim I consider as the call of heaven which would be blasphemery to

resist. My obedience in this point interrupts our happiness for the present in order to secure it more effectually. I maledict the Cause as much as any person but cant remedy it, tho I am lending my aid towards it. By the time you receive this Letter I suppose my Brother will be with you. But you need not set out to Stamford for I this day shall go to the Jersies with General Lee. The enemy have landed part of their force on the other side with an intent as we suppose of transacting the same affair at Fort Lee that they executed at Fort Washington, but I hope that will be prevented.[79] We shall endevor to get them into trobble [trouble?] which may God of his infinite wisdom Grant. The Congress have done nothing with Respect to the Settlement of the Artillery as yet, So that I shall be oblig'd to go to Philadelphia before I shall have the pleasure to be with you. I think the operations on the other side & the prospect of the settling [of] my department may take up 3 Weeks, 3 long Weeks or perhaps 4, & then if the enemy go into Winter quarters I think I may have a reasonable prospect of spending some considerable time with you. Consult your own happiness & care with respect to going to Boston. I must be a damn'd Brute certainly to wish you to do any thing inconsistent with your peace. However if my brother comes[?] [for you] at new Haven I most certainly [shall] have the pleasure to see him, but [do] not wish him to come [on] a wild goo[se chase] after me. I had rather he shoud [wait] awhile at New Haven, but . . . he may be govern'd by our success o[r lack of] success in the Jersies. . . . I shall endevor [to] Come to New Haven to have [the] pleasure of being with you—the Cas[e is][80] in so precarious [a] situation that no principle of prudence could justify your leaving this way. Much good may Mrs. P——[81] have in following her husband thro a flying Camp. I should have no love for you if I indulg'd such an Idea. The post officer is remov'd to Peekskill. I wish your letters to be directed to be with the Army in N. Jersey

　　　　adieu may heaven prosper
　　　　& bless you adieu my love
　　　　HKnox

The slaughter among the Hessians was great when the[y] storm'd Fort Washington.[82]

———————

HENRY KNOX TO LUCY FLUCKER KNOX, BUCKS COUNTY, PA,
SUNDAY, 15 DECEMBER 1776

> Bucks County about 10 miles above Trenton & 30 miles from
> Philadelphia, Decr. 15 1776

My dearest Love,

   Its an inexpressively great mortification to me to be obilg'd to write to
you at so great a distance from you. I feel most keenly for your anxieties
on my account. The Reports you hear must be so vague and uncertain
as to give you vast uneasiness. All these anxieties & uncertainties I most
devoutly wish to do away. The time will arrive my Lucy when your
Harry shall again be happy in the society of his Lucy, God hasten the
happy period. No prospect of ambition, or Interest could possibly keep
me from you, nothing but a most sacred attachment to the much injured
rights of my Country. These bear down everything & makes me sacrifice
the enjoyment of all present happiness to this fix'd principle. I trust this
principle will support & comfort me in hour of Death & be no bar to my
eternal happiness. The precarious mode of conveyance to you renders
it improper to write to you on public matters. Thus you may rely upon
that prospect which seem'd rather cloudy [but] is clearing up. But oh.
One dire stroke, the loss of General Lee who was taken prisoner a few
days since. This is a severe blow, but providence orders all things for the
better.[83] America must & will rise Triumphant—Much great happiness
must & will be in reserve for the virtuous part of America. Every thing
goes on right, all things will work for good. I wish the enemys being at
Newport might bring me to New England.[84] But I doubt of this. Kiss my
dear Little babe ten thousand times for me. May that Being who delights
in virtue bless you & forget not him whose whole soul is devoted to your
happiness. Give my love to Harry Jackson my brother &c. I'm in hopes
this may find you in Boston.

>   Adieu my Lila
>   H Knox

———

HENRY KNOX TO LUCY FLUCKER KNOX, NEAR TRENTON, NJ,
SATURDAY, 28 DECEMBER 1776

Delaware River near Trenton Decr 28, 1776
past 12 oClock

My dearly belov'd friend,

It grieves me exceedingly that I still date my Letters from this place, & that I am so far distant from the dearest object of my affections. This War with all its variety is not able to banish your much lov'd Idea from my heart. Whatever I am employ'd about, still you are with me. I often say to myself, no my Lucy, not so, your Harry will return as soon as the sacred calls of his Country will permit, will return with the permission of heaven and enjoy all the blessings of conjugal affection. I wrote you a few days past by Mr. Shaw.[85] It was short as my then hurry would not suffer me to do otherwise. You will before this have heard of our success on the morning of the 26th instant against the enemy. The enemy by their superior numbers had oblig'd us to retire on the Pennsylvania side of the Delaware by which means we were oblig'd to evacuate or give up nearly all the Jersies, [and] even after our retiring over the river the preservation of Philadelphia was a matter exceedingly precarious. This Force of the enemy [was] three or four times as large as ours. However the Enemy seem'd contented with their success for the present and quartered their troops in different & distant places in the Jersies. Of these cantonments, Trenton was the most considerable. Trenton is an open Town situated nearly on the Banks of the Delaware accessible on all sides. Our army was scatter'd along the river for nearly 25 miles. Our intelligence agreed that the force of the enemy in Trenton was from two to three Thousand with about six field Cannon and that they were pretty secure in their situation & that they were Hessians, no[t] British troops. A hardy design was form'd of attacking the Town by storm. Accordingly, a part of the army consisting of about 2500 or three thousand pass'd the River on Christmass night with allmost infinite difficulty, with eighteen field pieces. Floating Ice in the River made the labour almost incredible, however perseverance accomplished what at first seem'd impossible. About two oClock the troops were all on the Jersey side. We then were about nine miles from the object, the night was cold & stormy. It hailed with great violence, the Troops march'd with the most profound silence and good order. They arrived by two routes on roads at the same time about half an hour after day light <u>to within one mile of the Town</u>. The storm continued with great violence, but was in our backs & consequently in the faces of our Enemy. About half a mile from the Town was an advanced Guard on each road, consisting of a Captain's Guard. These Guards we forc'd & enter'd the Town with them pell-mell, & here succeeded a scene of war of which I had often conceived but never saw before. The hurry, fright & confusion of the enemy was unlike that which shall be when the last Trump[et] shall sound. They endevored to form in Streets, the heads of which we had previously the possession of with Cannon & Howitzers. These in the twinkling of an eye cleared the streets, the backs of the houses were resorted to for shelter. These prov'd ineffectual [as] the musketry soon dislog'd them. Finally they were driven through the Town into an open plain beyond the Town. Here they [re]form'd in an instant. During the contest in the streets, measures were taken for putting an entire stop to their retreat by posting troops and Cannon in such passes and roads as it was possible for them to get away by. The poor fellows, after they were form'd on the plains, saw themselves completely surrounded. The only resource left was to force their way thro [against] numbers unknown to them, strongly posted with Cannon. The Hessians lost part of their Cannon in the Town. They did not relish the project of forcing, & were oblig'd to Surrender upon the spot with all their artillery, 6 brass pieces, army Colors &c &c. A Colo. Rawle[86] commanded who was wounded. The number of prisoners was above 1200, including officers, all Hessians. There were but few kill'd or wounded on either side. The Hessians might have about 30 or 40 kill'd & perhaps a hundred wounded, our kill'd and wounded did not amount to more than 30. After having march'd off the prisoners & secur'd the Cannon, stores &c, we return'd to the place 9 miles distant where we had embark'd from. Providence seem'd to have smil'd upon every part of this enterprize; great advantages may be gained from it if we take the proper advantages. At another port, we have push'd over the River 2000 men. To day another body and tomorrow the whole army will follow.[87] The troops behav'd like men contending for every thing that was dear and valuable. It must give a sensible pleasure to every friend to the rights of America to think with how much intrepidity our people push'd the enemy & prevented their forming in the Town. These bugbears I hope will now be strip'd of their Lions skin. The people will see I hope that nothing but an exertion of their own strength is wanting to chase tyranny from this Country devoted to Liberty. His Excellency, the General, has done me the unmerited great honor of thanking me in public orders in terms strong & polite. This circumstance I should blush to mention to any other than to you my dear Lucy & I am fearful that even my Lucy may think her Harry possessed of a Species of little vanity in doing [this] at all. It is an exceeding great satisfaction to a mind of any sensibility to find approbation [when] succeeding [in] well-meant endeavors. I was in hopes I should have been on my way from Philadelphia to Hartford 'ere this, but this matter has prevented me for the present. My business will render my going there indispensable this winter & then I hope to have the happiness of being for a few days with my Lucy at N[ew] Haven or Boston. I wish to know at what place you are. I rec[ieve]d a queer note from Peter,[88] but it inform'd me neither of one thing or another. May that kind Being who presides over thee in quality of a Guardian angel, keep vigilant watch that no evils befall thee or thy babe & render the[e] safe to your anxiously tender Husband

Harry

1777

LUCY FLUCKER KNOX TO HENRY KNOX, CA. JANUARY 1777[89]

I am sick at heart, low spirited and almost indifferent whether I live or die. Had I no friends I suppose I should not take it so hard, but when I reflect that I have a father and a mother, sisters and Brother, and yet am this poor neglected thing, I cannot bear it. As for you, I love you. I underwent almost every distress for the sake of being yours, and you forsake me. My poor dear father I must never see again. When I reflect upon his excessive tenderness for me when a child, upon the thousand times he has helped me and prayed god to make me the comfort of his age, I am half distressed and yet believe me, dear Harry, I cheerfully remained the best of partners and would do it again and again to live to be with you. But this you refuse me. I have been confined to my room almost a week, have been alone most time, and have given myself up to the Horror of my situation.

HENRY KNOX TO LUCY FLUCKER KNOX, MORRISTOWN, NJ,
TUESDAY, 7 JANUARY 1777

Morris Town Jany. 7, 1777—

My dearest Love,

I wrote to you from Trenton by a Mr. Furnass which I hope you have
received. I then informed you that we soon expected another tussle; I
was not out in my conjecture.[90] Mr. Furnass had not been gone more
than two hours before we had intelligence that the enemy were advancing with considerable Force from Princeton 12 miles distant. We
immediately made a disposition for a Battle which, as the enemy did not
come on immediately, we afterwards varied in order to prevent their
coming in on our rear. About 3 oClock on the 2d of Jan[uar]y, which was
the same day on which Mr. Furnass went away & the same day of which
I'm writing, a Column of the Enemy attack'd a party of ours which was
stationed about one mile above Trenton. Our party was small & did not
make much resistance, the Enemy who were Hessians enter'd the Town
pell mell, pretty much in the same manner that we had driven [out] the
Hessians a few days before. Nearly on the other side of Trenton, partly
in the Town, runs a Creek which in most places is not Fordable & over
which thro Trenton is a Bridge. The Grounds on the other side are much
higher than on this and may be said to command Trenton completely.
Here it was [that] our army drew up with 30 or 40 pieces of Artillery
in front. The Enemy push'd our small party thro' the Town with Vigor,
tho not with much loss. Their retreat over the Bridge was thoroughly
secur'd by the Artillery, [and] after they had retir'd over the Bridge, the
enemy advanc'd within reach of our Cannon who saluted them with
great vociferation and some execution. This continued till dark when of
course it ceas'd, except a few shells we now & then chuck'd into Town to
prevent their enjoying the new quarters securely. As I before mentioned,
the Creek was in our front, our left on the Delaware, our right in a Wood
parallel to the Creek. The situation was strong to be sure, but hazardous
on this account that had our right wing been defeated the defeat of the
left would almost have been an inevitable consequence, & the whole
thrown into confusion or push'd into the Delaware, as it was impassable
by Boats. From these Considerations, the General thought it was best
to attack Princeton 12 miles in the rear of the enemy's Grand army and

where they had the 17th, 40th & 55th Regts with a number of draughts altogether, perhaps about 1200 men. Accordingly, about one oClock at night we began to march & make this most extra maneuver. Our Troops march'd with great silence & order & arriv'd near Princeton a little after day Break. We did not suprize them as at Trenton, for they were on their march down to Trenton on a road about a quarter of a mile distant from the one in which we were. You may judge of their suprize when they discovered such large Columns marching up, they could not possibly suppose it was our army for that they took for granted was coop'd up near Trenton, they could not possibly suppose it was their own army returning by a back road. In short, I believe they were as much astonish'd as if our Army had drop'd perpendicularly upon them. However, they had not much time for consideration [as] we push'd a party to attack them. This attack they repuls'd with great spirit & advanc'd upon another column just then Coming out of a Wood, which they likewise put in some disorder, but [with] fresh troops coming up and the Artillery beginning to play, they were after a smart resistance totally put to the rout. The 4th Regt us'd their Bayonets with too much severity upon a party they put to flight, but they now paid for it in proportion, very few escaping, near 60 were kill'd on the spot, besides the wounded. We have taken between three & four hundred prisoners, all British troops. They must have lost in this affair nearly 800 kill'd, wounded & taken prisoners. We lost some Gallant officers—Brig.r General Mercer was wounded & supposed to have been kill'd. He had three separate stabs with a Bayonet. A Lt Colo. Fleming[91] was kill'd & a Capt. Neil of the Artillery, an exceeding fine officer.[92] Mercer will get better. The enemy took his parole after we left Princeton.[93] We took all their Cannon which consisted of two brass six pounders, a considerable quantity of military stores, blankets, guns &c. They lost, among a number of other officers, a Capt. Leslie, son to the Earl of Leven & Nephew to Genl. Leslie. We brought him off & buried with the honors of War.[94] After we had been about two hours at Princeton, word was brought that the enemy were advancing from Trenton. This they did, as we have since been inform'd, in a most infernal sweat, running, puffing & blowing & swearing at being so out witted. As we had other objects in view to risk beating up their quarters, we pursued our march to Somerset Court house where there were about 1300 Quartered, as we had been informed. They, however, had march[ed] off & join'd the

Army at Trenton. We at first intend'd to have made a forc'd march'd to Brunswick at which place was the baggage of their whole army & Genl. Lee, but our men having been without either rest, rum or provisions for two nights & days were unequal to the talk of marching 17 miles further. If we could have procur'd 1000 fresh men at Princeton to have push'd for Brunswick, we should have struck one of the most brilliant strokes in all history. However, the advantages are very great already. . . . The enemy were within 19 miles of Philadelphia, they are now 60 miles [away]. We have driven [the British] from almost the whole of West Jersey. The Panic is still kept up: we had a Battle two days ago with a party of ours & 60 Waldeckers who were <u>all</u> kill'd or taken, in Monmouth County, in the lower part of the Jersies.[95] Another party of ours have routed the party of Tories there, kill'd and took two hundred prisoners. In short my Lucy America has a prospect of seeing this part of it entirely rid of her Foes. . . . They have sent their Baggage to Staten Island from the Jersies & we are very well inform'd they are doing the same from New York. Heath will have orders to march there and endeavor to storm it on that side.[96] There is a tide in the affairs of men such if taken at the Flood lead on to Victr'y.[97] For my part my Lucy I look up to Heaven & most devoutly thank the great Governor of the Universe for producing this turn in our affairs of America, & this sentiment I hope will so prevail on the Hearts of the people as to induce them to be a people chosen of Heaven, not to give way to despair, but at all times & under all circumstances never to despair of the Common wealth. Much is to be done by New England, great exertions must be produced by her. Heaven seems to have given her hardy sons replete with Health & Fortitude [text loss] be equal to battle all the efforts of tyranny. I wish something might or could be done with the enemy at Rhode Island. If God would so prosper our arms as to eject them out of America entirely, it would give Life & energy to the Formation of the new Army. I am not too Sanguine, I don't think, that the Army of America is established firmly. The Fate of War is uncertain. Victorious to day, defeated tomorrow. We shall shortly endeavor to make another stroke or two upon them. I repeat it again that New England must exert herself to the utmost for a new Campaign, and if she does much, very much may be expected. I most devoutly long for the happy day when War shall cease & restore me to my much lov'd Lucy. When I shall have the happiness of seeing you for a short time, I cannot with certainty say but I hope it will be in the course of six weeks or two months. May god preserve you & my sweet Babe.

Adieu my Love

HKnox[98]

───────────

Morris Town January 10 1776[99]

I yesterday had the happiness of receiving your Letter of the 25th of December by Major Frazier which gave me the greatest heartfelt Pleasure.[100] My Lucy's Fears lest the busy scene in which I am engag'd should in any measure diminish my Love for her are entirely groundless. Believe me my Love I live, move & exist only for you. In the greatest hurry & confusion of War, you are uppermost in my thoughts, my heart is yours altogether. My Country demands my poor pittance to endeavor to rescue her from Barbarity, Tyranny, & every misery consequent on an unlimited, uncheck'd power. Remember [the British have sent] Indians to massacre the back Inhabitants, to drench their peaceful habitations with the blood of poor defenceless Women & children, Negroes to poison & assassinate their masters, & Hessians, with all their other brood of mercenaries, to desolate & lay Waste [to] this Country, almost the only Country on earth where the Inhabitants have even the appearance of Liberty. Remember, these are the Acts of Britain, the boasted humanity of that people who calls themselves the mother Country! These are the Acts [of] Britain. What person with the least spirit, can tamely bear this can tamely suffer these horrid calamities to range without controul. Love, friendship and all the other generous passions & virtues which reside the mind and heart, call upon every person without exception to exert themselves for [this]. My Lucy, I'm well assur'd does not wish her Harry to be ignominiously inactive during this great contest, a Contest of Virtue with vice. My heart suffers pain, exquisite pain, in being separated from you. It sympathizes, feels & weeps with yours, & often pours forth a pious petition to the great author of all things to support & comfort you. Yes my Lucy our Love is I hope & perfectly believe mutual & will encrease & in one degree to another untill time shall be swallowed upon eternity. A Colo.

Stewart will deliver you this, please . . . dine [with] him. This is the handsome Stewart you have heard so much of. Take care of your heart.[101] Sure, I'm a good husband to write to you so often, but the pleasure I receive in doing it is as great as yours in reading it. I'm very sorry that you took my papers with you to Boston, as it will necessitate me to send a person there. [Please] find some Gentlemen who [will be able] to deliver them to me. . . . [T]hey are wanted immediately for the settlement of the Regt And are of the most capital Consequence to me.[102] I'm glad my friend Harry is at last determin'd to leave his God & Country & I'm happy in being able to provide for him agreeable to his wishes.[103] That May God bless & preserve you & your babe, is the very sincere prayer of your truly affectionate

    H Knox

HENRY KNOX TO LUCY FLUCKER KNOX, SPRINGFIELD, MA,
THURSDAY, 6 MARCH 1777

    Springfield March 6 1777

My dearest Love,

    The pangs which a disinterested Love feels at separation are not to be described.[104] I knew not untill now (shall I call it weakness) how dear you were to me and how necessary to my happiness. No, I do not and I will not call it weakness, it is not. Altho' every thing appears dull without you, it is a Love which it shall ever be my pleasure & duty to increase. How do you do, my Lucy. How [do you] bear the bitter pangs of parting with your Harry, who Laments this War as it occasions him to be from You. We arrived here about two oClock today and shall sett off tomorrow. The first day we got to [illegible] about 24 miles from Boston, the next day [illegible] 67 [miles], and arrived here 97 [miles from Boston]. Things here are in much greater forwardness than I thought them, so that my detention will be but short.[105] Give my Love to every body and believe me to be your

    Unalterable
    HKnox

HENRY KNOX TO LUCY FLUCKER KNOX, FISHKILL, NY,
WEDNESDAY, 12 MARCH 1777

Fish Kills upon Hudson River March 12, 1777—

My dearest Lucy,

After a most fatiguing Journey on account of the extreme badness
of the roads, We arrived here last evening. To Hartford the roads were
tolerable. There we were oblig'd to leave the slay [i.e., sleigh] and part
of my baggage, particularly my knives and forks plates and dishes. I also
left some at Springfield at which place I have order'd a field Waggon to
be built to be with me. I shall direct the person who brings it on to call at
the places where I have left any of my things to pick them up and bring
them on to me. I have arrived . . . [amid a] circle of Reports where, to
be sure, there are many, but the most considerable is of an action that
happen'd near Spank town where our people attack'd a foraging party,
defeated them, and kill'd and wounded five hundred. This is so well
authenticated that I am inclin'd to believe it.[106] I never suffer'd half so
much in parting with you my dearest Love as now, [and] I have almost
blush'd to my self at my total absorption of thoughts with respect to you.
Constant in my mind and clearly interwoven in my heart, you are ever
present with me and even the great objects in which I'm about to be
engag'd does not separate in the least your much, much lov'd Idea. I am
too unhappy to even express myself that I am oblig'd to be absent from
you and nothing but the great command of my country could oblig'd me
to it. The small pox is spreading thro Connecticut and will surely spread
its influence to your place. This gives me pain, but I hope my Lucy will
have the fortitude to chearfully take the advice of him who loves her
more than Life, which is that You with your little image be inoculated
immediately. Doct.r Rand[107] will provide you some clean commodious
building at Cambridge where you may have it conveniently. It will admit
of no delay and take care, my love, that you drink no wine or cyder or sit
by the fire while you have it [i.e., smallpox sores from the inoculation]
coming out for either of these circumstances will most inevitabley make
you have many more than a contrary conduct. Suffer me to conjure you
by every tye that bind us together not to put off to a distant day this important affair. I wish you well thro' it and would put the wish in a pious
form upon paper were I sure you would not continue to laugh at me for
my Religion.

Complete the affair respecting the attachment of the Land and Consult Mr. Bowdoin with Respect to eastern affairs. This is making you quite a woman of business. There is also another affair I most devoutly wish you to do and that is to get your Aunt Betty with you. There is a post office set up here, which is a post of Communication between head Quarters and you. Write me by every post & prod[?] my brother to do the same & the Colonel.[108] . . . Believe Me to love you as much as is possible for a Mortal to do.

    H Knox

    Mr. Eveleigh desires his Love to you.[109]

———————

LUCY FLUCKER KNOX TO HENRY KNOX, BOSTON, MA,
TUESDAY, 18 MARCH 1777

March 18th '77

How does my dear, dear, Harry. What is he thinking of, and how employ'd is he bustling in the busy world. Or [is he] pensive and alone reflecting upon the unhappy situation in which he has left poor me. If the latter is not the present case, and thro the hurry of business he for a while forgets his Lucy, yet in his more retired moments, the remembrance of what she suffers must some times extort a tear. My Harry is not above that proof of tenderness. His mind, tho equal to all dangers and all hardships, is still capable of the most refined & tender affections of the heart. We have never had a parting, nor ever an absence, that affected me like this. Think of some way, my only friend, by which it may be short'ned. I have heard nothing from you since you left Springfield, but I hope for a letter by the post, who is hourly expected. Do not neglect to give me the satisfaction of hearing from you often, [as it is] the only pleasure I can enjoy, save that of playing with my Harry's baby.

Mr. Smith has just called to invite me to the Peacock tomorrow.[110] Need I tell you I declined the invitation. No, sure, you know me too well. Billy[111] set out this morning for Newbury to purchase a cargo of stationary by which he thinks he shall make money. He is very anxious to perform the task you left him, [and] is much chagrined at Austin's bill of an hundred and ten pounds.[112] There is a petition now before the court to take of[f] the embargo upon the shipping. I know not what to wish as to its success, I do not like privateering. Could we confine it to those who have injured[?] us, it might do. But to take the property of innocent persons, who have nothing to do with the quarrel, appears to me to be very unjust. Mr. Jarvis has had another vessel come in, by which he will clear a thousand pound sterling as he says himself. He complains sadly for want of money from you. Says the business is at a stand for want of it. It is currently said that Lewis Gray is taken in a vessel going to the West Indies. Mr. Jackson is very uneasy on the account, as he thinks he will fare badly.[113] Colo. Crane goes on very slow. I am told he has not sixty men.[114] Yet what will become of us if the men do not turn out. My Harry, I think we are in a sad situation. . . . It greaves me to think you are embarked in a cause so wretchedly managed. Farewell my dearest hope. May the angels of heaven, guard, guide & protect you, may no evil by day or by night o'er take you, and oh my love, do not forget your Lucy. Remember the Sweet hours you have passed with her, remember the thousand proofs of affection we have mutually received, and also remember that she loves you truly, sacredly.

>Your
>Lucy Knox—

After I had finished the above, and taken a hearty cry, I took up Caspipinas Letters and opened to the following lines

>No more thy pleasing converse chears my soul,
>and smooths my passage thro lifes ragged way.
>thy smiles no more my wonted cures controul,
>and give new glories to the golden day—. . . .

>Soon may that power supreme, whose dread command
>can still the tumults of the raging main,
>thro paths of danger, with unerring hand,
>guide thee to me—and happiness again.

>In him my Harry, then thy trust repose,
>tis he alone—the joyless bosom chears,
>he sooths when absent—all our heartfelt woes,
>   At home our soft domestic scene endears.[115]

LUCY FLUCKER KNOX TO HANNAH FLUCKER URQUHART, CA. APRIL 1777[116]

The very sincere or tender affection that I entertain for you, my dear sister, induce[s] me to write you at this time, notwithstanding the great neglect with which I think I have been treated both by you and my dear Mama. To her, I wrote several times during the siege of Boston, but never obtained a line in answer, a circumstance that surpprised and grieved me not a little. Where she is now, I know not. I am not only deprived of father, mother, Brother & Sisters, but also denied the satisfaction of hearing of their wellfare. You, I am told, are at Halifax. If you are, it is probable this may reach you, and if it should, I beg of you to give me a particular account of my friends and relations. Is your little Boy living, is he well? Is Capt. Urquhart with you? When did you hear from him, [or] my Brother? Is Sally married or not? Where is she? I much wish to know all these particulars. For my father and mother I ~~love with~~ entertain the most Dutiful ~~and tender~~ affection. . . . Therefore [I] am greatly interested in the above particulars, the answer[s] to the above Querys. My dear Harry is well. He, my ~~dear~~ sister, is as when you knew him, the best and tenderest of friends. Never were two persons more happily united than we. We have a lively little girl. . . . ~~She is very like her gran-mama.~~ She looks vastly like our Mama, who I hope will one day see her. She will love her, I am sure she will. I am going at last to take the small pox, more for the sake of my little Lucy than myself. The Army and the country in general, having been innoculated, will make it dangerous for me to go from home without having had it, and in the present state of things, I wish to be in such a situation that I can go to all parts of America without danger. My Harry is not much home and I do not like to [be] from him. Oh, my sister, how horrid is this war, Brother against Brother and the parent against the child. Who were the first promoters of it, I know not, but god knows and I fear they will feel the weight of his vengeance. Tis pity the little time we have to spend in this world, we cannot enjoy ourselves and our friends, but must be devising means to destroy each other. The art of killing has become a perfect science. That man is most esteemed who has the best knack at destroying the human species. In our juvenile days, my Hannah, we little thought [that] this Barbaras [i.e., barbarous] art would so soon have reached America, but alas her fruitfull fields of war [have] been covered with the dead and dying of the heartfelt. The grief their sister and brothers must have suffered ~~can never be told~~

But enough of this. God send a speedy issue to this war and give us a happy meeting is the sincere wish and prayer of her who thro all the changing scenes of life never will cease to be your affectionate friend and sister

LK

———————

LUCY FLUCKER KNOX TO HENRY KNOX, BOSTON, MA,
TUESDAY, 1 APRIL 1777

Boston April 1st 1777—

My only love,

Thank you, ten thousand times, my dear dear Harry, for your kind affectionate letter by Mr. Shaw. Before I received it, I was anxious beyond expression for the fate of him whose welfare is the greatest concern of my life, having had no letters by the two last posts. I feared some evil had befallen him. At this cruel distance, how many such miserable moments I shall have. My heart does indeed witness that my love for my Harry is much much greater than it was three years gone. I am glad very glad that his reception was agreable to him. Would to heaven we had taken General Howe. It might have given us peace. You wish for the N[ew] England troops. I fear it will be a long time before any number of them are with you. There are a number of men raised, but I am told they have not a single necessary to take with them. By the return of Mr. Shaw, I will send you what you desire to Mrs. Hoffmans little daughter.

Now for the small pox—in the first place, Dr. Rand has no hospital under his direction, but I had applied to a Dr. Aspinwal at Brookline, and had engaged to go next week, but Genl. Heath has thought [it] best to order him to clear the house and to take the new inlisted soldiers. However, there is yet a chance that he will be permitted to take those he had engaged first. If he is not, there is another hospital at Salem, under the care of Betsy Davis's intended husband. Where I shall go if I am disappointed of the first. If I go to Brookline, Dr. Gardner[117] says he will see me daily. I have wrote to my Aunt, desiring her to come to me immediately, but have as yet received no answer. I will take the most effectual method to send you the things you desire. As to the affair with Mr. Hichborn,[118] I could wish my busy husband had seen to it himself. The paper that you left me with is thought insufficient. Therefore, [I] beg you would send me one properly executed. I will see Mr. Bodowin as soon as may be.[119] So much for your letter. Hannah is in NY.[120] I have wrote to her by Mr. Harbek[?], which I dare say you will approve of. I have taken care to say nothing but what the world may see. Poor girl, I fear her brute of a husband [who] does not make her proper remittances. Is it not very strange that he does not come out to her. My Harry, I believe there never were two persons more happily united that we. Could we, oh could we but live together. Give peace in our time oh lord. There is no petition in the whole liturgy that I offer with more energy than that.

For the present, farewell my all in all. May he without whose permission not a sparrow falls take you under his most gracious protection, may he cover your head in the day of battle, preserve your very precious health and soon, very soon, restore you to the Arms of your

tenderly Affectionate Wife
Lucy Knox

I meant to have copied this
but Speakman[121] cannot wait.
Lucy sends you a kiss. Burn it [i.e., the letter] for I shall be ashamed of it.

LUCY FLUCKER KNOX TO HENRY KNOX, BOSTON, MA,
THURSDAY, 3 APRIL 1777

Boston April 3rd 1777—

My Ever Dear Harry,

I wrote you yesterday by Capt. Speakman, acknowledging the receipt of your third wellcome letter and as I am fully convinced of your fondness for my scribbling, [I] shall not neglect to give Captain Treat a line also.[122] The affair of the house is compleated. I sent for Mr. Hichborn and finished it in half an hour. The demand is for the modest Sum of five thousand and fifty pounds. He said it would be right to put the regulated advance upon the goods, which Billy made [in an] amount to the above Sum. The present attachment is only upon the house, but should execution be granted, it will be extended to the Georges estate at least. This affair gives me pain (not that Papa will disaprove of it for he must certainly think it a wise step when he knows the circumstances) but for fear that it should be misconstrued on your part, who I know would part your last biscuit with him.[123]

I hope to take the Small Pox in a few days at one or other of the hospitals. I mentioned to you, in my letter of yesterday, I am very anxious to have it immediately, on many accounts. In the first place, it is my Harry's request. In the second, the season is growing worse, and third, the number of persons who have it here make it dangerous for me to move abroad. You will I am sure be very anxious for me, at such a distance and knowing my great dread of it. But alas, my love that will give you but a faint idea of what I feel for you. You desire me to procure for you a number of articles, which it is a pity you had not taken out of Austins store.[124] Cambrick [i.e., cambric fabric], I have but dimity, I fear I shall not be able to get in the town. You are not in actual want of it, as you have a number of these matters at N[ew] Haven, which shall be sent you with all possible expedition, and I will get more if I can.

Billy is delighted with his last letter from you. He has been very fortunate in raising the sum you required of him, [and] is impatient to know your mind as to the very few articles that will remain. I think it will be wise to send them to the country. I am very sorry to hear General Greene and you are parted. He has doubtless heard of the birth of his little Daughter, and that Mrs. Greene is well, or nearly so. Poor little woman, to have experienced the greatest of earthly miserys twice in his absence. Heaven preserve me from such an evil. The greatest distresses of human nature are in a great measure to be aleviated by the soothing tenderness of those we love. I have had frequent returns of that pain with which I am often afflicted since you left me, and he who made my heart, alone can tell how much I have lamented your absence. But I will not complain, I shall live, I trust, to see better days.

Miss Deblois has positively refused to listen to the Genl., which with his other mortification will come very hard upon him.[125] Mr. Jarvis has got himself some thousand pounds in debt already. I wish you may not get into a scrape about it. Treat Payne[126] tells him you had no right to employ him. They had like[ly] to have boxed yesterday in consequence of it. Is [it] not [that] these French Arms are a very great affair for us. It appears so to me. Do you credit the article in the [New] York paper under the Paris head[ing] concerning Dr. Franklin.[127] I wonder you mention nothing of Eveleigh.[128] I heard he got to camp before you. God be praised for the recovery of our worthy General. What a blow threatned us in his death. Is there any one that could have filled his place. I fear not.[129]

Good Night My Love. May your guardian angel keep vigilant watch that no evil befall you. Tho at four hundred miles distance, may you dream of your Lucy and be asured that she loves you and only you. God Almighty help you.

L.K.

If there is a post, what can be the reason you do not write by it.

L.K.

———————

HENRY KNOX TO LUCY FLUCKER KNOX, MORRISTOWN, NJ, SUNDAY, 6 APRIL 1777

Morris Town 6th April 1777

I leave [off] the usual address at the head of my Letter because I can fix upon none the thousandth part strong enough to convey the Idea of the strength of my attachment & love to you. I have received your [letter], No. 3.[130] My Lucy was very low spirited when she wrote it—small pox, absence, & Genl. Howes driving us thro' the Jersies, all dancing & hazing thro her brain at once were enough to crazy her. Most of the evils of Life my dear Girl are imaginary, ('tho an absent Love is by no means a fancied evil) which by examining, contemplating well & looking at disperse and vanish. Heaven will carry my Lucy & her baby [through] the small pox . . . & you may rely upon it for a fact that General Howe is not driving us thro' the Jersies into Pensylvania. These two evils will be remov'd, don't let them prey any more upon those spirits so essential to the health of my Love. Heaven in its own due time will restore us to each other with a full proportion of happiness to make up lost time. . . . The French from the fullest conviction of its being their interest will most undoubtedly assist us. I have seen authentic papers from France which removes the smallest doubt from my mind. Though they do not propose to declare War, yet they will open a Commerce with us and will defend that Commerce by force. This Cuts the matter short. France will trade & Great Britain will interrupt that trade by taking their Vessells. I am Chagrin'd to hear of Crane's ill success as he did not write me.[131]

From a thourough view of the mercenary tempers, narrow contracted views, [the] selfish and designing views of many of the people of America should be much less sanguine of the success of opposition against an invasion by a powerful, brave Army of Foreigners headed by a man of Genius and Capacity than I have been. Were it not that I have the most enthusiastic assurance of mind that it is the Will of high Heaven that America should be great, she may not deserve it. Her exertions have been small, her policy wretched, nay her supineness in the past Winter, would according to the common operations of things mark her for destruction. But we are contending with a people cruel indeed, that far from being enterprizing, far from being mark'd with scarce one Characteristick of Greatness, except a total debauch of morals be a mark of over refinedness of Manners, the consequence of ease and Luxury. Let them alone say you. I will, for I believe that God has let them alone.

By this time, I hope my Lucy has taken the small pox in such a way as to dissolve it of its terror. May God grant her every necessary [text loss] to go through it with safety [text loss]. Billey is so set upon going into the Army, but I have given my word to him and I must stand by it. Give my Love to him and tell him so.

> Adieu my Dearest blessing
> Adieu
> Henry Knox

LUCY FLUCKER KNOX TO HENRY KNOX, BOSTON, MA,
SUNDAY, 13 APRIL 1777

Boston April 13th 1777—

My dearest friend, my all, my Harry, where are you, are you Safe, are you well. Would to heaven I could see you for one half hour. Do you wish for your Lucy, do you think of me, do you ever shed a tear for me. Tis very very hard thus to be parted. Will it last long my love, or is the day at hand that shall reunite us. I hoped to have seen you at Springfield soon;[132] but you do not encourage me. What is the reason are you not to come there. Tell me you are, say something that shall clear my spirits.

I wrote you last Thursday[133] that I hoped to be inoculated that day for the small pox, but a rash breaking out in my arms induced the doctor to wait a little and dose me farther with the mercury, but he has just

Lucy Flucker Knox to Henry Knox, April 13, 1777. The Gilder Lehrman Institute of American History, GLC02437.00572.

now assured me he will finish it tomorrow morning. I own I have my fears that my spirits are not in a proper situation to carry me well thro it. Little dear Lucy grows the most engaging little rouge [i.e., rogue] that can be. She has learned a number of winning ways which would delight her papa, but alas. My Aunt is with me at present, but will not stay long.

She desires [me to give] her regards to you. She is going to marry an old fellow of sixty three and will not be persuaded of from it.[134]

On Tuesday next Colo. Jackson is to march for Providence with his company. Peter does not like it as it will retard his going to you.[135] In every other respect, I believe he is pleased with it. I know not, but I shall sett off for Morristown soon. I see no reason why I cannot as well be there, as Mrs. Washington, to whom present my respectful compliments. We have a vessel here, but eight weeks [ago departed] from Bristol who brings an account of that city having adressed his majesty, their king, upon the success of his arms in America. The captain, I am told, says that no [more] troops were coming, as they supposed long ever this Genl. Howe had made an intire conquest. Poor deluded people. I hear my brother is in [New] York, but hope it is not true. If it is, I will write to him and advise him to come home.[136] This is a horrid war, my dear Harry. I wish it had been protracted till my head was cold [so] that I might have spent the little time I have to stay in this world with him who is dearer to me than all that world beside. But, oh, he is taken from me to fight an inveterate enemy and perhaps to draw his sword upon my own and only brother.

I much wish to hear from you that the Army is full. I am almost discouraged at times fearing it never will be. Mr. Chester of Weathersfield who dined with me to day, says that even Colo. Webb, who had got the bounty, had few or no men raised. Two or three persons who have come from camp lately have brought me no letters. They say they either breakfasted or dined with you the day before, but you said you had lately wrote and desired they would tell me you were well. I am almost affronted at it as you know it would give me pleasure to hear from you, not only daily, but hourly. Mr. Jarviss[137] desires you will send him a waggon load of paper dollars, as he expects soon to give an equal weight of paper for lead, copper &c.

> Farewell, my dear Harry,
> your ever affectionate
> Lucy Knox

PS

I send you a letter which the famous Duchess of Brotenbourgs,[138] Princes[s] of Frankfort and cousin of the queen of Great Britain begs your care of. She brought it to me unsealed that I might give her my opinion whether it would offend his excellency or not. It is a very artful affair and may at least afford him some amusement. However, you will use your judgment, whether you wou[ld] deliver it or not. By Mr. Shaw I shall send you a few stocks [i.e., neckcloths] [and] will get some more, if I can, to carry with me to Springfield when I shall receive the wellcome summons to meet my Harry there. You will want to see me after the small pox I am sure. Will want to know if I look as I did or whether there is danger of your not liking me as well as you did when you saw me last. Peter has just come in in a great fret.[139] The Colo. has been telling them, that they are to do the duty of common Soldiers, to fetch their own pork and dress it, [and] when they have done [that], to stand centrys [i.e., sentries] and mount guards without distinction. It is very unhappy for me just at this time that Billy should be obliged to leave the town, as it will oblige me to shut up the house. But I am almost inured to misfortunes of this kind. May God Almighty avert the greatest of all evils and I will be patient under every other.

Adieu Adieu my Harry, love me one half as well as I do you, and if possible, lett me come to you.

> Your tenderly affectionate wife
> LK—

HENRY KNOX TO LUCY FLUCKER KNOX, MORRISTOWN, NJ,
SUNDAY, 13 APRIL 1777

Morris-Town 13 April 1777

My dear dear Wife,

I have received yours of the 1st instant, No. 4, for which I return you my unfeign'd Love. I am like those who receive the ninety favors and if the other is denied I in part am dissatisfied. How comes it to pass to you did not write me by the last post? Were you too busy? I can't admit that thought, because I live for you entirely and I hope you do the same for me. You must then have been gone to Brookline to have the Small pox. That is not probable otherwise Harry[140] would have written to me. Why then did you not write. Don't torment me again. I look for [the] post might as a devout Christian does to the expected moment when he shall receive some signal token of the pleasure of Heaven. I am pleas'd that Crane has at last a prospect of raising his men.[141] America trifles too

Henry Knox to Lucy Knox, April 13, 1777. The Gilder Lehrman Institute of American History, GLC02437.00573.

much with the high matters in which she is engag'd. An infinity of happiness or misery depends <u>upon the success or non success</u> of the present Contest, and yet the people are supine. Thank Heaven, the Inability of our enemy seem[s] proportion'd to our inertion— by the[ir] frequent desertions, [and] they are very sickly, [and] die fast. I yesterday was at Newark within 8 miles of New York. The Consequences of Trenton and Princeton affairs were very great, and yet their stay in the Jersies so long was much against us. It dissatisfied many people who were partly our friends, as we were oblig'd to give them up and they naturally embrac'd the power that was able to protect them. Their stay[ing] gratified the malice of the Tories who took every opportunity to impress upon the minds of the Common people an Idea of the magnitude of the power of Great Britain, and [many] did actually enlist for the Kings Service, very large numbers of the Nobility. Tho' the present mode of their assistance is but small, yet it's a very essential diservice[?] to us. A party of ours atack'd a party of seventy of these wretches to Humanity, routed them and took 5 prisoners. A party of these people are across the Pessaick[142] opposite to Newark. Genl. Howe seems to intend Philadelphia for his object & we at present judge from some circumstances that he will go partly by land and partly by water. That is, he will march some troops below Philadelphia and send his heavy baggage, Artillery &c round by Water. He does [not] look half so formidable this Year as he did last.[143] God Grant we may dispose these disturbers of Creation of that terror they carry to the women & Children. America owes every [one] of her past and present distress[es] to her sel[f and] the want of exertion . . . among her sons and daughters. Half the young married men in America [say they] "Cant go into the service because they are married and have families." I would annihilate such fellows, or transplant them to the Country that I hope one day to conquer.

> Adieu my love, may God
> Keep you and return you
> Safe to him who is affectionately
> Your H Knox

LUCY FLUCKER KNOX TO HENRY KNOX, BOSTON, MA,
WEDNESDAY, 16 APRIL 1777

April 16th 77

My dear dear Harry,

I had like to have wrote husband, and how you would have laughed, but laugh or not, be asured it is my greatest pleasure, and my greatest pride to call you by that endearing name, and I think upon the hour that made you such as that, when heaven bestowed upon me the greatest of earthly blessings. I am sensible that I have not been duly grateful to the author of all good and perhaps that is the reason why you are so cruelly torn from me. I wish my Harry knew how dear he is to me, but it is a subject that I cannot write upon. My heart over flows at my eyes. You are a sad boy to give me so much pain.

The packet which I send you was intended [to be delivered] by Colo. Lee, and my part of it wrote last Sunday. I was innoculated on Monday morning, as I expected. I wish Billy could have staid till I was well again, but how much more do I wish for his brother. I expect a letter to night by the post which I hope will raise my spirits. Do not neglect to give me that satisfaction as often as possible. There is a Letter to Sam Pitts, dated April 1st [and] signed H Knox. I cannot suppose it came from my Harry Knox, as his last to me was March the 31st.

I send three stocks by Mr Shaw [and] shall send as many more in a few days, with a very handsome waistcoat if the price is not too high. I have not heard it yet. I send Miss Hoffmans shoes. There are some pretty Callicoes to be opened to morrow where I hope to get something which will make her a pretty frock.

> God bless you my love—think of me &
> pray for me Your ever affectionate
> L Knox

Lucy sends you a kiss. She has learned several words, very plain.

———

HENRY KNOX TO LUCY FLUCKER KNOX, MORRISTOWN, NJ,
SUNDAY, 20 APRIL 1777

Morris-Town 20th April 1777

My dear Lucy,

I wrote you a short note by the post to day least [i.e., lest] Capt. Speak-man by whom I write this should not arrive so soon as the post, and give you the same disagreable sensations which I feel when the post brings no letters from my Love. I have always written by the post, & had done so the day when Gab. Johnnot[144] din'd at Head Qtrs., and I beg that you also would write by it as it is now conducted with some regularity. In your Letter of the 10th you inform me that You were to take the small pox that day by innoculation. Heaven guard my Love and her babe thro' that distemper and dissolve her of her fears on that account. If you were then innoculated, it must have broken out by this [time]. I hope you will have one or two or as many as you have a mind to in your face. Pray, can't you by force of Imagination, as in other cases, have them where you please. If so, [you] have to have one over each eye brow and one [on] each Cheek and one on yr Chin. Don't let my little baby have too many or too few. She may bear a considerable number. I will pray that you may have it in such a way as will not prejudice yr Health in future. Have I acknowledged your two welcome Letters by Capt. Treat and the post. I don't know how many Letters this makes which I've Written to you but think 8 or 9. I shall consider it as the latter and number [them] accord-ingly. I had wrote you 5 [as of] the 1st instant. . . . Let me beg of you not to omit writing while the small pox is upon you, and send them by the post as usual. Colo. Gabriel Johnnot must have given you an account true [of the military situation in New Jersey] as he Conceiv'd it, but I assure you we by no means think ourselves Despicable. Force arrives almost every day. Sir William[145] has protracted his movement to the present and perhaps will not move under[?] a Week. Philadelphia, imperial Philadel-phia, is his object. Ships have been in the Delaware but gone out again. A few days ago a fleet sail'd from N[ew] York but with out troops. I believe their Course from the Hook[146] S E, perhaps for Philadelphia and perhaps for the West Indies. Your brother Tom must be in Augustine as the 2d Battalion of the Royal Americans are there.[147] We have lately a Vessell arriv'd from Gothenburg in Sweden laden'd with military stores. Its said Mr. Deane[148] is gone to the Hague, and that Prussia, Sweden &c have desir'd that Ambassadors may be sent from the United States of N. America. Matters ripen in France as fast as we could wish. . . . I think matters look as favorable as possible after an unfortunate Campaign. Write me often and, as I am call'd, God bless You my dear Lucy.

    H Knox

    . . . Gen: Greene sends his Compliments and hopes you to get well thro the small pox[149]

––––––––––

LUCY FLUCKER KNOX TO HENRY KNOX, BROOKLINE, MA,
THURSDAY, 1 MAY[?] 1777[150]

    Brookline April 31st 1777—

My dearest dear friend,

    In what words shall I convey an idea to my Harry how dear he is to me or how much I want to see him. Indeed, indeed we must not live so. I am unhappy and that I am sure will make my H. so. Join with me my love, in humble gratitude to him who hath preserved your Lucy and her sweet babe: and thus far carried them thro the Small pox. No person was ever more highly favored than I have been since it came out, but before for three days, I suffered exceedingly. I have more than two hundred of them, twenty in my face,[151] which is four times as many as you bid me have. But I believe none of them will leave a mark. Lucy has but one, and has not had an Ill hour with it. Both hers and mine have turned and are drying away. And now for a jaunt to Morristown. What hinders my coming with Peter.[152] Only think my love of his being absent all this time. He writes me he has no prospect of returning soon nor do I know how to manage upon my return [home]. [Our] Man Tom (who prevailed upon my compassion to take him back) has inlisted,[153] nor is there a man to be hired under 10 dollars a month. Boys are not to be had as they can earn much more by working in the forts, and standing ocasional centrys. In short, I am in a very disagreable Situation and unless you will take me under your wing, I know not what will become of me. I thank you ten thousand times for your kind letters, eight of which I have received, but alas, not one encouraging word of meeting soon.

    I must describe the place I am in at present. It is called an officers room and is to be sure some degrees better than the common ones.

When I first came, which was last Wednesday, it was enlightened by one chearful window of about 2 foot square. But it was glass. There were two others of boards which were some bigger, neither clapboards upon the outside nor plastering within, but a few rough planks was my guard from the weather, which answered very well when the wind was calm. Two soals [i.e., soles] of old shoes served for hinges, the door on which was chalked the cloven footed gentleman upon his head. In short, I was never so horror struck in my life. But presuming upon my connection with the military, [I] sent for the barrack master who gave orders that the carpenters should obey my directions by which means I am much more comfortable.

I have no glass [i.e., mirror], but from the feel of my face I am almost glad you do not see it. I don't believe I should get one kiss, and yet [the] Dr.[154] tells me it is very becoming. He, the Dr., has been very kind and attentive for which I desire you will write him a letter of thanks and not call me by the formal name of Mrs. K. I want an answer to a very saucy letter I wrote you before I was sick by a Mr. Spooner, wherein I returned you a part of one of yours for an explanation. What you meant by it I cannot tell, unless it was to rally me upon a subject which is too delicate to be played with.

I have just come from a scene my Harry which has roused my very soul, in gratitude to my bountiful benefactor. A man who was inoculated at or about the time I was lay in the last agonies, his pock proved the purple sort and he poor soul must die. His brother had just arrived from his wife, who was near [to] laying in [i.e., giving birth] and very impatient for his return. And, as a proof of her affection, had sent him some good things such as he might venture to eat. He sent for Mr. Gardiner (who is in the next room to me) to make his will, and I had curiosity to go. He is just now dead. What a stroke will it be to that poor miserable woman. But oh my God, my own situation will not bear reflection. How do I know to what the dear partner of my Soul is at this minute exposed. Indeed, my Harry, I am serious, I cannot live at this distance from you. What has become of Springfield, have you no prospect, you sure[ly] are not indifferent about it? If you are, you are greatly altered since

you parted from your LK

———————

HENRY KNOX TO LUCY FLUCKER KNOX, MORRISTOWN, NJ,
SUNDAY, 4 MAY 1777

Head Quarters Morris Town, 4 May 1777

My only Love,

I received yours of the 19th ultimo & I am sorry to say it gave me but little pleasure for I was unhappy that my Lucy should take a resolution not to write to me untill I had inform'd her of my meaning in a certain Letter respecting an enigma as she took it. Consider my dearest Girl that had I been faulty, you had determin'd to be in the fault too and make me unhappy for at least one month. This was cruel. But as I live only to Love and make you happy, I will indevor to explain what to me appear'd and still appears to be self evident. Your Words are "I wish to know what always passes in your heart." The answer I meant to convey to this was wholly in your favor. It suppos'd my Heart to have your belov'd image engrav'd in so many places and had taken so full a possession of it, that Could You look there, you would see no other image than your self and no other passions than that of Love to you. As to the term "oh fye," it was only a piece of facetious[ness] at my dear Girl, under the Idea that the representation of your ever dwelling in my heart was perfectly under-stood by you. I am much mortified at your not taking what I thought a very pretty piece of Love. [Just] as the person . . . who repeated the story which had made the whole company laugh when it had been told, but found the effect not so great when he told it, and repeats in a suprize, "why dont you laugh, it was a good story when I heard it," so I must [illegible]. I thought it clever when I wrote it, but so much for this Eclarisesment [i.e., éclairissement, or enlightenment].[155] How does my Love, has she return'd to Boston. You[r] Doctor Gardiner kindly inform'd me that you were out of danger and that the erruption was complete, and that you had not above thirty and our little pledge of Love not so many. How does the dear little thing, can she speak? Can she walk, do you teach her to call papa. I bow with reverence and gratitude to the Great Father of Love for his kindness and protection to you in giving you the distemper so kindly and giving you the near prospect of being rid of that eternal fear which must ever have hung on your mind. My Lucy writes me something about the house and that the Court had pass'd some resolve about the effects of persons in the same predicament with your papa but what that resolve is you do not write.[156] I am pretty certain Mr. Bowdoin will do his utmost to serve you. Its so unreasonable that you should not have the full proportion of your papa's estate that no person in their senses can pretend to dispute it, but I wish no step to be taken but with Mr. Bowdoin's advice. I am very sorry that Billey should have been oblig'd to leave you as you were going to take the small pox.

The enemy have lately made a manoevre, presuming that their former successes had awestruck the people, they expected to have destroyed the stores there, as there were no Continental troops, without opposition. But they were mistaken. Nearly the same rage animated the people near Danbury as at Lexington, and I believe the enemy must have suffer'd as much or more loss than there. Our loss in stores in Danbury was very amply made up in the store ship lately taken and carried into Dartmouth.[157]

What think you of the late arrival of Cannon and stores from our good Ally, the King [of] France[?]. [One-]third are arrived and more are expected, but a bird in the hand is worth two in the bush. Mr. Howe has by this late manoevre puzzled us much. It would appear by it that his design was for Philadelphia and not for the Hudson River, the most probable place of damaging us and absolutely necessary for him and Genl. Carleton[158] to make a junction. Our intelligence from the other side of the water is that Howe is bound for Philadelphia, Carleton, Ticonderoga & Burgoyne, to push for the puissant and renown'd Town of Boston. How true this may turn out is uncertain, but I think if Billey has raised any thing near 1200, You had better have the [bookstore's] Goods remov'd out of the Town and the reason, not given as of fear, but that it may possibly happen and likewise I wish you to get a house provided [it is] in some part of the Country where it may be the most agreeable to you.[159] What would you think of Hartford, [or] Springfield, but at any rate you will have some time to take yourself away into the Country. I have no other desire but this. You should be in the way of my Letters, and on the Way of the post.[160]

LUCY FLUCKER KNOX TO HENRY KNOX, BROOKLINE, MA, THURSDAY, 8 MAY 1777 [MORNING]

May 8th, 1777

My dear Harry,

I did not expect to have wrote you again from this place, but Heaven ordained it be. I write you, by the past post, that we had got thro the worst of this terrible distemper and in a day or two could return home, but how greatly was I mistaken. My little innocence was suddenly taken very ill. She lay two days, without noticing any one and I may say without life or motion, and on the third broke out with the small pox, as the Doctors tell me, in the natural way. She poor little soul is covered from head to foot with it. She has upwards of eighty in her sweet face, but it is a fine sort and the Doctors say will not leave a mark [and] tis now upon the turn. My Harry, shed one tear, at thinking what an anxious mother feels at such a crisis. The partner of my Soul is gone, he who would share and sooth my cares is far far away, and when I again shall see him, not I, but heaven and he can tell.

Billy has returned from Providence, but in such a condition that he has not been to see me. His hands and arms are continued sore, so bad that he cannot use them. He is at the place where he used to board. As I shut up the house when I left it, I am very desirous to get to town upon his account, but must wait [until] the recovery of my little darling.

Col. Jackson has got his affair thro the court, and means to begin recruiting immediately, but General Heath tells me there is an order for his and Lees regiments to remain in Boston. If so I believe tis but a finesse, to take in the men to inlist. The people in Boston are all mad, moving out as fast as possible, for fear of Genl. Burgoine. For my part, I shall not stop short when I go, which will not be till there is real danger. They say he is now at Nashua, with ten thousand men, means to land at Braintree and march to us. I do not doubt but half the number might march thro the country, but all my hopes are that they will not try. After the affair of Danbury, I think we have nothing to hope from militia. Are we not excellent politicians to place our stores in the midst of our enemys. I remember to have heard frequently (when I was in Connecticut) that there was scarce a whig in the place.[161]

Poor Uncle Winslow, my Harry. What an unhappy step was his going away for [i.e., from] his poor family. Now he is dead what will become of them I cannot think what they will do.[162] I expect a long letter from you tonight. Oh that you may tell me to come to Springfield, that I may once more see you. I have ten thousand things to say to you. Tis very hard, but I will not complain. I would write more but my spirits are agitated and my heart heavy. God bless, my dearest life, think of me and pray

for me, yours entirely,

Lucy Knox

LUCY FLUCKER KNOX TO HENRY KNOX, BROOKLINE, MA,
THURSDAY, 8 MAY 1777 [EVENING]

My Dearest only Love,

I wrote you My Harry this morning, but as I sent my letter by an
unknown hand to town, I fear it may not reach you, and as you kindly say
it gives you pleasure to receive my scribbling [so] I will not be affraid of
tiring you with it. I told you that your dear little babe had got the small
pox in the natural way. It is now upon the turns and this afternoon, she
is very lively, playing about the floor. The Dr. says she will do well and I
trust he is not mistaken.

I got Mrs. Pollard to take out of my trunk at N[ew] Haven such of
your things as were worth sending and to leave them with Colo. Mason
at Springfield.[163] She has been to see me and says she left in his hands 8
waistcoats & 4 pair of breeches which he promised to forward. When I
return to town, my first care shall be to get you some more of these articles with the handkerchiefs stocks &c.

I have no company here but Madam Heath[164] who is so stiff it is impossible to be sociable with her, and Mr. Gardner, the treasurer,[165] so that
you may well think what I feel under my present anxiety, out of which
if I am not soon relieved I fear I shall be sick myself. What would I not
give to see my dear Harry. When we parted, my Love, I felt what words
will not cannot tell, but did I think after ten weeks absence, there would
be no prospect of our meeting. No, no, no, My dear boy said, in six weeks
my Lucy shall be restored to my arms. Do you remember it. Do you also
remember that you shed a tear at leaving me. If you have forgot it, I have
not. But [if] tomorrow morning brings me a letter, which were I in town
I should receive to night, who knows what it contains. I will hope for
that, and in that hope again [I may] take my leave. May all good angels
> guard him who is dearer to me than life itself is the prayer
> of a fondly anxious wife by the name of
> Lucy Knox
> Sewals Point May the 8th—eight Oclock in the evening

The Perils of War II

THE PHILADELPHIA CAMPAIGN OF 1777

"There is such a thing as equal command"

Although Lucy Knox desperately sought to be with her husband in 1777, the protracted campaign around Philadelphia kept them apart even longer than in 1776. Letters written during the military operations around what was then the American capital demonstrate how the Continental army and the Knoxes' marriage each continued to develop in crucial ways. As is well known, the American army faced numerous challenges throughout 1777, including recruitment shortfalls, a dearth of supplies, and growing exhaustion as the war stretched on, seemingly without end. Yet Henry's letters also reveal that American soldiers and officers were gradually becoming a more disciplined and effective fighting force, with men and commanders gaining valuable battlefield experience. The couple's correspondence during the year also illustrates that, once the Knoxes came to grips with the Revolutionary War's scope and magnitude, their relationship and marriage developed in the direction of greater parity. Each spouse became more dependent on the other as the year progressed, in order to sustain both the war and home fronts. Equally as important, Lucy fully recognized her contributions to the overall struggle and insisted that her husband acknowledge her as an equal partner in their marriage.

Military operations began that June when British general William Howe ordered his army's forward units to withdraw eastward across New Jersey, in the direction of New York City. Although Washington's forces followed cautiously, the American commanders were baffled in trying to discern Howe's overall intentions. Henry wrote to Lucy in July that British pickets "gave out" to their Continental counterparts that they were soon to march northward to link up with General John Burgoyne's army, which was then pushing south through the Hudson Valley toward Albany, New York. Instead, Howe's men set off from New York City by sea in late July. After a month-long voyage that ultimately took them to the Chesapeake Bay, the British landed at Head of Elk, Maryland, on 25 August. Marching south with the Continental army in order to protect Philadelphia, Knox and other American generals continued to be puzzled at Howe's strategic objectives. In one letter, Henry sarcastically wondered if the British were afraid of tangling with American forces again.[1] After the Royal Navy had been spotted inside the bay, he then speculated that the enemy might wish to land on the Delmarva Peninsula, due to its large Loyalist population and plentiful supplies of food and forage.[2]

Despite Knox's predictions, Howe's army marched northward from Head of Elk, toward what was then the nation's capital, Philadelphia. The campaign's two major battles outside the city, at Brandywine (11 September) and Germantown (4 October), proved that the Continental army's capabilities had improved considerably since the disasters in New York, twelve months before. Although American forces lost both actions in Pennsylvania, the soldiers in the ranks fought long and bravely. The Continental army's junior officers and field officers, furthermore, provided effective leadership and maintained discipline over their men. The army had come a long way. Knox himself fully understood and appreciated their improved capabilities. As Henry explained to Lucy two days later, although he was disappointed at the defeat along Brandywine Creek, the men had fought well and inflicted considerable losses on the enemy. The army's withdrawal, moreover, had been conducted with such skill and order that the British dared not pursue them. As for Knox's artillery corps, the troops had performed magnificently, behaving "like men contending for everything."[3]

Nevertheless, the two battles revealed that the Continental army's commanders were only slowly learning their craft, since they continued to make near-disastrous mistakes. At Brandywine, for instance, Washington left his right flank open (repeating a similar mistake he had made on Long Island). As a result, Howe's regulars fell upon the exposed American troops and soon forced the entire army to retreat. The defeat also paved the way for the British to capture Philadelphia in late September. At Germantown, Washington devised an overly complex plan to retake the city. When fog at dawn unexpectedly blanketed the battlefield, his widely separated columns got lost and stumbled into one another. The army's other officers also demonstrated shortcomings. Knox himself contributed to the defeat at Germantown in this respect. At the battle's height, and with the enemy falling back before Continental assaults, he became obsessed with an isolated British detachment that was barricaded inside a stone mansion known as the Chew House. Rather than simply bypassing the hundred or so troops inside, Knox drew on his military reading from before the war, which taught that an attacking army never left an enemy force in its rear. During a hastily convened council of war, he convinced Washington to assault the house, even though the detachment posed no serious threat to the main body of the Continental army. Not only did the attack fail, but it disrupted the overall momentum of the American offensive. The British, therefore, recovered from the surprise attack and ultimately won the battle. Still, given the performance of the men in the ranks and their "prodigious Spirits" after both of these actions, Knox and other officers felt a growing confidence in the Continental army, as well as in their own ability to command.[4]

The men's spirits also rose throughout the autumn of 1777, because of news from upstate New York. When British general John Burgoyne invaded the Hudson Valley that summer, the assault had looked like another American disaster in the making, especially after the fall of Fort Ticonderoga. In mid-October, however, reports arrived in Pennsylvania with glorious news. The northern army, Henry wrote to Lucy, had decisively beaten the British invaders, and everyone expected that they would soon capitulate.[5] Still, the campaign outside Philadelphia dragged on throughout the autumn and into the winter as both armies fought over two American-held garrisons along the Delaware River, Forts Mifflin and Mercer. Because the British needed to capture these strongholds in order to resupply their forces inside Philadelphia, the fighting was long and intense. Thus Henry remained with the army and away from his family.

The period during the Philadelphia campaign proved to be long and tense for Lucy Knox, especially as she never stopped thinking or worrying about her husband. Though always reassuring regarding his own well-being, Henry did occasionally write about the battlefield's grimmer details. He finished his letter about Germantown, for instance, not only by observing that "Gen. [Francis] Nash had his thighs taken off by a Cannon ball," a wound from which Nash would die several days later, but also by stating that many other officers had fallen that day.[6] Such information could only have heightened Lucy's fears and anxieties concerning her husband. As a result, she returned her previous habits from time to time. She complained in several letters about loneliness and pleaded with Henry to let her join him with the army. Where else, she asked, could she and their child be safer than under General Washington's protection?[7] Yet despite her periodic complaints, Lucy was not the same person she was the year before. Her letters in 1777 generally focus less on herself and more on her work in maintaining their home. In other words, her actions point to a 21-year-old woman gradually gaining confidence in her ability to deal with the many challenges of war. While occasionally depressed, she nevertheless had come to realize that the American Revolution's changes were permanent, and that she had to find ways to cope. Thus, in addition to assuming control of her parents' Boston home and property and undergoing a smallpox inoculation, Lucy worked with her brother-in-law, William, to get Henry's bookstore repaired and reopened for business. Furthermore, she obtained and shipped clothes, foodstuffs, wine, and other supplies to Henry during his time with the army. In June 1777, she chided her husband for his multiplying requests from the front, stating that "My Henry writes to me as if I lived in a land of plenty." Wartime inflation, widespread shortages, and profiteering, she explained, had made many items nearly impossible to obtain. His demands for green tea, for example, led her to state that none could be procured in Boston. The one merchant who had some "refuses paper money," and that was the only kind she now possessed. Still, she promised to keep looking.[8]

Lucy scolded Henry, moreover, for relying too heavily on his brother instead of her in business matters. For instance, when William sold two of the family's horses to raise money (per Henry's instructions), he had insisted that they be sold as a pair. Lucy had told her brother-in-law that the horses would bring in far more cash if sold separately, but William refused to budge. When the pair fetched only £75 (much less than expected), Lucy lectured Henry, insisting that she could have done better and, therefore, that he would do better to rely on her in future financial dealings. She assured Henry that "I am quite a woman of business." Lastly, Lucy continued to raise their daughter on her own, with neither her husband nor other family members to assist her. Updating Henry on little Lucy's development and health, she wrote in June that their daughter had only five smallpox marks remaining on her face after her bout with the disease, "which make her still prettier (if possible)." Her father, moreover, would be enchanted by the child when he saw her, particularly because "she is proud—and pleased as she can be."[9] Lucy understood that her work in sustaining the family on the home front was crucial, and that her efforts had moved her marital relationship toward one of equality. For example, in August 1777, speculating about Henry's postwar career, she openly worried that his military service, especially his long habit of command, would make him "too haughty" for commerce and trade. She further asserted that such an attitude would not only be unacceptable in a man of business, but also intolerable in a husband. Therefore, she pointedly explained, he must not consider himself "commander in chief" of their household, for, unlike the army, there *was* "such a thing as equal command" within marriage.[10]

The year 1777 ended on a sour note, yet one that reveals the ongoing evolution of the Knoxes' marriage. Frustrated by the campaign's protracted operations and her husband's long absence, in late November, Lucy wrote to express renewed doubts about Henry's commitment to their family and again called on him to leave the army and come home.[11] Stunned by her accusations and demands, coming as they did at the end of a grueling campaign, he angrily defended himself. Indeed, he fumed, Lucy had written words that "will long be the source of unhappiness to me."[12] Sending the letter off immediately, he soon went to bed. Henry awoke the next morning in a calmer frame of mind and once more took up his pen. Although he remained "exceedingly unhappy," he confessed his own sorrow at having sent the previous day's note, knowing it would give her pain. He realized, furthermore, that Lucy had written such sentiments in a moment of weakness and depression. Above all, Knox understood that his wife had legitimate grievances that he could hardly dismiss. Lucy had made "capital Sacrifices" for the cause, perhaps even greater than his own. Not only had the war deprived her of his love and company for over two years, but she had "lost her Father mother sisters and brother in this contest." She therefore understandably wanted him home. But he pleaded with her, saying that he could not and would not prove his love by deserting the American cause. Such an act would render him "eternally infamous" in the eyes of all those whom he respected. Thus she must not ask him again to abandon the army. But, he vowed, the remainder of his life would be dedicated entirely to her happiness. With the year's operations about to end, he also promised to come to Boston as soon as possible, to be with her and their daughter. Lastly (and perhaps best of all to Lucy), Henry pledged that when the next year's campaign commenced, he would have his wife as near to him as possible. In short, their long separations were almost over.[13]

1777

LUCY FLUCKER KNOX TO HENRY KNOX, BOSTON, MA, CA. 18–24 MAY 1777

Boston, May—

As I can think of no address that would convey an idea of my affection and esteem, I will it omit intirely rather than do injustice to my heart, a heart wholy absorbed in love and anxiety for you. I cannot at this time tell where you are nor form any judgment where you are going. We hear both Armys are in motion, but where their rout[e] is, we cannot hear nor have we yet been able to conjecture. What a situation for us who am at such a distance. How much more we suffer for you than you for yourselves. All my hopes are that it will not, cannot last. A french general, who stiles [i.e., styles] himself Commander in Chief of the Continental Artillery is now in Town. He says his appointment is from Mr. Dean, that he is going immediately to the headquarters to take the command, that he is a Major Genl. . . . Who knows but I may have my Harry again. This I am sure of, he will never suffer any one to command him in that department. If he does, he has not that Soul, which I now think him possessed of.[14]

Billy is very unwell. He has a terrible breaking out which Dr. Bull-finch[15] says is very like a leprosy. Dr. Gardiner thinks it is the itch, which has lain so long in his blood as to corrupt it to that degree that the care [i.e., cure] will be difficult.[16] He is as thin as Gabriel Johnnot was but in good spirits, and says he has an appetite, but that he is not permitted to indulge. I am very anxious about him, and at times fear we shall lose him, or at least that the humour in the blood has taken such deep root, as to embitter his future days. This will be handed you by Capt. Learjent[?] who will also deliver [to] you your box of pickles. I have seven yards of linnen for breeches for you. Am afraid to have it made up here, for fear it should be spoiled, as it cost twenty shillings per yard. Sure[ly] there must be a tailor in Morristown. If there is not, dont scold at me. Seven pound lawful for a two pair of breeches is a great deal of money, too much not to have them made neat. The pretty waistcoat I wrote you of, upon ex-amining, I found to be painted, that the first washing would have spoiled, but I will be upon the lookout for you. I wrote you last Thursday by Col. Henley,[17] and the same day by the post. Can you get some covers franked [i.e., letters that are officially marked, so they can be mailed for free]? It would save us a very great expence, an object at this day when the price of everything is so exorbitant. Indeed it is difficult to get the neccessarys of life here at any price. The evil increases daily. Beef is at eight pence a pound. If you will take half an ox neck, skins and all, you may get it for seven pence. For butter we give ten shillings a pound, for eggs two pence a piece, and for very ordinary Lisbon wine, twenty shillings a gallon. As for flour it is not to be had for any price, nor cyder nor spirit. A pretty box we are in. This and the behavior at our town meeting has almost made me a tory. Will you believe me when I tell you that Mr. Ewing is among the number who they have passed a vote to confine in close jail untill they can determine what further is to be done with them. This upon the suspicion of their being torys. I do not mean to blame them for ridding themselves of those persons who in case of an attack would take a part against them, but their meddling with that old gentleman who has been superanuated this ten years, [I] can take from [this] as their motive [is] but to share his estate. The colonels—Crafts, Revere, & Sears[18]—

are the three leading men of the place. The first of these motioned to dissolve the meeting and lett the people revenge their own cause. Quite military was it not? In short, the mob have so much the upper hand at present that there was a man to have been shot on Thursday next. The gent[lemen] dare not execute him for fear of the consequences. He is the brother to Dr. Oliver's wife, son to Col. Barye of Salem. But so much for the present. My hand trembles to such a degree that it has been as much trouble to me to write what I have, as it will be to you to read it. I believe my nerves are much weakened by the mercury I have taken. In the true meaning of the word

> Adieu
>
> your own
>
> Lucy Knox

Our lovely baby sends her pap-par- (as she calls him) a kiss

I want much to know if your soup is good for any thing. Do not mortify me by saying no.

HENRY KNOX TO LUCY FLUCKER KNOX, MORRISTOWN, NJ,
TUESDAY, 20 MAY 1777

Morris-Town 20th 1777

My much belov'd Lucy,

I wrote you from Peekskill by the last post a short Letter expecting to meet the post on my return to this place when I intended to have written you more fully.[19] I went to the posts in the Highlands in Company with General Greene upon public business, was gone one week and return'd last evening. Mr. Wm.[20] continues yet quiet in his quarters, but we have still reason to think he intends to evacuate the Jersies, tho our information is not very perfect as I believe he has pretty much the act of keeping his intentions secret. I have heard nothing further about Mr. Burgoynes going to Boston, but from some indirect circumstances it rather appears that they are disapointed of the German recruits they expected and that their Generals in America must operate with what forces they have in America with some additionals from Europe.[21] How far this may be true, I cannot at present determine, but from the present information it appears that America will have much more reason to hope for a successful

Campaign the ensuing summer than she had the last. Our forces came in pretty fast and are disciplining for the War. We are well supplied with arms and Ammunition of all species, these with the blessing of heaven will assist us much. But I am sorry to say it, we seem to be increasing most rapidly in impiety. This is a bad omen but I hope we shall mend, tho' I see no immediate prospect of it.

Were it possible, my dearest friend, I would endevor to acquaint you [with] how much and how earnestly I long for the sweet society of my Love, but it is not. The time will arrive, my dear Girl, when We shall be united not to be separated, & I very devoutly pray it may not be far off.

Where's my stocks [i.e., neckcloths] and other little matters I wrote You about. General Greene desires you would also send him half a dozen, as he is much in want of them. Have you yet return'd to Boston and how are you accommodated? Billey I hear has return'd to Boston, but not a word from you or him by the last post. I don't relish this well. Is there any pain or trouble to you in writing to me? Have you no time for the purpose. Why I think my whole Life too small for Your service. I cant endure the thought that it was thro' negligence or disinclination. The Letters must have miscarried. Pray don't let me have any more complaints on this head.

How stands Billey's inclinations to go into the service and how far has he . . . complied with his instructions, the performance of which [is essential for] him to enter the service. I wish him to go into the service, though then I see <u>his & my own Lucrative desires crush'd by the measure</u>.[22] You mention'd to me in the last Letter that the Court had pas'd some resolve or act which had embarrass'd you about the house.[23] I wish you had enclos'd it for I wish to know what process they intend ag[ains]t. the estates of people in the predicament of yourself.

Have you ever heard any thing more about your sister Hannah's being in New York or your Brother. Where can Capt. Urquhart be? I think I have heard the regiment was draughted into others and therefore sent home. Mrs. U. continuing in America looks as if she expected her husband. Altho' your parents are on [the] opposites Side from your Harry, yet its very strange it should divest them of humanity. Not a line, my god, what stuff is the human heart made of. Altho' father, mother, sister and brother has forsaken you, yet my Love your Harry will ever esteem you the best boon of heaven. . . .

Your own faithful and loving Husband HKnox

LUCY FLUCKER KNOX TO HENRY KNOX, BOSTON, MA,
MONDAY, 26 MAY 1777

My ever dear Harry,

Indulge me, my only friend, in venting my sighs and unburdening my heart to you, after sitting some hours alone giving vent to tears and heart felt grief. A young man came in, who said he left you, but last Thursday. My heart leaped for joy from the dear hope that a kind letter from you, of so short a date, would divert the train of my gloomy ideas. But this was a pleasure too great for me to enjoy. Four days only said I, where are my letters. I have none. You have none, is he sick and are you come for me? No, he was well he desired me to tell you so, but busy. I could not help it, my Harry, I answered him by bursting into tears. Nor are my present feelings unlike the agony of distress I felt at [our] parting.

Happy Mrs. Washington, happy Mrs. Gates. In short, I do not recollect an instance like my own. Mrs. Greenes, you will say, is similar. But it is not. Mrs. G and myself were not cast in one mould. If I lose this Summer, the only season when I can go from home with convenience, I never may expect to be with you again. Out of the last ten months, we have not spent six weeks together. Boston is called a place of danger. Nor do I know the place that is not, save under the wing of General Washington. If you will suffer me to come to you when Billy does, I can dispose of every article I have to great advantage. Mr. Jarviss would come into the house, and I (even if I could not be much with you) should be happy in the reflection that you were willing to gratify me, even against your own opinion. At any rate, I insist on being answered seriously, and if (which god forbid) you will not make me happy, give me so substantial reasons why you refuse me. I shall impatiently wait your answer. Do not be rash. Remember that I have no friends here, that the complaints of last Summer were not mine, for I solemnly declare, I was pleased with the inconveniencys of which that very foolish woman complained.[24] Nor would you ever have known from me that I wanted even the luxuries of life. But in this, you may believe me, I would compound to taste nothing, but bread and water half my time, might I but live within twenty miles of you. Now, it [is] romantic, but a serious truth.

Billy is much better. He has applied the external remedies, as his disorder proves to be a scotch one. Lucy is well. She is a lovely Child. I have parted with her maid which has attached her more to me. I will

bring her to see you. Can you deny yourself that pleasure? No, sure you
will not,

> in which pleasing hope I will compose
> myself to sleep. Do you ever dream of
> me my Harry? If never before, do tonight.
> LK
> Boston May 26th 1777—

HENRY KNOX TO LUCY FLUCKER KNOX, CAMP MIDDLEBROOK, NJ,
SUNDAY, 1 JUNE 1777

Camp Middlebrook[25] 1st June 1777—

I wrote you in the morning by the post, but lest I should fall into the
same error as when Capt. Lt. Lillie went,[26] I embrace the opportunity
by Major Trescot[27] first to tell you that I am well and love you infinitely.
I am exceedingly fatigued having return'd from a jaunt of 8 or 10 miles
out and the same in a most broiling sun, sweltering under a thick cloath
Wais[t]coat. This is a hint for my summer cloaths, an effective one I hope.

We had yesterday a Capt. and ten men cut to pieces by the enemies
Light horse.[28] Send me all the things which I have so repeatedly written
to you for and love me as I do you

HKnox

LUCY FLUCKER KNOX TO HENRY KNOX, BOSTON, MA,
TUESDAY, 3 JUNE–THURSDAY, 5 JUNE 1777

Boston June 3rd 1777—

My dearest dear friend,

This day, three months, I parted with the dear partner of my Soul,
happy was it for me that I did not then know how many moons would
revolve, ere I was again blessed with the sight of him. He bid me hope
our absence would be short, but alass, after three months, the prospect
instead of brightening grows darker daily. The absence of lovers I ever
thought one of the greatest evils of life. But when attended with constant
anxiety for the safety of the person beloved, tis almost insupportable. I
wish I could look in upon my Harry at this time and see him at dinner

among his friends, now interrupted by business and now by a wish for his companion, his friend, his Lucy. Do you not often wish for me, my love. Say that you do, I beseech you, and tell me honestly and sincerely when you expect to see me. Our dear little girl goes alone.[29] You would be delighted to see the little tottler. She is proud, and pleased as can be. She has five pitts of the small pox in her face, which make her still prettier (if possible), than before she had them. My arm remains troublesome yet owing to my own imprudence in attempting to heal it too soon, but Lucys is quite well.

Mr. Russell[30] yesterday brought me a letter from you of the twenty fourth of May refering to one I shall receive tomorrow by the post. I am heartily sorry for your loss which I fear will be irreparable. But if there is cambrick to be had in Salem, Newbury or Portsmouth, you shall have it. I think you were to blame to trust a person of his appearance with your Cloaths. I thought they were to have been Johns care. Did he take your [illegible] with him and tell me honestly how many paper dollars you are the worse for him.[31]

My Harry writes to me as if I lived in a land of plenty. Six pounds of best green tea is what I have endeavored to the utmost of my power to procure. I wrote you last week that I expected some, but it belongs to Bill Turner and he refuses paper money for it.[32] However, you shall have a couple of pounds by the first opportunity tho it were my last gunie [i.e., guinea] that purchased it. The horses fetched but seventy five pounds owing to your not entrusting me with the sale of them. I wished to have had them sold separate, but master Wm was of a different opinion nor could he be persuaded. You had better make me your future agent. I'll assure you, I am quite a woman of business, but good bye for the present. I am going to drink Tea with Mrs. Russell in hopes to hear some particulars of you.

Will continue my letter tomorrow—

LK

June 4th

I drank tea last evening at Mr. Russells and had the pleasure to hear that my Harry is well, in good spirits, but not a word of sending for me. Do you remember your going to Newbury my love, how unhappy you were to leave me for two long days. We daily expect your waggon in town, which will take you some choice madeira, some good old [i.e., well-aged] spirit, some loaf sugar, and some other little matters. Billy intends to send his baggage by the same opportunity. He is still low in flesh and spirits, lives intirely upon milk, and is in my opinion very unfit for a campaign. Pray, if you see General Arnold, make my Comp[limen]t to him and ask him what he would have me do with those things that he left with me to be presented to Miss D.³³ Tell him Mr. Blodget³⁴ says he will part with them, which if he will do, Mrs. Genl. Greene will be glad to have one of them. I beg to have a scarf which is in the trunk, if he will part with them. Desire him to send the invoice either to Mr. Blodget, who is his agent, or to me. But at any rate, I must not relinquish the scarf, as I cannot get any thing to make me one. Farewell my love may

>angels guard and keep you and soon
>restore you to your afflicted Wife
>L Knox

June 5th

I last evening received three letters from you by the post. For the first of them I will not say I thank you, as (tho pretty long) it contained not one tender expression but was a continued scold from beginning to end. In the first place, you resent my little raillery of your horses, and take revenge upon poor old Romeo.³⁵ You then attack me about your Brother, and unkindly say it would have been but decent in me to have wrote you whether he was dead or alive. To this I answer that when I wrote the letter you refer to, your Brother . . . should also write to you. Nor did I know till some hours after it was gone that he did not. . . . I do not think I am answerable for him. You often talk much of your affection for him as if I had objected to it. So, my Harry, be assured I la[ment] the loss of much [i.e., many] near connections to wish to deprive one so dear to me of the enjoyment of [that.] [I] hope that your affection for him is not quite so great as what you feel for me, who I must think have a right to the greatest love. In him, you will soon be happy, as he is determined to sett out in one or two weeks, but for me I see no end to my friendless unprotected state again. Adieu my all in life

>your LK

Mr. Russell says you complain I do not date my letters, I did not think my Harry would have made me look so little.³⁶

Boston, June 19th 1777

Dearest, best of men,

Is it possible, is there a dawn of hope, may I expect to be again blessed with him who forms a part of my very soul, whose presence I esteem the greatest good that this world can afford. Yes, it is possible, my Harry says it is, and I am happy. But should he yet disappoint me, should he stoop to be told he is unequal to his command and must take a partner, how mortified and wretched should I be. But I speak of an absolute impossibility, my dear Harry has too great a Soul. Yet I have another dread, should General De Coudier accept of a command . . . to the Artillery, my fall would be like phaet[h]ons.[37] My love would perhaps remain as he is and poor I must still want a protector, a friend, a husband.

Our little darling gives me many an anxious hour being subject to short breathing upon taking the least cold. She is now unwell, but Dr. Gardiner tells me it is owing wholly to her breeding teeth. Pray to heaven to spare her to us. She is a lovely desirable child, and I trust will one day make our hearts glad. I wrote you some time since that she went alone, she speaks but few words but those very plain. Billy is gone to Salem. He will I expect be back before the post goes out. If not, be satisfied from me that he is almost well. I thought at one time we should lose him but now, by the help of a milk diet, I think him quite out of danger. I meant to have wrote you a very long letter, but my old pain in my stomach prevents. In the dear hope that o[v]er three weeks, I shall call you mine. I commit you to the care of heaven.

Yours, wholly yours
L.K

Your wagon set off on Sunday last with a cask of excellent Maderia, one of port and one of Lisbon, a barrel of spirit, three loafs of sugar, three pounds of best green tea, one dozen of chocolate, a box of coffee, three pounds of pepper, and a case of very fine brandy, sweet meats, a very elegant black Silk coat lined with white, two pair of neat breeches, six stocks, three pocket handkerchiefs, a black ditto, three pounds of [gun]powder in a bag. A Lieut. Proctor who has the care of the wagon is to receive at Springfield the other matters which blundering Mason[38] has kept all this time. But I hope to see them all again soon. Many of the articles are not to be had

here for any price. Therefore I wish my Harry to order them back. Should
he come himself, which believe me would give me more pleasure than his
being created a prince, my present state of suspence has almost deprived
me of reason. You will I am sure release me from it as soon as possible, but
be sure you do not disapoint me. If you do after raising my hopes to such an
height, I shall be more unhappy than I have ever been yet.

HENRY KNOX TO LUCY FLUCKER KNOX, CAMP MIDDLEBROOK, NJ,
SATURDAY, 21 JUNE 1777

Camp Middlebrook 21st June 1777

There is no describing the pleasure which I receive from the perusal
of my Lucys Letters, the dear partner of my Soul. I have her Letter beginning the 3d & ending the 5th instant now before me. Language cannot
convey my thanks to you for it, my Life shall be devoted to you and you
alone. All my Affections center in you. Ah Harry, say you, why then are
you absent. My Lucy knows the reason, and high Heaven knows that no
other earthly inducement would have been sufficient to effect it. Yes,
my Love, I miss you and my heart stalks sulkily alone. Tho surrounded
by numbers, wrapt up in itself, it gloomily surveys what it gives up for
the present. But my darling babe, fully grown, presents itself in a suppli-
cating posture for help from some British barbarian who is just on the
eve of ravishing her! Some prostrate young widow beleft [i.e., beset], or
her affectionate husband by some Herk or Jessenes for refusing his wife
to their brutal Lust, some mournful old widow whose husband died in
prison because he nobly stood forth in opposition to their cursed tyranny
and whose children they have sold for Slaves, all present themselves, and
in the names, the sacred names of virtue, religion and God by me to lend
a helping hand to rescue them from these most tremendous of human
Miseries. These motives my dearest Girl are the only ones which keeps
your affectionate Harry from you. I most devoutly pray God, that all
impediments may be speedily remov'd to our happy meeting.

I have written a pretty particular account to Harry of the operations
of the enemy since my last note to you.[39] I then expected that the enemy
would oblige us to come to some capital action with them, but poor fellows, from all the intelligence we are able to collect, their views are very
different at present in this place from fighting.

The militia pour'd in to our assistance and had they [i.e., the enemy] attempted to have gone to the Delaware, we should probably [have] ruined[?] them. These hectoring Gentlemen who a few days ago were swearing they would go to Philadelphia, God willing or not, are at this very instant making the best of their way out of the Jersies. We are harassing them much. We have the most respectable body of Continental troops that America ever had, no[ne] going home to morrow to such, hardy brave fellows who are as willing to go to heaven by the way of a Bayonet or Lance as any other mode. With the blessing of Heaven, I have great hopes in the Course of this Campaign that we shall do something clever. I think in five days there will not be an enemy in Jersies. But I fear they will go up the North River[40] where perhaps they may plague us more. The Inhabitants here appear'd as one man and as people actuated by revenge for the many rapes and murders Committed on them. While I am writing this a party of four thousand are going after the enemy, & this afternoon there will be as many more.

I have this instant received your beloved Epistle of the 12th instant,[41] and am exceding sorry that the want of my cloaths should make you so very unhappy. You have done all in your power I am sure, but that old scoundrel who had the management [of them] I shall not forgive in a hurry. Yes, my Love, our hearts are riveted so firmly to be happy, when absent every hour brings me fresh proof of it, and yet the great duty one owes to their Country. The Congress have taken some previous steps with Respect to Mr. De Coudre. They have resolved that Mr. Dean has exceeded his Commission and that they cannot ratify his treaty with Mr. De Coudre. Pretty this, to bring a Gentleman 1200 Leagues to affront him. . . . Under all circumstances and at all times I am your devoutly affectionate

Henry Knox

HENRY KNOX TO LUCY FLUCKER KNOX, MIDDLEBROOK, NJ,
SUNDAY, 29 JUNE 1777

Camp Middlebrook 29th June 1777

My dear Lucy,

I have the pleasure of yours of the 19th instant for which I most tenderly thank you. Pity it is that Lovers so exceedingly attach'd to each other as we are should be separated by the horrors of war, but then, my dear Lucy, your Harry is free and will in time join you again. This expression as occasion'd by the british barbarians tearing the tender Husband from the affectionate wife by the most unrelenting, unfeeling hand of power. They have made almost a perfect defect of every thing in their late excursion. I write you that on last Sunday they retreated to Amboy with precipitation where they were busily employed in transporting their baggage, tents, Waggons, Horses, Heavy Artillery and a great part of their troops. Amboy is approachable only by one Road. The left flank is sever'd by the Raritan River and the right by the sound of Staten Island. On Tuesday morning last we push'd down part of Lord Stirlings division to reconnoitre them, but found them so strongly posted as not to be attacked and numbers on our side would answer no purpose. Lord Stirlings party retired to Ash Swamp, distant from Amboy about 6 miles. A large part of the Army took post at [illegible] Town below the heights which our army have occupied for some time past and about 4 or 5 miles in the rear of Lord Stirling. On Thursday morning the enemy, having in the night preceeding brought back all their force from Staten Island, push'd out without tents or baggage, having only light Artillery with a view of suprizing Lord Stirling's division. . . . Maxwells and Conways[42] Brigades, under the Command of Lord S., were posted on two main roads leading from Amboy to the heights. The enemy came in a bye road between the two large roads and effectually separated the two brigades, and for some time put them in a very critical situation. However, Lord Stirling's, who was with Maxwells brigade, after a severe action with 9 or 10 times his number, was oblig'd to retire to the Field with the loss of three pieces of Cannon and some men. . . . Lord Stirling retir'd to Westfield and Conways [brigade] retir'd to the main body. Upon the retiring of Lord Stirling's division, the enemy push'd for our left flank with great Industry, which occasioned our Army to occupy their old ground only more inclined to the left. . . . The enemy finding we had taken possession of our strong Grounds again, retir'd to Westfield, plundering every thing before them, and destroying and burning Houses in [a] manner scandalous to Humanity. They stay'd at Westfield on the night of the 26th and the next day [went] to Morris Town, stripping the County as they went as far as was in their power. Yesterday, the 28th, they retir'd to Amboy. We had large parties of light troops continually on their flanks to prevent the plundering [of] the unhappy people who were near to them, and have taken a number of prisoners from them. Our Camp is so

Strong & must put an enemy under such very great disadvantages if he attacks it, that His Excellency thought [it] proper not to descend to the plains to fight them. Had we made this mannoevre, so much wish'd for by Mr. Howe, he would have immediately taken possession of it and put us under the very disadvantage that we had him under. Their officers, superior and inferior, are very abusive, frequently damning and swearing "they had given the Americans every opportunity to fight and they would now attack their Camp." But this action, this very honorable and worthy set, declined him [i.e., Washington] from very prudential motives. They give out they are going to New England, but we suppose the North River to be their object.[43]

Had they not taken the 3 pieces of Cannon, their last blustering trip would have made the modest men on that side blush. I dare say they will find some mode to make it appear a very capital measure. Our business is to defend the Country, their business is to attack us [and] they were within one mile and an half of our left flank. Why if they were so exceedingly anxious to fight did they not attempt it. Droll policy to retire and push off two or three hundred miles to attack the Americans when they could find them within one and a half mile in full sight and view. Sr. Wm. Himself, its said, was very free with his epitephs as if we were oblig'd by any turn[?], human or divine, like Don Quixot[e] to descend into the plain to take a lusty boxing match with him. If he laughs at us, we can [in] return laugh at him and shall in the course of two days laugh him out of one of the finest provinces in the World. The next Letter you will receive from me will perhaps be on our march to Hudson's River or perhaps to New England. The Waggon which my Lucy has loaded with good things and sent on to me is not yet arriv'd. I never enjoyed a better state of health than amid the bustle and fatigue I undergo. God preserve you.

HKnox

LUCY FLUCKER KNOX TO HENRY KNOX, BOSTON, MA,
MONDAY, 30 JUNE 1777

Boston June 30th 1777—

My Only Love,

Did my Harry lett the 23rd of this month pass by unnoticed or did it occur to his mind that it was the anneversary of his wedding day, was he so much engaged in publick business, perhaps in scenes of horror and distress, as not to spare one sigh for me. Tell me dear and tell me truly, did you think of me, did you reflect upon the vast difference in my situation, at this time & at that. Oh, my Love, the world did not then afford a being more happy than myself, but from what cause did that happiness arise—from the dear prospect of spending my life with you, from the pleasing idea that you were wholly mine, from the dear the blessed hope that in you I should find a constant protector, a tender and indulgent companion, a fond and affectionate friend, to share with me for life, in all my joys, and all my troubles. But oh alass, how great is the reverse. Instead of spending our lives together, how far and how long have we been asunder, and deprived of you, I am at once deprived of my protector, my companion, and my friend. Far from sharing my troubles, you cause them all by exposing your precious life. Oh, my Harry, did you know the distress of my mind, I cannot think you would suffer me to be thus afflicted. I am not without hopes that the affair of Mr. De Coudre may produce happy effects yet, tho so long a delay. Perhaps they want your assistance in the present exigence, but as soon as that over, they will shew what they are.[44] Billy is very anxious for the event—he wishes much to go to the army provided you remain there, but not without. We are

    Genl. H B Knox[45]

HENRY KNOX TO LUCY FLUCKER KNOX, POMPTON PLAINS, NJ, SUNDAY, 13 JULY 1777

    Camp Pompton plains[46] 13th July 1777—

My dearest friend,

    I have received yours of 2 & 3d July[47] and thank you most sincerely for the same, tho' I confess [to] you the dearest partner of my soul, that the shortness of Your two last letters were not very agreable to me. As long as Providence has parted us for a time, I wish to hear as much and as often from you as possible it is the only alleviation our state will admit.

    We have received the most chagrining news of the evacuation of Ticonderoga, pregnant in my opinion with the most disagreable consequences of any thing during the war. As we have not heard Genl. St. Clair's account of the matter, we suspend our Judgement with respect to the propriety of the evacuation.[48] Tho we Dread the Consequences, we shall send some reinforcements to Genl. Schuyler.[49] This event must rouse N[ew] England to a man, or they must submit to have their frontiers bath'd in blood. Burgoyne publishes a kind of manifesto in the style of a Gascoon [i.e., gascon, or a boastful, swaggering person]. If he does not succeed, he will appear most ridiculous indeed. I have received the valuable Cargo you sent me in the Waggons for which I hope to give you ten thousand kisses. Beg Mr. Jarvis to send me a Bill of the wine as Genl. Greene is Copartner and I want to settle with him.

I suppose Master Billey to be so military mad as to have set out before this. I confess to you, my dear Lucy, it is much against my will he enters, upon your account but no other, for while he staid [in Boston] you had a disinterested friend and protector in him. If he has not yet set out, I wish him to stay to see what Course Genl. Howe will take with his army, which is on the point of a move, having been all embark'd for some days. We pin him to the north River as being the most rational plan of forming a Junction with . . . Burgoyne. I will try about the Muslin you desire me to get, but I am one hundred miles from Bethlehem. Therefore, it will be some time before I can get them.

My Lucy regrets that she is not with her faithful Harry, so does he most sincerely. Mrs. Greene arriv'd here two or three days ago & must again part with her Genl., who is now on his way to the North River, as we all are. Mrs. Bland has been at a distance from Colonel Bland for a long time.[50] Mrs. Washington or no other Ladies but those I've mention'd are any ways near.

The Letter which I wrote to congress to know whether they had appointed the Mr. du C—— has in Conjunction with the Letters of Generals Sullivan & Greene produc'd a Resolve, purporting the said Letters to be an infringement on the Liberties of the people, as tending to influence the decisions of Congress, and expecting that we make acknowledgements to them for so singular an "impropriety." The Letters and resolve I will inclose you at some other time. Conscious of the rectitude of my intention, . . . I shall make [no] acknowledgements whatever. Tho my Country is too much press'd at present to resign, yet perhaps this Campaign will be the last.[51] But I am determined to contribute my mite to the defence of the Country in Spite of every obstacle, and I shall be happy to set it in peace, which I hope will be in the course of this Campaign.

May God preserve You adieu

HKnox

LUCY FLUCKER KNOX TO HENRY KNOX, BOSTON, MA,
THURSDAY, 17 JULY 1777

Boston July 17th 1777—

My All in Life,

Thank you, my dear Harry, for your kind letter by last evening's post.
It gave me great pleasure, tho I was much disapointed it did not tell me
for certain whether I shall see you here or not. If I do not, I am resolved
nothing shall prevent my coming to you early in September but your pos-
itive refusal, in which case, I will try to be as indifferent as I shall then
think you are.

Billy set off on Friday last, and will without doubt reach you long
before this will. I miss him more than I expected. The Colo. is so much
engaged with military matters that I do not see him once in a week,[52] and
as for Jarviss, [s]he is as mad as ever, she fancys that Sr. Wm. is coming
this way and is very unhappy in consequence of it. Poor girl, she is near
laying in.

I did not need an inducement to kiss my sweet little girl, but depend
upon my executing your comission, for which I shall expect my pay.
Do you know, my Love, that you have been absent from me almost five
months. I am affraid you will fall into the usual error of absent lovers.
That indifference will take place of that refined affection which you have
entertained for me. If it should, ah me, what shall I do.

By a letter from Mrs. Tyng[53] to Aunt Waldo, we learn that papa enjoys
his three hundred [pounds] a year as Secretary of this province. Droll,
is it not. I will not say a word of Ticonderoga, for fear I should be saucy,
nor of the retaking of the fox frigate.[54] The former, I wish to hear your
opinion of. Oh that my Harry would return home and earn something
for his little Girl. Tis true your present pay is a genteel support, but you
will not lay any of it by the prospect to me if you stay in the army. So very
gloomy, but you know what you are about. Good by to you my dearest
blessing.

> May heaven continue to protect you prays your
> tenderly affectionate wife
> LK—

Billy left with me free of incumbrances [and] eighty six pounds—

———

HENRY KNOX TO LUCY FLUCKER KNOX, "20 MILES FROM
PHILADELPHIA,"[55] PA, TUESDAY, 12 AUGUST 1777

Camp 20 miles from Philadelphia 12 Aug.t

I received your letter from Newbury port of the 29th ultimo.[56] It gives
me great pleasure that my dear Lucy went in such agreeable Company
and to a place for which I have a peculiar respect. The Gentlemen there,
with whom I am acquainted, are in my opinion some of the most virtuous, public spirited, patriots on the Continent, and when I do return to
my Lucy again I may have some serious thoughts of settling there. I am
glad of the happiness which results from the Connection you find with
Mrs. Smith & family. Mr. Howe took his departure from these Capes on
the 31st instant, nor has been heard off [i.e., of] untill 2 days ago an express arriv'd with news of his being off Sinepuxent county[57] to the South
suppos'd for Cheasapeak Bay. This if true, (which I am much inclined to
disbelieve) [it] must be a feint, either the N[orth] River or Philadelphia
must be his object. I should suppose if he pursued his true interest that
the post of N[ew] York[?] to be the immediate design of his attention. But
he reasons for himself, and its my opinion that this summer he reasons
himself out of America.

We were going up to Corryells Ferry supposing the enemy were gone
eastward, but we are now stopp'd until we hear further. The season here
is infinitely hot, too hot for good Whigs. It almost makes me believe the
materiality of Fire. Tis a Sweet consolation my Love that our two Souls
are so firmly rivetted to each other. Yes, I am attach'd to you by all the
powers of my mind for life. Mr. Burgoyne will push himself untill he
finds a stone wall to break his head against. I hope that will not be too
soon untill all parts of the Machine may harmonize which is to work his
destruction. If the Genius of America Guards her [in] this Campaign,
all of the misfortunes which we have all felt [will] be only blessings in
disguise. How does Mrs. Jarvis and her Whig Gallant. Give my love to
them. Master Bill bears the fatigues of the Campaign like a Soldier, and
they are not very few, for we live like soldiers, though not to the greatest
hardships. . . . Both ships the Tatar and Hero are out. You do not like the
scheme. I am sorry for it. I do [like it] if it succeeds, if not, I shall dislike
it. War is nothing, and I can see no reason why individuals may not make
war as ever on his own account as to assist it on account of the public.[58]

I must sincerely and devoutly pray the great Governor of the World to
take you into his kind keeping, and am your

>unalterably affectionate
>Harry Knox

LUCY FLUCKER KNOX TO HENRY KNOX, BOSTON, MA,
SATURDAY, 23 AUGUST 1777

>Boston August 23rd 1777—

My Dearest Friend,

I wrote you a line by the last post just to lett you know I was alive
which indeed was all I could then say with propriety for I had serious
thoughts that I never should see you again, so much was I reduced by
only four days of illness. But by help of a good constitution I am surprisingly better today. I am now to answer your three last letters in one of
which you ask for a history of my life. It is my love so barren of adven-
tures and so replete with repetition that I fear it will afford you little
amusement. However, such as it is, I give it [to] you. In the first place, I
rise about eight in the morning (a lazy hour you will say, but the day after
that, is full long for a person in my situation). I presently after[wards]
sitt down to my breakfast, where a page in my book, and a dish of tea,
employ me alternately for about an hour. When after seeing that family
matters go on right, I repair to my work, my book, or my pen, for the rest
of the forenoon. At two oclock I usually take my solitary dinner where
I reflect upon my past happiness when I used to sitt at the window
watching for my Harry, and when I saw him coming my heart would
leap for joy, when he was all my own and never happy from me, when
the bare thought of six months absence would have shocked him. To
divert these ideas I place my little Lucy by me at [the] table, but the more
engaging her little actions are, so much the more do I regret the absence
of her father who would take such delight in them. In the afternoon, I
commonly take my chaise, and ride into the country or go to drink tea
with one of my few friends. They consist of Mrs. Jarviss, Mrs. Sears,
Mrs. Smith, Mrs. Pollard and my Aunt Waldo. I have many acquaintances
beside these whom I visit but not without ceremony. When with any of
the former, I often spend the evening, but when I return home, how shall

describe my feelings to find myself intirely alone, to reflect that the only friend I have in the world is at such an immense distance from me. To think that he may be sick and I cannot assist him. Ah poor me, my heart is ready to burst. You who know what a trifle would make me unhappy, can conceive what I suffer now. When I seriously reflect that I have lost my father, Mother, Brother and Sisters, intirely lost them, I am half distracted. True, I chearfully resigned them for one far dearer to me than all of them, but I am totally deprived of him. I have not seen him for almost six months, and he writes me without pointing out any method by which I may ever expect to see him again. Tis hard my Harry, indeed it is. I love you with the tenderest, the purest affection, I would undergo any hardships to be near you and you will not lett me. Suppose this campaign should be like the last, carried into the winter. Do you intend not to see me in all that time. Tell me dear what your plan is.

I wrote you that the Hero sailed while I was at Newbery. She did, but has been cruising about from harbour to harbour since, to get met. She is now here, and will sail in a day or two for France.[59]

I wish I had fifty guinies to spare to send by her for neccessarys, but I have not. The very little gold we have must be reserved for my Love in case he should be taken, for friends in such a case are not too common. I am more distressed from the hott weather than any other fears. God grant you may not go farther southward. If you should I positively will come too. I believe Genl. Howe is a paltry fellow, but happy for as that he is so. Are you not much pleased with the news from the Northward. We think it is a great affair and a confirmation of St. Clairs villainy baseness. I hope he will not go unpunished. We hear also that Genl. Gates is to go back to his command. If so, Master Schuyler cannot be guiltless. It is very strange, you never mentioned that affair in any of your letters.[60] What has become of Mrs. Greene, do you all live together, or how do you manage. Is Billy to remain with you, payless or is he to have a commission. If the former, I think he had much better remained where he was. If he understood business, he might without a capital [outlay] have made a fortune. People here, without advancing a shilling, frequently clear hundreds in a day. Such chaps, as Eben Oliver,[61] are all men of fortune, while persons who have ever lived in affluence, are in danger of want. Oh that you had less of the military man about you, you might then after the war have lived at ease all the days of your life. But now I don't know what you will do. Your being long acustomed to command will make you too haughty for mercantile matters, tho I hope you will not consider yourself as commander in chief of your own house. But be convinced, tho not in the affair of Mr. Coudre,[62] that there is such a thing as equal command. I send this by Capt. Randal[63] who says he expects to remain with you. Pray how many of these lads have you. I am sure they must be very expensive. I am in want of some square dollars, which I expect from you to by me a peace of linen, an article I can do no longer without having had no recruit of that kind for almost five years. Girls in general when they marry are well stocked with those things, but poor I had no such advantage.

Little Lucy who is without exception the sweetest child in the world, sends you a kiss but where shall I take it from say you, from the paper I hope. But, dare I say, I sometimes fear that a long absence [and] the force of bad example may lead you to forget me at sometimes. To know that it ever gave you pleasure to be in company with the finest woman in the world, would be worse than death to me. But it is not so, my Harry is too just, too delicate, too sincere, and too fond of his Lucy to admit the most remote thought of that distracting kind. Away with it. Don't be angry with me, my Love. I am not jealous of you[r] affection. I love you with a love as true and sacred as ever entered the human heart, but from a diffidence of my own merit, I sometimes fear you will Love me less after being so long from me. If you should, may my life end before I know it, that I may die thinking you wholly mine.

Adieu my love LK

HENRY KNOX TO LUCY FLUCKER KNOX, DERBY, PA,
MONDAY, 25 AUGUST 1777

Derby, 7 Miles below Philadelphia 25 Aug 1777

The post not having arriv'd at Camp, I have it not in my power to acknowledge the receipt of the Letters of <u>my Lucy</u>. I was in hopes by this post to have acquainted you that I was coming nearer to you, as a remove of the army had been determin'd upon towards the N[orth] River. But after we had march'd a few Miles, an express arriv'd informing [us] of the enemy being in Chesepeak Bay near 300 miles up from the Capes of Virginia, the design as suppos'd to possess a neck of Land from Christeen River[64] to the head of Elk river, 12 miles across by which they would separate seven Counties of Delaware and Maryland, and two of Virginia. The inhabitants of these counties or at least a great number of them are disa-fected, and capable of supplying Sr. Wm. with provisions in plenty. Others again suppose that he intends to land there & march to Philadelphia.

Both of these conjectures are in my opinion, almost totally wrong. I believe Philadelphia may be his principall object, but it is not by the way of Chesepeak. The plain natural way by the Delaware will be his route. The Army will take post below Wilmington about 16 miles from this place and on to which they are now on their march. Two divisions will be there to night and two others with the Park [i.e., collection] of Artil-lery will be there tomorrow night.

The army Yesterday march'd thro the City of Philadelphia. Their excellent appearance and marching astonish'd the Tories, who are very downcast in the respectability of the army. I was so unhappy as to [be] absent at this time, when we lay at Bucks County and the Army had determin'd to move to the Jersies. Genl. Greene and my self begg'd the favor of his Excellency's permission to pay a visit to Bethlehem, to purchase some things for my dear dear Lucy, distant about forty miles. The weather was extremely hot and we set out 4 oClock in the afternoon and arriv'd at Bethlehem next morning at 9 oClock, where an express from the General was waiting for us with orders to return immediately. He had rode all night, however we first visited all parts of this singularly happy place, where all the inhabitants seem to vie with each other in hu-mility and brotherly kindness. I inquired for the suit you desired me, but they inform'd me that Gauze was so extremely scarce that they have not even a pair of ruffles, but that if you would send Gauze for any things you might want, they should be done as soon as possible, which indeed will be pretty quick. I have no conception of the quickness with which the Girls execute their tambour [i.e., a type of embroidery] or flowering, an Inch a minute for certain. I shall reserve myself the pleasure of returning [to] this place untill I have the ineffable pleasure of seeing you. When that will be I cant say but please God at all events before Christmas.

We joined the Army after a most fatiguing Jaunt of 100 miles Yester-day about an hour after they had pass'd thro Philadelphia.

The news of the militia at the Northward under General Stark must give you singular satisfaction, indeed, it was a noble stroke for the oldest troops, but the achievement by Militia doubly enhances the value of the action. America will ever be free if all her sons executed themselves equally.[65] The violence which I am oblig'd to exert [every effort to] restrain myself from bursting every tye of obligation [to] my country, and uniting myself inseparably to my dearest Love is past description.[66]

We were made for each other's happiness, and I most sincerely execrate the wretches who have been the Cause that we were even a moment asunder, and Consider it as time lost to happiness. I love you purely and devoutly, all other affections whether of Brother or friend is nothing to the order of affection I have for you. May God soon bring us together again & I sincerely beg him to bless you and your babe.

> I am my dearest Love
> Your truly affectionate Husband
> HKnox—

LUCY FLUCKER KNOX TO HENRY KNOX, BOSTON, MA, 28 AUGUST 1777

Boston August 28th 1777

My Dear Harry,

Not a line not a word from my Harry by the post. What can be the cause, is he Sick, no, god forbid, or has he forgot me, that would be equally bad. What shall I think, that he was out of the way. That he is well I will hope he is and that a variety of Philadelphia beautys have not rivaled his little girl I will also hope.

I wrote you a long epistle this week by Capt. Randal, who said he was going direct to you, be you where you might. The other day Capt. Bliss called to see me and beged I would mention him in my letters.[67] He says he wrote you frequently upon the subject of his exchange but has never obtained an answer. Pray write him or do something for him if it is in your power—for his familys sake. . . .

Your Man Jacksons wife is very unhappy that she hears nothing from him as is Johns father. Having over slept myself this morning, I have not time to say more than that your little girl and myself are well, and to refer you for the state of my mind to my last [letter].

> May he who is able and ready
> to help you send his blessings unnumbered
> upon you—Adieu, my Love, Adieu, your
> tenderly affectionate
> Lucy Knox

LUCY FLUCKER KNOX TO HENRY KNOX, BOSTON, MA,
THURSDAY, 28 AUGUST 1777

August 28th

Capt. Randal not going so soon as I expected, I have the pleasure to add another line. I forgot to tell you how much I am mortified at having received an epistle from you wrote upon the second of this month wherein you take no notice of it being your Lucys birthday. Such apparent trifles are not over looked by persons who tenderly Love, but it was the hurry of business, it was not, it could not be want of affection.

Colo. Jackson tells me that he writes all the news, therefore you will excuse me upon that head, he has doubtless informed you of our great rejoicing for the late advantage gained at the Northward. The bells were rung, guns fired, the people shouted in the streets, there were fireworks of various kinds and to compleat the scene every man you saw, from the fine gentleman to the porter, were as happy as liquor could make them. I will leave you to make your own comments, for my part I thought it highly ridiculous.[68]

From the first commencement of this horrid War, I never felt as distressed with regard to you, as I do now. The extreme heat of the climate, the dread of your going farther southward, the fatigue you must undergo, make me truly unhappy, and what is still worse, I can look forward to nothing to relieve me. Did I know that you were determined to see me at any certain period, even tho it were not so soon as I wish, yet I should have the pleasure of counting the hours till it arrived. But now I have nothing to look up to and if this winter must be spent like the last, my Soul, what will become of me.

You have no idea what the sufferings of the people will be in this town this winter. Wood, there is none. Salt, little or none, and common butchers meat at eighteen pence p[e]r pound. Butter is half a dollar, little candles are six pence a piece, and all other things in the same proportion. In short, I am ashamed to tell you what I have spent since Billy left me, lest you should charge me with what I do not deserve. Wood is now ten dollars a load, in the heat of summer. If I am with you this winter, it will be hundreds in your pocket. My horse, if here, will cost a little estate and I cannot be without.

Billy has wrote the Colo. a letter as formal as mine.[69] Tell him when he can write less [formally] as he behaves, I shall be happy to correspond with him, but I would give a farthing for a hundred such letters as his last. He never once mentioned my Harry thro the whole of it, and what care I for any other subject,

> but this is imposing upon good
> nature—good bye take care of yourself and remember
> your
> Lucy Knox—

HENRY KNOX TO LUCY FLUCKER KNOX, CAMP NEAR SCHUYLKILL, PA, SATURDAY, 13 SEPTEMBER 1777

Camp near Schuylkill 13 Sept.r 1777—

My dearest Life,

Most willingly would your Harry relieve all Your cares and anxiety on this and on every other account, chearfully would he take them on his own shoulders for the sake [of] you whom he loves more than Life. I received your kind Letter I believe by Mr. Livingston, altho deliver'd to me by another hand. The irregularity of the posts has prevented my writing in proper time to you. But my heart did not omit communicating with yours. I always console myself with the conversation of my Love. War, nor none of its concomitant Honors, is sufficient to put my Lucy from my mind for a moment.

My dear Girl will be pleas'd to hear of her Harry's safety. Yes, my Love, heaven who is our guide has protected him in the day of Battle. You will hear with this letter of the most severe action that has been fought this war between our army and the enemy. Our people behav'd well, but Heaven frown'd on us in a degree. We were oblig'd to retire, after very considerable slaughter of the enemy. They dar'd not pursue a single step. If they advance, we shall fight them again before they get possession of Philadelphia, but of this they will be cautious. My corps did me great honor, they behav'd like men, contending for everything thats valuable.[70] Except my writing You a long letter, inclos'd you have the account which I have sent to the president of the Council. I shall have the happiness to be with you in two months most certainly. I regret it to be so long but its impossible to quit. I am with the utmost attachment that the human heart is capable of Yours most Affectionately

> HKnox

LUCY FLUCKER KNOX TO HENRY KNOX, BOSTON, MA,
THURSDAY, 18 SEPTEMBER 1777

Boston Sept.r 18th 1777—

My Dear Harry,

The situation of the Army at this time renders it unsafe to unbosom myself by letter, lest it should fall into wrong hands. Therefore, [I] shall only inform you that your wife and Daughter are both alive, and in tolerable good health.

I omited writing until this morning in hopes to have received something from you by the post, but to my great disapointment, I had not a line. I rec.d a few words by I know not who on Monday last which informed me you were well on the first of this month.[71] But alass where and how you are now, I cannot tell, my anxiety is not to be expressed by words. Oh, my Harry, will you not send for me to save me so much pain.

I would write more had I time, but you have no reason to complain as in the last fortnight I have forwarded six or seven letters. May he without whose permission not a sparrow falls, preserve you—Adieu my Love.

Your LK

———

HENRY KNOX TO LUCY FLUCKER KNOX, POTTSGROVE, PA,
WEDNESDAY, 24 SEPTEMBER 1777

Pottsgrove 24th Sept.r 1777—

My dearest hope and only Love,

I have received your letter dated somewhere about the beginning of this month, it was short because my dear Girl had lyen [i.e., lain] too long in her bed and the post was about going. I wrote you from near Schuylkill on the 13th giving you an account of the Battle of Brandywine on the 11th instant. The same day I wrote you, we cross'd the Schuylkill in order to try the Issue of another appeal <u>to him who directs all human events.</u> After some days manoevring, we came in sight of the enemy and drew up in order of Battle, which the enemy declin'd, but a most violent rain coming on oblig'd us to change our position, in the course of which nearly <u>all</u> the musket cartridges of the Army that had been deliver'd to the men were damag'd consisting of above 400,000. This was a most terrible stroke to us, and owing entirely to the badness of the cartouch[e] boxes [i.e., cartridge boxes] which had been provided for the army.

This unfortunate event oblig'd us to retire in order to get supply'd with so essential an article as cartridg's, after which we forded the Schuylkill in order to be opposite to the enemy. Accordingly we took post opposite to them at a place call'd Flatland Ford. A defensive war is the most difficult to guard against because one is always oblig'd to attend to the feints of the enemy. To defend an extended River when it is unfordable is almost impossible, but when the River is fordable in every part, it becomes impracticable & nothing is more easy than to cross it. This we well knew and the enemy knew it full well too. On the afternoon of the 21st, they made a most rapid march of 10 or 12 miles to our right, this oblig'd us to follow them. They kindled large fires and, in the next night, march'd as rapidly back and cross'd at a place where we had but few Guards and immediately cross'd and push'd towards Philadelphia and will this morning enter the city without opposition.[72] They have declin'd to combat our army and have taken possession of the prize for which we both contended. We fought one battle for it and it was no deficiency in knowing[?] that we lost the day. We fully intended to have tried the efficacey of another day which we intended should have been well fought, but heaven interposed. They boastingly gave out that they wish'd not to go to Philadelphia for two months to come, but have taken the first opportunity to give us the slip. Philadelphia it seems has been their favorite object, and for which they have made some bold pushes. Their shipping has not join'd them there. They will first have to raise the Cheveux de frize [i.e., chevaux de frise, or portable spiked barricades] on the Delaware and defeat the naval force there which is considerable, tho perhaps nothing near equal to what they can bring against it. We likewise met with another misfortune. General Wayne and Genl. Smallwood, who were on the Westside of Schuylkill, were attack'd in the night of the 20th and oblig'd to retire after having done every thing that was possible.[73]

The troops in this excursion of 10 days without baggage suffer'd excessive hardships, without tents in the rain, several marches of all night, and often without sufficient provisions. This they endur'd with the perseverance and patience of Good soldiers. Gen[era]l.s Smallwood, Wayne, McDougal and a considerable body of militia will join us to day and tomorrow. This day we shall move towards Philadelphia in order to try the fortune of another battle in which we devoutly hope the blessing of heaven. I consider the loss of Philadelphia as only temporary [and] to be recover'd when expedient. It is no more than the loss of Boston, nor in my opinion half so much [important] when the present trade of the latter be considered and the difficulty of interruption be consider'd, compar'd with the stoppage of the trade of the Delaware, where one or two frigates is sufficient. It is situated on a point of land form'd by the Rivers Delaware and Schuylkill so that it would [have] been highly improper to have thrown ourselves into it. Had we have taken both these and been unsuccessful in our action we should have been ruin'd having no retreat. If the enemy do not get their shipping up soon and go into Philadelphia, they will be in a very ineligible situation. I do not under the present circumstances consider Philadelphia of so much consequence as the loss of reputation to our army, but I trust in God we shall soon make up that matter. Billy is well and undergoes the hardships of this Campaign surprizingly well, and they are neither few nor small. I am perfectly well and. . . .[74]

———————

HENRY KNOX TO LUCY FLUCKER KNOX, ARTILLERY PARK CAMP, 25 MILES FROM PHILADELPHIA, PA, MONDAY, 6 OCTOBER 1777

Artillery Park,[75] Camp, 25 Miles from Philadelphia 6th Octb.r 1777—

My dearest Lucy,

I expect the post will arrive this day by which I shall have the happiness of hearing from my dear Girl. A Mr. Bates is going off to Hartford. By him I could not help writing to you, altho' I am by no means certain it will reach you so soon as the post who will go perhaps to morrow or next day.

I wrote you on the morning of the 3d Inst.[76] by the post and inform'd you that I was in hopes I should be able to give You some pleasing intelligence before Christmas. Indeed I expected it the next day, but I did not write my Lucy so partly for fear of alarming her and partly because it was dangerous to send a Letter of such a nature on the road as the success of the enterprise depended upon secrecy. We form'd a design to attack the enemy and to put in execution next morning. Accordingly, we began to march at 6 oClock in the evening and march'd all night, being distant from the enemies encampment from 15 to 20 miles. The Columns arriv'd nearly about the same time and made the attack with an impetuosity that would have done honor to old Soldiers. The enemy retreated two miles in front and about a mile and an half on their right. All things were in a most happy way [with] the enemy retreating from every part, when a fog which was but moderate at first became so thick from the continued firing of Cannon and musquetry that it absolutely became impossible to see an object at yards distance. To this cause and this in conjunction with the enemies taking possession of some stone buildings in German Town is to be ascribed the loss of the victory which we had been in possession of for above two hours. The action lasted 2 hours and forty minutes. At last we were oblig'd to give way in our turn and retreat which was conducted in such order that we did not lose a single piece of Cannon and lost very few prisoners. We brought off the greater part of our wounded. We might have kill'd and wounded about 500. Our troops are in prodigious Spirits at being able to drive nearly the whole collective [force] of the enemy so far. God who orders all things for the best gave us not the final Victory, perhaps he will the next time.[77] It will not be long before we have another tryall [i.e., trial] of skill. We retreated beyond our former Camp about 3 miles. I am sorry that it is not in my power to write you more fully, but the Gentleman who takes this refuses to stay one moment. Excuse me to Harry, but shew him this Letter. My Brother behaved with Spirit. Genl. Nash had his thighs taken off by a Cannon ball,[78] he was the only Genl. Officer wounded though we had a large proportion of officers killed and wounded.

> I am Dearest Lucy
> Your most Affectionate
> H Knox

HENRY KNOX TO LUCY FLUCKER KNOX, ARTILLERY PARK CAMP, 24 MILES FROM PHILADELPHIA, PA, WEDNESDAY, 15 OCTOBER 1777

Camp 24 Miles from Philadelphia 15th Octb.r 1777—

My dearest and only Love,

I have received your short Letter by Doctor Lulling[?], but am extremely sorry to observe that two posts have arrived here by whom I have not received a single Line. It is impossible that my Lucy should have known of the circumstance of the posts going from Boston, otherwise she would have written to the man who adores her. Nothing gives me half so much pain as not hearing from you by the same medium which other people hear from their friends in Boston. I mean not to complain, but hope you will not give me the least reason for [i.e., in] the future. I send you this by Capt. Randall who has the misfortune to be again made a prisoner after being slightly wounded in 7 or 8 places.[79]

I sent you early in the summer a certain Gold watch. You never have mentioned to me whether you received [it], which induces me to believe that something unfair has happened with it. The matter you mention about rations cannot be complied with, and I thank God I have too much reliance for his divine providence to have any of those misgivings and forebodings of which my dear Lucy seems so apprehensive. I trust the same divine being who brought us together will support us.

The enemy have not yet reduc'd our obstructions in the river Delaware below Philadelphia and consequently have not got their shipping up to the Town. They have made several efforts, but hitherto in vain, in one of which we took 2 officers & 56 privates prisoners.[80]

If the enemy cannot get their shipping up, Philadelphia is one of the most ineligible places in the world for an army, surrounded by rivers which are impassable, and an army above them. We have been pretty quick since the action of the 4th, but we have yet tolerable prospects and hopes to winter in Philadelphia, I mean our army. For however clouded the prospect may be, yet I have sanguine hopes of being able to live this winter in sweet fellowship with the dearest friend of my heart. However, I cannot as yet point out the Way.

Ere' you receive this you will receive the Account of the loss of Fort Montgomery, which I own to you is in my opinion exceedingly heavy, but it must stimulate us to much greater exertions.[81] America almost deserves to be made slaves for her non exertions in so important an affair, an affair of the most infinite consequence to ourselves and posterity. Observe, my dear Girl, how providence supports us [with] the advantages gain'd by our Northern army, altho we have not yet heard the minute particulars. Yet we have, in General and very authentically too, [a report that] gives almost a decisive turn to the contest. For my own part, I have not yet seen so bright a dawn as the present & I am as perfectly convinc'd in my own mind of the kindness of providence towards us, as I am of my own existence.

I most earnestly wish the contest finished that I might return to the arms of her who I flatter myself loves me equal to my love for her. Without this hope, I should, Lucy, me [i.e., be] the most miserable of the human species. Kiss my dear babe & pray for it. Give my love to Mr. & Mrs. Jarvis and all other friends. I have to complain that I have not received a Line from [Harry] for those two posts past, nor from any other person in Boston.

I am my dear Lucy with the utmost purity of affection your Harry Knox

---

HENRY KNOX TO LUCY FLUCKER KNOX, CAMP 10 MILES FROM PHILADELPHIA, PA, WEDNESDAY, 29 OCTOBER 1777

Camp 10 miles from Philadelphia 29th October 1777

My dearest Lucy,

I am unhappy that I do not hear from you. Post arrives after post and no letters from her I love to distraction. I have made so many conjectures upon this subject that I am weary of them and shall not give myself the trouble to write them to you. When we were on the other side of Schuylkill, the letters were irregular, but on this side the post has arriv'd as punctual as in peace time.

Since my last to you which was on the 21st, the Enemy attempted to storm a redoubt of ours at Red bank on the Delaware. A Count Donop[82] commanded the party which consisted of 1200 or 1300 principally Hessian Grenadiers. A Colo. Greene from Rhode Island[83] with two r.gts from that place defended the redoubt. The action was severe for 40 minutes where the enemy gave way in all parts, leaving more than a 100 dead on the spot, [and] 100 [wounded] most of them mortaly wounded among which was Count Donop himself, a man of great Consideration among the enemy. The remainder retreated with the utmost precipitation to Philadelphia with the loss of more than half the party. The next morning, the 23d instant, 6 of the enemies ships came up the river and three of them engag'd our Gallies and battery at Fort Mifflin for 6 hours during which time there was a most infernal Cannonade. The enemy were beat back and two of their ships, the Augusta, a 64 Gunship & a frigate, [I] cannot learn her name, ran aground & were burnt, to the great joy of the Americans. The rest retreated pretty quick and have made no advance

since. The operations on the river grow more more important every
moment. If the enemy do not get possession of the river, they cannot stay
in Philadelphia with any ease. Their convoys will be liable to be cut off &
they blockaded. They must attempt to get possession of the River at any
risque, and if they are again foiled, they will probably depart. The Lustre
of the northern Army quite eclipses us, but we have done our best.
"Great Garrick can do no more."[84]

If the people of America makes a proper use of the advantages put
into their hands and exert themselves in proportion to the magnitude of
the object, the next campaign will probably terminate her troubles. Do
you know, if God spares me, that I am determin'd to see you this winter
at all events, if it can possibly be consistent with my duty? Yes, & I think
my duty will doubly call me to Springfield. May God bless you my dear
& your babe. Write me I beg you often. Billey is well and a saucy dog for
not writing you.

> I am with the utmost purity of affection, your faithful
> HKnox

———————

HENRY KNOX TO LUCY FLUCKER KNOX, WHITEMARSH, PA,[85]
MONDAY, 3 NOVEMBER 1777

> Camp Nov.r 3 1777—

My dearest Love,

I have but ten minutes to write to her whom I love with all the power
and faculties of my soul. Colo. Cary[86] is just setting off.

I have received no Letter from you Since the 3d ultimo altho' I have
written regularly by the most [i.e., post] and as often by private hands as
was in my power. Write me the reason of all this my Lucy.

I yesterday read a Letter from Harry, informing me of the horrid
abuse of all property in Boston—the horrid prices demanded by the
traitors renders it immediately necessary for the Legislature to execute
four [out] of 5 of the principal rascals. No stone shall be left unturn'd for
me to see you this Winter, if consistent with the public good, but this
said public good will demand it of me and my private good too. I have no
doubt if God spares me to see you by Christmas or New Years, at least
that is my present determination.

We have no material news here. Indeed, the all glorious event to the northward so far exceeds any thing in our power that we Feel quite small. However we have done more perhaps than providence dictated. We fought two General actions and pretty toughly too. Yet they would not avail. We were oblig'd to march without obtain'g our wish & with some bloody noses.

We are waiting for some favorable opportunity to give them another blow & if possible to dispossess them of the redouted city of Philadelphia. The enemy have not yet been able to drive our Gallies away or storm or batter our ports with success. We have lately had a storm which has ruin'd their Batteries and works erected against fort Mifflin. Since they had their two men of War burnt on the 23d in the river and were defeated the 22d at Red bank with the loss of 5[00] or 600 with Count Donop prisoner and who is since dead of his wounds, they have appear'd quite silent in deeds but not so in words. They have been very angry for our feux's de Joy [i.e., feux de joie, or celebratory rifle salutes] which we have fir'd on the several victories over Burgoyne, and say we bye & bye shall bring ourselves in Contempt with our own army for propagating such known falsehoods. Poor fellows, nothing but Britain must triumph.

Had we retain'd but [Forts] Clinton & Montgomery in the highlands of New York, we should this day have been in the most puissant situation [during] this War. Indeed as it is, I believe, it is still better. The loss of men in the storm of Fort Montgomery is such that they have dearly bought the advantage obtain'd, especially when Considered they cannot keep it.

> Rejoicing in the sweet hope of being with You speedily I am
> Your Most affectionate
> H Knox

I hate Billy for not writing. Wrapped up in the contemplation of his own sweet person, all the World beside is a blank.

My All in life,

I wish to write my Harry a very long letter by this post, but it is not in my power. I was last evening seaised [i.e., seized] with that afflicting pain at my stomach, which obliged me to go to bed, where I lay the greatest part of the night, in the most extream distress immaginable, and am this morning too ill to sitt long.

You again in this letter of the 22nd of October, acuse me of neglecting to write by three posts, and impute it to pleasure or negligence. My pleasures, God knows, are very few, and neglecting you is a thing I never shall be guilty of. The reason of my not writing by those posts was that they brought no Letters from the army.

I immagine by this time that you have almost forgot my very looks and, if perchance my name is mentioned, you cry what have we to do with women. Out of the last sixteen months we have not been six weeks together, and it is now eight months since we parted, a circumstance which I dare say you never think of or you would some times mention it in your letters. But, alass, what a change from the happy days I have seen. Begone my foolish tears, why should I wish for his company who is indifferent, whether he lives at four hundred miles distance or not.

We have a report that Genl. Howe has met the fate of Genl. Burgoine. If that is true, do you think you can content yourself to return to my arms. If you can, may god almighty soon place you there is the prayer

of your unhappy wife

L K

Boston November 6th

HENRY KNOX TO LUCY FLUCKER KNOX, WHITEMARSH, PA, FRIDAY, 7 NOVEMBER 1777

Camp near Whitemarsh Church, 7th Nov.r 1777

My dear dear Lucy,

Altho' I wrote you yesterday by the post and altho' I do not expect this Letter will reach you very soon yet I cannot forbear writing by a Mr. Richards whom I send to Boston on some public business.

The happiness your Last letter of the 25 Ultimo[87] gave me was almost infinite, after not having had a line from you for a month. Did you know what pleasure and satisfaction Your Letters did me, you would spend much of Your time in writing and send them when you had opportunity.

That kind providence which brought us together did not do it before our souls were previously form'd for our mutual happiness.

The authors of this War on the British side receive my maledictions, which hardly square with the forgiveness recommended in the Gospel. But yet my dearest Love I chearfully entertain the hope that we shall sweetly enjoy the Society of each other again, and the blessings of it richly enhanc'd by knowing the afflictions of absence.

Should this or any similar Letter fall into the hands of people who [I] love less than my Lucy, they will make a scoff at it. Let them ridicule, [as] I have a witness within me like the Christian and our happiness of which their nigh dull souls never tasted. Man was form'd for Bliss, which thro the depravity of passions, few arrive. The great bulk of mankind give themselves up to the pursuit of improper objects, the obtaining of which disgusts and palls the mind.

I bless the day which heaven made You mine and I hope that providence which brought us together will give me an opportunity by a long connection of convincing you with a pure ardent affection how much I love and esteem You.

Give my Love to all friends. I shall hope to see you by Christmas or the beginning [of] January. God bless you & your babe

H Knox

HENRY KNOX TO LUCY FLUCKER KNOX, WHITEMARSH, PA, FRIDAY, 14 NOVEMBER 1777

Camp 14th Nov.r 1777—

My dearest Lucy,

I received your kind letter by the last post dated October 30. The pleasure it gave to me was almost infinite. Yes, my dearest Girl, I love you and your sweet babe with all the conjugal and parental tenderness possible & I hope I shall have the opportunity of enjoying the happiness of being with you some part of the ensuing winter.

I am this instant going out on some service which obliges me to write to you because the business will take me up two or three days in the interim of which the post will arrive and depart. Fort Mifflin after having most nobly sustain'd a fire of Batteries within [illegible] 500 yards for near 50 days, is at last evacuated.[88] The different Garrisons in it (for it was at last relieved several times) have acquir'd never ending[?] applause. I lost my worthy Capt. Treat who was kill'd with a cannon ball to my very great Grief. There are few young men existing of greater virtue & bravery.[89] Several other officers and men were kill'd & wounded. The enemy at last dismantled and ruin'd every single piece of Cannon in the Fort, and work'd their ships so near as to kill every man who appear'd on the platforms. We hope yet to prevent [the] enemy from bringing their men of War up to the City.

I am my dearest Lucy with the utmost purity and sincerity of affection

Your

HKnox

HENRY KNOX TO LUCY FLUCKER KNOX, WHITEMARSH, PA, TUESDAY, 25 NOVEMBER 1777

Camp 25th Nov.r 1777—

My dearest dear,

I receiv'd your two Letters by Colo. Crane[90] & Dr. Mark[?] of an old date but none by the post. I am unhappy to the last degree that you should suppose in the least that my affection for you is diminished. My God knows how much I suffer for Your sake, how much anxiety I go thro. This you may rely upon my dearest Love that I have no other affection on earth that bears the least Competition with that I have for you, that my being in the service is part of that affection. I have said so much on this subject of my being in the army that it is impossible I should add any thing further on the subject. I am yours wholly and entirely, and Wish to have no other Love. The greatest happiness I have is the Contemplation of when I shall enjoy in the [illegible] of my lovely Lucy. Be assur'd, my dearest Girl, that no earthly object shall ever seperate me from you after this matter shall be once happily settled. I shall by the Grace and permission of God see you this Winter when I shall endever to convince you with all[?] my ardency, I am your affectionate Harry.

I am call'd off by an immediate summons to attend the General.

That may heaven protect & bless you in the ardent prayer of your unalterable

HKnox

HENRY KNOX TO LUCY FLUCKER KNOX, WHITEMARSH, PA,
TUESDAY, 2 DECEMBER 1777

Camp Whitemarsh 2d December 1777

I have received your two Letters by the post one dated the 13th and
the other 20 Nov.r.[91] The post will set off in the morning, by him I shall
write a Letter. I have in every former Letter express'd the true genuine
feelings of my heart in the most tender expressions of which I was capable, nay I have lamented most exceedingly that no language of which
I was Master was in any means adequate to the warmth of my affection.
I have in every letter which I have written to you lamented with the
utmost sincerity the cause of my being absent so long from You. I have
counted the tedious days and hours since I was with you with a regret
that hardly, very hardly, squar'd with the profession of arms. I have reck-
on'd the probable movements that must revolve with an anxiety that, had
it have been fully known to those around me, might have been attributed
to a very different motive (to a wish to be distant from Danger). In short,
my Lucy, no man on earth seperated from all that he holds Dear on
earth has ever suffer'd more than I have suffer'd in being absent from
you whom I hold dearer than every other object. I have told you this so
often and with all the sincerity which God ever infus'd into the human
heart. I am unhappy at the Contents of your Letter and am very sorry
to say that unhappiness will still lay [with] me until heaven shall bless
me with your society. To answer the Letters would be improper least it
might miscarry. I shall therefore keep the Letters to shew them & have
an explanation from you. This truth you may rely upon & I dare call the
Supreme omniscient Judge to witness. That there never was a purer and
more ardent[?] affection than what I profess for you, and that I carry this
delicacy of affection so far as to be very indifferent indeed to all the rest
of your sex, even to a degree not justifiable by good manners. I wish you
my dearest Love to reflect seriously on what I have written and believe it
as seriously as part of the Gospel of Jesus Christ. But however much you
have pain'd me I should be extremely unhappy to give you the least pain,
but in one moment of inadvertence you have written [words] which will
long be the source of unhappiness to me.

The situation of our army on account of Cloathing is such as to render
a Winters Campaign impossible, without [which] we have a mind to put
an end to the War by starving all the soldiers.

I therefore expect to be able to set out for Congress when the army goes into Winter Quarters. After doing the business of my department with them, I shall set out for Boston, and do expect to be there in one month, or nearly so from this day. Yes my Lucy, I love, I adore you far infinitely more far than any other mortal but I confess that my chagrin is exceedingly great and that my happiness in seeing you will be Allay'd were I to believe that you lov'd me less than I have ever flatter'd my-self You have done. Gods that she in whom my soul is completely and entirely absorb'd should ever doubt of my affection. The thought almost drives me to desperation. You have often spoken of Mrs. Greene and urg'd it with much warmth that I wish'd to conceal her situation from you, a situation which you almost seem'd to envy. Mrs. Greene [is] in a very unpleasant season of the Year. With much difficulty, and in an ill state of health, [she] reach'd Mr. Lotts[92] about 7 Miles nearer to Boston than Morris Town. Genl. Greene saw her there and was with her for three days, at which time the army march'd southward and he has never seen her since nor has he been with her one moment. Mr. Lotts family is undoubtedly an amiable family but he is too much of a Gentleman to take any Compensation from Genl. Greene for Mrs. Greene's being there, for the servants and horses. At one hundred & fifty miles distant from [illegible], I think the delicacy of my Lucy's mind would be much wounded by being in such a situation. I am certain mine would be, and I think my friend is in the same situation of mind. However that may be, I am nearly determin'd to have my Lucy in some situation near me if I shall serve another Campaign. Her unhappiness is so great that I am determin'd to sacrifice every inferior consideration to remove it, even if She like Mrs. Reidsal should be taken prisoner.[93] This and other arrangements will probably be the Consequence of my being with You.

Continue to love me and . . . if any part of it should have depreciated (which God in mercy to us both, forbid) endeavor to rekindle the flame of sacred Love and friendship in your bosom.

I own I am chagrin'd beyond measure, and therefore hope my friend Harry will [not] . . . open this Letter. God bless You and the dear pledge of our Love I am your truly affectionate and faithful HKnox—

I have not written to Harry supposing him to have set out for Camp. . . . The detachment for the Boston reg.ts are the best cloathed men in Camp.[94]

HENRY KNOX TO LUCY FLUCKER KNOX, WHITEMARSH, PA,
TUESDAY, 3 DECEMBER 1777

Camp near Whitemarsh 3 December 1777

I yesterday wrote the best belov'd of my heart by Colo. Rejoicer[?],
and inform'd you that I had recieved your two Letters of the 13th and
20th Nov.r. I gave my dearest Love my sentiments with that freedom I
ever wish to preserve with so dear a connection. I was half sorry after I
had sent the Letter least it might give her pain. I consider that I ought
to bear with her little feebleness, when they are contracted with those
qualifications and loveliness which have captivated and which still hold
my heart.

I have observ'd with pleasure since our union that our Love increas'd
for each other every hour, each moment gave to each other such proofs
of sincere affection that could not but endear the connection. I am exceedingly unhappy to hear the least hint from You that my Love should
have in the least diminish'd, an assertion so totally different from reality,
that it pains me much. Believe me thou best belov'd of my Soul, were it
possible to transport me back to that situation in which I was before our
union, & I could know half the amiable lovely and enchanting disposition [of] my now dearest wife with permission to wedd her without a
single friend or fortune but herself, and the whole world contracted in
the opposite scale on condition of not doing it, I should spurn the offer,
and embrace her who I hold much dearer than life.

But does my Lucy really want a proof of my Affection, is there nothing
in this world that will satisfy her but deserting the cause in which I am
engag'd and render'd my self eternally infamous and all my connections
by resigning at a time my Country may stand in need of my little assistance. God Forbid.

I attribute her feelings by no means to such a cause. I believe she
is chagrin'd and unhappy to have lost her Father, mother, sisters and
brother in this contest, and her husband full knows she has made such
capital sacrifices at too great a distance for [him] to support her under
this consideration of such great afflictions. Believe me my only and dearest Love (if your affection is not diminished), what a thought! that my
Life shall be spent to make you happy. This matter I have often assur'd
you, but alass have not always [been] so happy as to have it believed.

I shall have the happiness to be with You in about one month. This is my expectation and wish, but some matters may turn up which will render the time longer, and yet my Love, for you remain as ardent as ever, I not only long to see you but Your sweet babe, which by every account is a sweet child—God protect [her] and its mother. . . .

> Adieu My dearest and only Love, continue to believe me your truly Affectionate HKnox

I do not write to my friend Harry as we expect him here every hour.[95]

HENRY KNOX TO LUCY FLUCKER KNOX, VALLEY FORGE, PA,
SATURDAY, 27 DECEMBER 1777

Camp great Valley 27th December 1777

My dearest and only Love,

I wrote you two days ago by the post[96] and then inform'd you that it was my unhappiness that I had not then set out for Boston. I also inform'd you that the obvious urgency of the public business would in my opinion induce his Excellency not to permit, but to order me to proceed to make such arrangements in the ordnance department as would answer the probable great demands of the next Campaign.

I am certain my dearest Lucy wants no inducements to believe my anxious desire to see her <u>at all events,</u> but in one of her Letters she appears hurt that I should make use of the argument of public business, co-operating with my own private sentiments and wishes, to establish the certainty of my being able to come to Boston. I should most certainly see you this winter if within the compass of human possibility, but it will most assuredly be much better for my own reputation that I should have the honor of doing public business and, at the same time, the pleasure of being in the society of her with whose happiness my own is intimately interwoven and connected.

I have had some conversation with the General on the business, he seems inclin'd to wait [for] the arrival of a Committee expected from Congress. If so, it will detain me sometime, ten days perhaps. How long and how tedious [how]soever the time may be before I shall arrive to my dearest joy, not one moment shall be protracted by me, but I am really fearful it will be as late as it was last year before I shall reach you. But then perhaps I shall stay longer and perhaps, when I come away, I shall bring a certain little charmer with me. But this will be according to your wishes and desires on that heart.

My Brother has been ill for some time owing to much fatigue and being expos'd a[t] nights in an uncomfortable hut. He is out of Camp and I have not heard from him for some days. Your not having any remarkable fondness for him and viewing him, tho very unjustly, as a kind of rival will induce me to leave him behind. Indeed, I believe it his wish.

Genl. Howe has been for some days past drawing forage from the meadows near Philadelphia, we are at such a distance from him that I believe not much more will be done than harass him with small parties.

[I] Shall think every hour tedious untill I have the pleasure, the superlative pleasure to see you. May God grant that nothing turn up which may prevent [this]. Kiss my Lovely little daughter, & beg heaven to bless her in the name of her Father. I am my dear Girl with the utmost purity of affection your own HKnox[97]

CHAPTER FIVE

Enduring the War (1778–1783)

"Swords into ploughs[hares]"

The Revolutionary War dramatically changed course in 1778. Although the Continental army struggled through a difficult winter at Valley Forge, soldiers and officers remained in camp and under arms despite cold, hunger, and disease. In February, moreover, the men began drilling under the direction of a recently arrived Prussian officer, Baron von Steuben. George Washington, meanwhile, worked with both Congress and his generals, including Knox, to reform and strengthen the army's system of administration and supply. Thus, by spring, the American forces were stronger, better trained, and more confident in their abilities. Across the Atlantic Ocean, Benjamin Franklin used the victory at Saratoga to convince Louis XVI's government to enter into an alliance with the United States, an act that soon led Britain to declare war on France, its ancient foe. Franklin's diplomatic achievement fundamentally altered the American Revolution and forced George III's ministers to scale back their operations in North America.

The war changed in an equally dramatic fashion for Lucy and Henry Knox. In January, Knox left for Massachusetts, to recruit additional men for the Continental army. Arriving in Boston in February, he, as usual, spent most of his time on military matters. But he finally got to see Lucy and his daughter again, after nearly a year apart. Not only did the couple rekindle their relationship, but they also mapped out another family survival strategy for the coming year. They renewed their efforts to reopen Henry's bookstore, with his brother William to be in charge of its daily operation. In fact, carpenters began work on repairs while Knox was still in Boston. The couple also discussed Henry's promise of the previous December, which was to have Lucy as near to him as possible. Although he needed to return to the army in March, Knox arranged for Lucy and their daughter to join him in Pennsylvania later that spring. In early May, the pair left Boston, and, by the month's end, the Knoxes were together once more.[1]

The war briefly but forcefully intervened the following month to cause yet another family separation. On 18 June, the British army's new commander, Sir Henry Clinton, marched his men out of Philadelphia, headed for New York City. France's entry into the war had forced the ministry in London to order the withdrawal, as part of an overall consolidation of its military positions on the North American continent. Wishing to strike a blow to a retreating foe, Washington ordered the Continental army to set off in pursuit. At a 24 June council of war, the commander ordered an attack on Clinton's rearguard, near Monmouth Court House. The campaign culminated four days later, close to that rural hamlet's crossroads. After a confused dawn assault by American forces, the two armies fought bitterly for nearly twelve hours, under a blistering sun, until physical exhaustion halted the action. The British retreated during the night, and the next day, Washington declared the fight an American victory. Following the battle, Henry himself penned a long and detailed letter to Lucy, describing his part in the engagement, where he was active with his artillery regiments. He called the battle "very splendid" and delighted in the enemy's hasty withdrawal, under cover of darkness. Although his corps' casualties were many, Henry himself had once more emerged unscathed. With American scouts reporting that Clinton's men would soon reach New York, via Sandy Hook, Knox told his wife that he expected field operations to conclude shortly, and that he would rejoin her soon.[2] As he foresaw, the campaign ended within the week, and Henry was back with his family several days later.[3]

The Knoxes' brief reunion at Valley Forge and the subsequent Monmouth campaign marked the start of the final, and longest, stage of the American Revolution. Unlike the war's initial phases—the first, characterized by giddy excitement and success, and the second, by great perils and hardships—this last stage required the couple to endure a conflict of which they were heartily tired and yet still had no end in sight. Nevertheless, they lived together for most of these years in various American encampments and, as a result, wrote relatively few letters to one another. But those missives that they did exchange—whenever Henry maneuvered with the army or inspected Continental outposts—unmistakably reveal the conflict's altered state. Discussions about the American Revolution and its causes, as well as Henry's military contributions to the effort, mostly disappear. Rather, family members, finances, and the couple's future together become the dominant themes of their written conversations. Although happy to be together, they often expressed fears that the war would stretch on forever. And an ongoing conflict, even one of maneuvers, kept Henry in the ranks and prevented the family from making concrete postwar plans. Therefore, they desperately longed for peace and domestic normalcy.

Soon after the battle of Monmouth, the mid-Atlantic theater settled into an extended war of movement as Washington sought to keep the Continental army intact, as well as to guard New Jersey, the Hudson Valley, and southern New England from possible British assaults. With outposts scattered across Connecticut, the Hudson Highlands, and central New Jersey, the Americans kept a close watch over and occasionally skirmished with enemy units scattered throughout the lower Hudson Valley. During this period, Knox periodically travelled with the army and participated in several minor actions. He focused the bulk of his time, however, on improving the size, organization, and capabilities of his artillery regiments. Toward this end, he established what came to be known as "the academy" in Pluckemin, New Jersey, a dozen or so miles from the main encampment at Morristown. Inside a large and open barracks, he and other officers instructed the men in gunnery tactics, as well as in the care and operation of the army's 200 field guns, mortars, and howitzers.[4] Knox even found time to organize several elegant balls, in order to relieve the general tedium of camp life. For instance, in February 1779, on the one-year anniversary of the French alliance, he (probably with Lucy's assistance) planned what one observer called a "splendid entertainment," attended by 300–400 officers and at least 70 ladies. The evening included fireworks, cannon blasts, and an elaborate dinner, and it culminated with a formal ball that began when George Washington, having "for his partner the lady of General Knox," opened the first dance.[5]

Despite ongoing military responsibilities and occasional diversions, the couple focused the bulk of their written correspondence on peace and the familial themes of home and children. In June 1779, for instance, Henry told Lucy, "I pant after domestic happiness" and wished to "turn our swords into ploughs[hares] and pruning hooks." Lucy wrote to Henry in a similar vein. When staying at Mount Vernon during the Yorktown campaign, Martha Washington's hospitality only made Lucy long for her own home.[6] Children, above all, were the letters' key topic during these years. The couple almost always discussed little Lucy Knox, mentioning her developing personality, physical growth, health, and well-being. When traveling, Henry invariably asked for news of his daughter. Not surprisingly, additional children entered the Knox household within this period. In late March 1779, a second girl, Julia, was born to the couple. Her adoring father wrote to William Knox that the infant was "a beautiful daughter" and "a divine child."[7] Julia, however, died just three months later. Being away with the army at the time of her death made

Henry's grief all the more difficult to bear. Heartbroken by the loss of his daughter, as well as by his inability to be with and comfort Lucy, he could only write of the terrible pain they both felt.[8] Less than a year later, Lucy gave birth to a son, who was named after Knox's close friend, Henry Jackson. While Knox's letters almost always asked his wife to kiss the children many times for him, his mind turned toward their educations as they grew older. When little Lucy was just three years old, for instance, her father started to demand letters from her. He closed one note instructing his wife to order the child to write a letter to him or else face stern consequences.[9]

The Knoxes also began to think more seriously of Henry's postwar career plans. In fact, some of the couple's face-to-face conversations on this topic seem to have found their way into their letters and revealed anxieties about the future. On the eve of the Siege of Yorktown, for example, Henry began one note by again lamenting the ongoing war and expressing his ardent desire for peace. After hostilities ceased, he hoped he and Lucy could then "tutor . . . the young minds of our sweet babes, and . . . sit and prepare ourselves for a glorious eternity." Knox realized, though, that such sentiments were far too speculative for his wife. Lucy Knox seems to have developed an acute dread of poverty during the war, perhaps due to the hardships she had experienced since 1775. Therefore, he penned her likely response to such musings: "Too enthusiastic my Harry!" Possibly repeating words he had actually heard from Lucy herself, he continued in her imaginary voice: "Endeavor to obtain a permanent fortune for yourself & children. You are always flying off into some eccentric path, and instead of improving your time like other rational mortals, you are suffering that to elapse which can never be regain'd." Sensitive to his wife's deep-seated fears, Henry promised to exert every effort to render their future circumstances easy.[10]

The Continental army's three-year war of maneuvers ended with the Yorktown campaign, in the summer and fall of 1781. Planning for the complex combined operation began that July, as American and French forces prepared for an overland trek to the Chesapeake Bay, in hopes of bagging Lord Cornwallis's southern army. As Knox organized his artillery train for the march, Lucy traveled northward with the children, visiting several friends in the Hudson Valley and Albany, New York. As always, however, Lucy really wanted to be with her husband. The fact that she was three months into her fourth pregnancy probably added to her wish. Referring to Henry as "My only love," she explained in a 26 July letter that she had remembered the previous day was his thirty-first birthday. Therefore, she asked God to bless the couple with many more birthdays, which might all be spent together.[11] Henry replied in a similar vein. Because joy and contentment came only when they were in each other's arms, he confessed how "totally unhappy" he was not to be with her.[12]

While Lucy continued to remain in the north, Knox received news from his brother in Boston that Thomas Flucker Sr. apparently lay gravely ill in London and was not expected to survive. Since migrating to England in 1775, Lucy's father, with his family, had lived primarily in the British metropolis, where he had become associated with the "Brompton Row Tory Club," a group of New England Loyalists residing in London. While Flucker continued to collect his annual £300 salary as a colonial royal secretary, the cost of living in that city had greatly strained his finances. Thus Knox told William that, if Thomas Sr. died, "the family in England would . . . have their distress extremely increased by so awful an event." He especially worried, however, that Lucy "will be afflicted by [the news] beyond moderation."[13] Henry was about to depart for Virginia, and, with Lucy nearing the midpoint of another pregnancy, he now became concerned about her health. Feeling the competing pressures of public and private duties, he lamented to his brother that the army's movement to the south had entirely "derange[d] my little family" and created stress that only a father and husband could feel.[14] To solve his dilemma, Knox apparently went to General Washington himself and asked if Lucy and the children could travel with him and the army to Philadelphia. Washington not only agreed, but he also invited Lucy to "spend her time at Mount Vernon" with Lady Washington.[15] Throughout August 1781, therefore, the Knoxes, as well as the army, traveled southward. When the couple arrived in Pennsylvania, they placed little Lucy under the care of a prominent Philadelphia merchant and former Continental officer, Clement Biddle, and his wife, Rebekah Cornell Biddle. The Knoxes' daughter would be educated at a well-known boarding school within the city. After settling the child with the Biddles, Lucy Knox and her son, young "Master Hal," then traveled onward to George Washington's great estate on the Potomac River. At the same time, Henry and the Continental army marched farther south, to deal with the British at Yorktown.[16]

By the end of September 1781, the Knoxes had completed their various journeys, and Lucy and Henry again started to write to one another. On the 29th, Lucy took up her pen and enumerated Martha Washington's many kindnesses to her and their little boy. Such hospitality, however, had reawakened in Lucy all of her longings for peace, domestic tranquility, and, especially, a permanent home of her own. Not knowing that the war's final major operation had already commenced, she told her husband there was only "one possible way to obtain one [i.e., a home]," and added, "you know my meaning," probably an oblique reference to

Lucy's long-standing desire that Henry leave the army. She clearly still wished him to pursue a more profitable mercantile career.[17]

Martha Washington's son, John Parke Custis, delivered Lucy's letter to Henry two days later. Arriving at the Continental army's camp outside Yorktown to serve as a civilian aide, Custis told Knox that he had just seen 18-month-old Hal at Mount Vernon and called the boy "a monstrous fine fellow." Delighted at the compliment about his son, Henry immediately wrote the first of four letters he sent to Lucy that October. Ignoring her renewed suggestion that he resign from the army, he instead appeared thrilled to be once more in the midst of an active campaign and cheerfully described the allied armies' fine prospects. Two weeks later, he seemed even more exultant as he shared news of the successful French and American assaults on British redoubts 9 and 10. With the military noose clearly tightening, Knox saw that a successful end to the battle was approaching. Still, he promised Lucy that he would take care of himself and look out for his own safety.[18] On 19 October, at precisely 8 a.m., Knox once more took up his pen. Although short on sleep and pressed for time, he wanted to be the first to tell "the Charmer of my soul" that Lord Cornwallis and his British troops would that day lay down their arms before General Washington and the allied forces. Explaining some of the details surrounding the surrender negotiations, he triumphantly noted that British bands would *not* be allowed to play "Yankee Doodle." Knox then heard a knock on his tent pole and scribbled that Washington needed him at headquarters immediately. He finished with some news he had recently learned about little Lucy in Philadelphia and rode off to see the general.[19]

Details regarding the processing and distribution of captured British cannon and other ordinance kept Knox in Yorktown for several additional weeks, but he reunited with Lucy and young Hal at Mount Vernon in early November. The Knoxes only briefly stayed together at the mansion, however, due to the untimely death of the commander's stepson. Custis caught a "camp fever" when visiting the allied encampment and died on 5 November. In addition to not wanting to intrude on the Washington family's grief, Henry and Lucy also wanted to see five-year-old Lucy in Pennsylvania. After the couple arrived in Philadelphia, they decided to remain there for several more months, so Lucy could safely deliver her fourth child. On 10 December 1781, she gave birth to a boy, whom the couple named Marcus Camillus.[20]

As Lucy convalesced from childbirth, she and Henry endured what most likely was their final separation during the American Revolution. In late March 1782, Knox accompanied New York congressman Gouverneur Morris to Elizabethtown, New Jersey, where they attempted to negotiate an exchange of prisoners with the British. Soon after his arrival at the conference site, Henry confessed to Lucy that being apart from his family made him feel as if he had set off on another campaign. Although her husband faced no enemy guns, Lucy also wrote of her grief at yet another separation. The Knoxes' Revolutionary War letters consistently demonstrate both the enduring strength of their love and their ardent desire to be together, and these final letters were no different. Yet they also reveal how the war had enormously altered their circumstances and their place in the new republic. For instance, Lucy told her husband how pleased she was that the Continental Congress had finally done him "justice" by approving the one-time bookseller's promotion to major general in the Continental army. Though pleased at their extraordinary rise in American society, the youthful excitement expressed in their first letters was now entirely gone. These final missives instead reveal a fully mature couple, deeply devoted to one another and anxious for peace. Above all, as Henry wrote on 31 March 1782, they wished to be surrounded by "our sweet children."[21]

The Knoxes' wartime letters end that spring. Henry's service in the ranks, however, continued until the Continental army's demobilization, a year and a half later. Military obligations thus continued to direct the course of the family's life. In May 1782, for example, Henry rejoined the main army in the Hudson Valley Highlands, with Lucy and the children dutifully trekking northward with him. Four months later, in September, Knox took command of the American fortifications at West Point, and once again the family followed, though, sadly, little Marcus Camillus died soon after they had all arrived at that posting.[22] In addition to overseeing West Point's daily military operations, Henry kept busy throughout this period with other matters. He repeatedly wrote to the Congress of the Confederation to secure adequate postwar pay for the men in the ranks. With the end of the conflict clearly approaching, Henry also helped to establish the Society of the Cincinnati, to serve as a fraternal organization for the army's officer corps. Although the society later proved to be controversial, Knox and his brother officers hoped it would preserve the camaraderie and fellowship they had all forged during the struggle for independence. Finally, Knox worked with George Washington in March 1783 to defuse the famous Newburgh conspiracy, where some in the army wished to threaten the Confederation Congress with a military mutiny, in order to secure their postwar pensions.[23]

In the weeks following the Newburgh controversy, reports arrived from Europe with the news that preliminary articles of peace had been signed in Paris. Another packet ship reached America that spring, bringing a personal letter to Lucy from her brother, British Captain Thomas Flucker Jr., the first piece of correspondence she had received from her family since the Battles of Lexington and

Concord. Though that missive has not survived, it contained the news that their father had died in London, after an extended illness. Henry and Lucy both immediately penned letters to Lucy's mother, Hannah Waldo Flucker, to express their sympathy, but she and other family members in England maintained their complete silence. Indeed, the Knoxes' letters went unanswered, nor was there any further correspondence from Captain Flucker. On the evening of 24 November 1783, however, Henry decided to reach out to his London kinsmen one more time. In a brief letter to his mother-in-law, he explained that he had written to her the previous May about her tragic loss, and that Lucy had written twice. Almost pleadingly, he said that he hoped this "part of your family . . . is still dear to you," and that he and Lucy would welcome any news from them.[24]

The very next day, Knox led the Continental army's military honor guard into New York City, as American forces finally reentered the place from which Henry and his comrades had fled in disarray seven years before. On 4 December 1783, with the bulk of the army demobilized and heading home, Washington himself took his final leave of his generals and aides. Inside Fraunces Tavern, the commander-in-chief embraced Henry Knox first among all his subordinate officers, before riding off to the Confederation Congress to resign his commission. Ten days later, right before Henry and Lucy also left New York for Boston, he happily wrote to his friend and fellow general, the Marquis de Lafayette, "The English have at last left us to ourselves."[25]

1778

HENRY KNOX TO LUCY FLUCKER KNOX, MONMOUTH, NJ,
MONDAY, 29 JUNE 1778

June 29th 1778 near Monmouth Court House

My dearest Love,

I wrote you some few days ago that a day or two would determine whether we should have an engagement with the Britons.[26] Yesterday at about 9 oClock A.M., Our advanced parties under General Lee attak'd their rear while on the march towards Shewsbury upon which their whole army except the Hessians came to the right about and after some fighting oblig'd him to retire to the main Army under his Excellency G. Washington, which was about two miles distance. The Enemy advanc'd with great Spirit to the attack and began a very brisk Cannonade on us who were form'd to receive them. The Cannonade lasted from about eleven untill Six oClock at which time the Enemy began to retire in all quarters and left us in possession of the field of Battle. We have several field officers kill'd and a Considerable number of others. Colo. Ramsay,[27] Mrs. Ramsays husband was taken prisoner and this morning releas'd on his parole. I have had several Officers kill'd and wounded. My brave Lads behav'd with their usual intrepidity & the Army give the Corps of Artillery their full proportion of the Glory of the day. Indeed upon the whole it is very splendid. The Capital Army [i.e., the main army] of Britain defeated, and oblig'd to retreat before the Americans who they despise so much. I cannot asscertain either our or the enemies Loss, But I really think they have lost three times the number we have. I judge from of the field of Battle which to be sure is a field of Carnage and Blood, three to one of the british forces lie there. The Britons confess they have never received so severe a check. Colo. Monckton who commanded their first Battalion of Grenadiers[28] and a considerable number of other officers belonging to them were left dead on the field of action.

The Enemy took a strong post about a mile of[f] the place of action. To dislodge them from which, as it was dark, would cost too many men, and by which they cover'd the retreat of their Army. After having been fighting all day, one of the hottest I ever felt, they decamp'd in the night and march'd off with the utmost precipitation, leaving a great number of their wounded, both officers and men, in our hands. We have sent out large bodies in pursuit but I believe they will not be able to come up with the main body. They intend to embark at Sandy hook, and as soon as we have collected our parties in and given over the pursuit and refresh'd our men, we shall begin our march for the North River. The number of deserters since they left Philadelphia must exceed eight hundred, this march has prov'd to them a most destructive one and is very ill calculated to give Sir Wm Clinton any éclat. He may storm Fort Montgomery, but is very ill calculated in my opinion to be at the head of a large Army. My friend Harry[29] cros'd over from Philadelphia & was in the unfortunate part of the day. I saw him once on the field for a moment, he appeared much fatigu'd. His regiment had a few killed and wounded and is reported to have behav'd well. I hope in a few days to have the superlative happiness of being with you. Give my most respectful Compliments to Mr. & Mrs. Lott, Mrs. Livingston and the Young ladies and present to them my congratulations on our Victory.[30]

[unsigned]

1779

HENRY KNOX TO LUCY FLUCKER KNOX, NEW WINDSOR, NY, TUESDAY, 29 JUNE 1779

New Windsor 29th June 1779

Good Heavens, my Lucy, what affliction did your Letter p[e]r Ridland[?] inflict upon me. Julia, poor innocent,[31] is not in half so much pain as its unhappy mother and, to add to her & my distress, I am absent, unable to assist her, personally to support the fatigues attended on the situation of her babe. To be absent at such a time [is] excruciating pain indeed! Yes, my dearest Love, I lament that it is not in my power instantly to fly to share with you all the anxiety of a tender parental affection and to endever to lessen such as will admit of alleviation. I long to see you to be assur'd from your own lips that you are getting better daily. I long to hear the little prattle of my lovely Lucy[32] and to see the expressive countenance of Julia. I pant after domestic happiness and most heartily wish the time arriv'd when we shall turn our swords into ploughs[hares] and pruning hooks.[33]

We have reason to believe that the principal Force of the Enemy have gone down the river, leaving a Garrison of six regiments in the Works which they have erected at Kings Ferry. The [out]posts here are too strong, especially when guarded by the Army, to admit even of an Attempt much less a storm. Probably Sr. Harry[34] waits for a more favorable opportunity when our Army shall be at a distance and in the meantime intends an operation that may draw us away and harass us [through] long marches.

Give my Love to Cousins Eliza and Sally[35] and assure them of my tender affection. I believe Billey sailed last Thursday.[36] God preserve you and grant your sick baby to recover. I have sent you by Doctor Brown some paper but have no quills. The Geese of the neighbourhood must supply them. I am, my dear Lucy, with the most perfect affection Your
    HKnox

HENRY KNOX TO LUCY FLUCKER KNOX, WEST POINT, NY, MONDAY, 8 AUGUST 1779

West point 8th August 1779

I embrace the opportunity by Doctor Craik[37] to write to thee my Lucy, my friend, my only love, <u>my all</u>. I have not had the happiness to hear of you since your Letter of the 28th by Mr. Pollard.[38] I entreat if you have opportunities that you would embrace them and confer that pleasure on your Harry of informing [him] of your health, your health which is so inexpressably dear to him. I wrote you by Major Bauman[39] that I hop'd by September to be so far inform'd of the Enemies intentions and designs as to determine to have you nearer to me than at the present. I still entertain that hope though I am possess'd of no more materials than at that time to form a judgement. I long with the utmost devotion for the arrival of that period when my Lucy and I shall be no more seperated, when we shall set down free from the hurry, bustle, and impertinence, of the World, in some sequestered Vale where the Education of <u>our children</u> and the preparation on our own parts for a pure & more happy region shall employ the principal part of our time, In acts of Love to men, and Worship to our maker. Our Brother William had not sail'd on the 29th July but <u>expected</u> to in a day or two, which would bring it about the 1st Instant the day on which 4 large Men of War sail'd from New York to endever to intercept our little Navy at Pe-nobscott, so that that I think the chances are in favor of the poor fellows being made prisoner.[40] However, even if that should happen, and to be sure it would be a most adverse event indeed, I should not dispond [i.e., despair]. That Being who has hitherto conducted [us] will I hope still support us.

Lady Kitty really kept her own Secrets uncommonly well. I think she must not have entrusted it in many hands.[41] We did not suppose that she was married at the time we were at Baskenridge. Mr. Duer inform'd a gentleman of it not long after my return from you. I thought it pretty good authority to be sure, but did not know but it might be in jest. The day before yesterday I was mentioning the affair to Colo. Hay[42] of Fish-Kill who said he believed it was true that they were married, for that the night before <u>they had slept together</u> at his house. This was convincing to me for though it was possible Mr. Duer might, in jest, say that he was married. Yet I did not believe that Lady would merely for the sake of the jest and without any Counter security <u>go to bed</u>, even to [i.e., with] Mr. Duer.

If you are [at the home of] Colonel Ogden,[43] give my love to him and Mrs. Ogden, Mr. & Mrs. Lott and all the Beverwyck Family,[44] Cousin Eliza, and every body else that you think proper, not forgetting my lovely little Lucy. Tell her papa will flog her if she does not write him a Letter. I want to see some of her performance.

Believe me my dearest love to be with the utmost affection your,

HKnox

1780

HENRY KNOX TO LUCY FLUCKER KNOX, RAMAPOUGH [NOW RAMAPO], NY, THURSDAY, 29 JUNE 1780

Ramapaugh 29th June 1780

My dearest and only Love,

I arriv'd at this place yesterday morning and found the army halted here. The Enemy have no intention of investing [i.e., besieging] West point. They are in the vicinity of Phillips Manor and Kings-bridge. I believe we shall stay in this neighbourhood for some days. If so, and I shall know more about it tomorrow, I will make an appointment to meet you at Colo. Ogdens towards the latter end of the week. Believe me my Lucy, you are my only happiness, and absence from you is in every sense of the word a deprivation of pleasure. Kiss my sweet babes a thousand times for me. You well know by the discharge of my old debts of this kind that I will amply repay you.

Heaven preserve You and your little family

HKnox

1781

LUCY FLUCKER KNOX TO HENRY KNOX, LIVINGSTON MANOR, NY, THURSDAY, 26 JULY 1781

Manor Livingston[45] 26 July '81

My Only love,

I dine this day with Mr. P R Livingston[46] and am happy to find that his son is to sett off for Camp in one hour & [I] retire from table to inform the dear partener of my Soul that his Lucy & his dear children are well.

Not one line from my Harry in all this time, how shall I account for it.

Sure he is not unmindful of my distressed state of mind. Pray, my love, be attentive to it, and write me by every possible opportunity.

Your birth day was yesterday. May the Almighty bless us with many repetitions of it, but may they not all be days of absence. Thursday next will be <u>mine</u>. I wish my Harry as deeply affected by it as I by his.

I would write much more but the time will not permit. Hope you have rec'd my letter which I forwarded by Colo. Lewis[47] and that I shall have a long epistle by his return. I shall sett off tomorrow for Albany but make a very short stay, as I find there is no chance of hearing from you and am of course very discontented.

Be civil to the bearer of this as an acknowledgement of the great politeness of his family to your

Lucy Knox

HENRY KNOX TO LUCY FLUCKER KNOX, PHILLIPSBURGH [NOW SLEEPY HOLLOW], NY, THURSDAY, 26 JULY 1781

Camp Phillipsburg 26 July 1781

It is only for the few of similar sentiments and who love with the Zeal of my Lucy & I to conceive of the anxiety and distress of being separate, especially when the purest affection has been crown'd with such charming pledges as our little celestials. Although it is painful, to suppose my Lucy will not be displeas'd at the confession that I have never found my absence from her so truly insupportable as the present. I am alone amidst a crowd, and unhappy without my companion. Haste happy time, when we shall be no more seperated, when we shall justly be the shadow of each other and when every emotion of our hearts & minds shall be to render our happiness complete, employ'd in the ravishing care of tutoring the young minds of our sweet babes, and endevoring to sit & prepare ourselves for a glorious eternity. "Too enthusiastic my Harry! Endevor to obtain a permanent fortune for yourself & children. You are always flying off into some eccentric path, and instead of improving your time like other rational mortals you are suffering that to elapse which can never be regain'd." Indeed, my sweetest tye to mortality, I will exert myself in every laudable pursuit to render you easy in your circumstances, as soon as this vile War shall cease. Vile I call it because it is a War upon the affections of humanity. It has deprived us of the right enjoyment of six

years, long years of our Life, a period infinitely too long to be engross'd
by other objects than the business of Love.

I know not what to say about the prospects of the campaign. The
number of men which were to have been furnish'd fall vastly short. We
have lately been down to the grounds adjacent to York Island,[48] with
a view to reconnoitre the points of attack, and where the Enemy were
most vulnerable. Our view was satisfactory, and amounted to a conviction that with a proper force, the possession of both Islands would not be
so difficult as has hitherto been imagined. I speak now, even if we should
not have a superior fleet. That event, combined as above, could render
our success certain & complete. But we have the fullest evidence that
the enemy intend to recall the greatest part of their forces from Virginia, and that the British fleet sail'd from the Hook on the 4th to convoy
them hither. This, tho it was part of our original plan, will prevent our
operations in this quarter provided the reinforcements which shall be
brought, amount to a large number. Time, the great developer of human
events, will shew us how far we can go.[49]

Some of the Marquis's troops under General Wayne have had a re[n]
contre with the Enemy under Lord Cornwallis in which we suffer'd
some, and lost 2 pieces of Cannon. But it will have no consequences to
it as the Enemy continued to pursue their plan which was to retire to
Plymouth [i.e., Portsmouth] that they might have the liberty to send
troops this way according to exigencies.[50]

General Greene, after having the best prospects of expelling the
Enemy from all the upper country of South Carolina & Georgia, has
been oblig'd to raise the siege of ninety six when just within the grasp of
victory. This was owing to a reinforcement of about 1500 men receiv'd by
the Enemy from England. But previous to this event he had taken all the
other [out]posts of the Enemy.[51] His conduct has exhibited him a great
man, and established his reputation beyond the powers of malice to
ensure it lastingly.

I yesterday received a message from Colonel Livingston by Colonel
Webb,[52] informing me that he had prospects of obtaining two rooms for
you in Doctor Darbys house provided he could get out a family which
was on the point of going away, and which was expected hourly. That he
would write me by the post. By this, it does not appear that the persons
he mention'd vzt [i.e., namely] Mr. & Mrs. D could make it convenient to
take you. However we shall know more about it in a few days.

I am at a loss to know where to direct this. I shall send it [by] Colonel Hughes[53] with a request to send it to Colo. Duers & for him to send it to the place where you may be. Write me, I beseech You, and let me know where you [are] & whether you are pleas'd [with] your Servant. I want to know whether if I can get Cato, you will exchange him for William. You know my reasons for this and they operate forcibly for this exchange. When you get fix'd, black Jace may answer, and then others can join me.

Kiss my dear little Girl & boy and assure them next to Mama papa wishes to see them of all people on earth. With the most[54]

HENRY KNOX TO LUCY FLUCKER KNOX, DOBB'S FERRY, NY, FRIDAY, 3 AUGUST 1781

Camp near Dobb's Ferry even[in]g. 3 Augt 1781.

I have the happiness to acknowledge your three favors, my life, my love, my all, dated one at Claremont the 23d of July by Colonel Lewis, one from the manor of livingston of the 26th July by a young Mr. Livingston also, [who] I had not the pleasure to see, and the last of the 30th by Express from Albany.[55] I shall not attempt to describe the pleasure they gave me, but be assur'd that my happiness is so interwoven with yours that I am totally unhappy in being absent. The longer the War lasts the more sick am I of it and sigh for domestic felicity with my Lucy. I am glad that you have found some amusement in your Journey. Upon your return to Colonel Duers, you will certainly find a long letter from me written some time ago. It is morally impossible I can forget you for a moment. Yesterday was y[ou]r birth day. I cannot attempt to shew you how much I was affect'd by it. I remember'd it, and I humbly petitioned heaven to grant us the happiness of continuing our union untill we should have the felicity of seeing our children flourishing around us, and ourselves concern'd with virtue, peace and Years, and that we both might take our flight together secure of an happy immortality. These were not momentary effusions, but they were the settled principles of the day.

I have heard nothing from Colonel Livingston in Jersey, notwithstanding what I wrote you last. I wish to know how long you intend to stay at Colonel Duers & whether you will make any stay at our friend Ellisons at New-Windsor.[56] If you send to the care of Colonel Hughes at Fish Kill, I shall receive it soon. Were you at New Windsor, I could write you every two days, and possibly might make a jaunt up to see you, at least it is possible that I might have business that would call me. Notwithstanding my anxiety, make your own convenience the rule of your actions.[57] I don't conceive I could go up at any rate under ten days and possibly not then.

Colonel Duer will relate our situation here. All is harmony and good fellowship between the two armies. I have no doubt when opportunity offers that the zeal of the french and the patriotism of the Americans, will go hand in hand to glory. I cannot explain to you the exact plan of campaign. We don't know it ourselves. You know what we wish, but we hope more at present than we believe.

My Brother writes me from Boston that a Mr. Winslow & family are going to England & as a cartel and would be glad to take your Letters. Write, I pray you, some very long letters, and don't forget to tell them how much I love, not to say adore you.[58] And I need not urge you to mention your several babes Kiss them; bless them for me, & assure yourself of the most perfect and unalterable affection of your

HKnox

Give my compliments to Lady Kitty & Miss Brown, also my love to Mrs. Blair. Enclos'd is a letter from Mr. Blair,[59] which Doctor Craik gave me a few days ago. I could wish him to join [us] as soon as his health will permit.

LUCY FLUCKER KNOX TO HENRY KNOX, "MR. DUERS,"
SUNDAY, 12 AUGUST 1781

No. 6

I am at a loss whether to write you or not, four posts have passed without a line from you, and general Lincoln,[60] who came immediately from your quarters brought no token of remembrance. This is what I am so unused to that I scarce know how to behave under it. If it is meant to mortify [me] it has answered the purpose admirably.

I wrote on Thursday last,[61] and forwarded my letter by Colo. Lewis, am very anxious for an answer that I may know how to proceed. Expect his return on Tuesday next.

We hear nothing of the movements of the Army, and poor [me] I am constantly Sick with anxiety. Oh horrid war, how hast thou blasted the fairest prospect of happiness, robbed of parents, of Sisters, & Brother, thou art depriving me of the Society of my husband, who alone could repair the loss.

But I am too low spirited to write, and lest I should infect you will conclude

>May the best of heavens blessings be yours.
>LK
>Mr. Duers 12th August

HENRY KNOX TO WILLIAM KNOX, PHILADELPHIA, PA,
TUESDAY, 4 SEPTEMBER 1781

Philadelphia 4 Septr 1781

I wrote you my dear brother from Kings Ferry about a week past, & informed you some movements were about take place but it was improper for me to specify what they were. One object is now developed and known to be Lord Cornwallis. Our measures are such that if the respective parts harmonize, we hope to do something handsome and we extend our views pretty far south.

This manoeuvere, though much thought of by me, deranges my little family and creates a distress known only to domesticated minds. The General & Mrs. Washington prefers Mrs. Knox to take a trip to Virginia and she seems inclined to accept of the offer for several reasons.[62] Our little daughter at any rate will be left in this Town at a eminent boarding school. Master Hal will be the companion of his mama, who is six months in[to] her fourth pregnancy.

In hopes of the arrival of the Amsterdam,[63] the other Vesell, and for reasons which you can easily imagine, I have been constrained again to draw upon you for purchase [of] about 100 dollars, and I have put it at ten days sight. The money belongs to a Mr. Somebody at Salem, and is here in the hands of Mr. Hodgdon[64] who can find no opportunity to send it.

I shall set off tomorrow from this place and Lucy, who if she goes to the southward, will also set off for her destination in a few days afterwards. She is in now in this City, and, if she does not go as before, suppos'd will probably remain here. Give my love to all friends

>I am your most Affectionate Brother,
>HKnox

LUCY FLUCKER KNOX TO HENRY KNOX, MOUNT VERNON, VA,
SATURDAY, 29 SEPTEMBER 1781

Mount Vernon Sept. 29 1781

Last evening I was so happy as to receive two lines from my dearest friend which were wellcome coming from him: tho I must say I wish he would bestow a little more time and pains upon the only pleasure I enjoy in his absence.

I wrote you on monday by Mr. Custis[65] and informed you that Lucy was fixed with Mrs. Bredo[?] in philidelphia. Colo. & Mrs. Biddle[66] have promised to see her every Sunday and to write by every mondays post. I directed them to forward their letters to you which I repent having done, as the communication between us, is much less frequent than I expected. I beg you will write him by the first opp[ortuni]ty and thank him for his great kindness & friendship to me and I need not ask you to forward any letters which mention the dear little girl, with all possible dispatch to her anxious mother. Will the time never come when we shall have a house of our own and our Children about us. If not, life is not desirable.

I mett a very kind reception from the good Lady of this place but my circumstances lead me ardently to wish for a home, and I see but one possible way to obtain one. You know my meaning. I wish for nothing inconsistent with your happiness and future peace. But could you reconcile it to your feelings, I think it would make me happy

Harry has been very troublesome to me since he lost his nurse. He will have nothing to say to the new one, but is in my arms day & night a circumstance not very agreeable at this t[ime], but I must not say who is to blame.

We have a report of an important action fought by Genl. Greene but fear it cannot be true as you do not mention it in your letters. Pray write me all news that may be communicated and believe me to be as ever

Yours

LK

———

HENRY KNOX TO LUCY FLUCKER KNOX, YORKTOWN, VA,
MONDAY, 1 OCTOBER 1781

Camp before York, 1 Octbr 1781

I was made happy my dearest and only love by your letter by Mr.
Custis which I received Yesterday. I am pleas'd with the disposition you
made of our little daughter, and to hear of the health of master Hal who
Mr. Custis says is a monstrous fine fellow.

We came before York on the 28th, on the 29 nearly completed the
investiture, but Yesterday the Enemy evacuated their out posts which
gives us a considerable advantage in point of time.[67] Our prospects are
good & we shall soon hope to impress our haughty foe with a respect
for the combined arms. I have been perfectly well since I have been in
Virginia. I pray You to present my respectful compliments to Mrs. Washington.

> I am my dearest hope
> Your affectionate
> HKnox

LUCY FLUCKER KNOX TO HENRY KNOX, MOUNT VERNON, VA,
MONDAY, 8 OCTOBER 1781

My ever dear Harry,

I promised you a long letter by Mr. Blair[68] but not having received a
single line from you since the 23rd Ultimo,[69] am led to conclude that you
could not spare time for the perusal of such an epistle. Never was I so
anxious as at this moment nor ever less able to bear it.

I send W[illia]m[70] for several reasons. The principle one, as it respects my own feelings, is that he may return to me with the earliest
news of any important event. Pray my only love, be attentive to me in
this instance, and as soon as any new lights are thrown upon the matter,
dispatch him to me express.

Mrs. W. proposes setting off this week for Williamsburg. Her return is
very uncertain. Lett me know when there is a ray of hope that I may see
you and why you do not write by the post.

You will find Mr. Blair an histeric [i.e., hysteric] companion. To him I

refer you for farther particulars, as my pen is infamous, and myself not
well.

Adieu in the true sense of the word

LK—

Mount Vernon October 8th 1781

LUCY FLUCKER KNOX TO HENRY KNOX, MOUNT VERNON, VA,
TUESDAY, 16 OCTOBER 1781

Mount Vernon October 16th 1781

Mrs. Washington & Mrs. Custis have just been made happy by the
receipt of long letters from their husbands, while I poor unhappy girl,
am not worthy of a line. It is not possible for any person to be more
low spirited than I have been for more than a week past, heavens that I
should be neglected at such a time. If you were so immersed in business
that not a moment could be devoted to my peace, surly Major Shaw[71]
has goodness enough to lett me know that you live. The generals letter
to Mrs. Washington is dated the 12th, wherin he informs her of every
manuvere however trifling, which has taken place since the opening of
the trenches. In consequense of these letters, she with Mrs. Custis setts
off tomorrow morning for Williamsburg in full expectation of being in
camp very shortly.

I shall remain here, probably ignorant of what is passing at the place
where my all is at stake. My last account from you was a few lines of the 6th
instant left at Alexandrie,[72] by Capt. Peirce.[73] On the same day I received a
letter from Mrs. Biddle informing me that my little girl was well and toll-
erably contented. I miss her more than I could have immagined, her little
prattle has diverted many an hours chagrin, but now when I retire to my
room I have no companion but my little Boy, who I hug and weep over.

Mrs. Washington will inform you of my reasons for not accompany-
ing her if you have forgot them, and will either deliver or forward this.
When you can spare time to write, lett me know when you intend to
come to me

Why you do not write.

I mentioned a bag to Major Shaw which was put into the waggon at
N.W. If Wm. can bring it I should be glad.[74]

HENRY KNOX TO LUCY FLUCKER KNOX, YORKTOWN, VA, TUESDAY, 16 OCTOBER 1781

Trenches before York 16 October 1781

My love,

I have only one moment to write by an express, which Colonel Humphreys[75] informs me is just going from Head quarters, to inform the best beloved of my soul that I am well & have been perfectly so. The night before last we stormed the enemies two advanced works with very little loss.[76] The fate of the enemy draws nigh. I hope in ten or 12 days, we shall with the blessing of heaven terminate it. I shall take care of Your Harry for Your sake. I shall send William to you tomorrow or next day at furthest when I shall be more particular.

I am my beloved
Your truly affectionate
HKnox

HENRY KNOX TO LUCY FLUCKER KNOX, YORKTOWN, VA, FRIDAY, 19 OCTOBER 1781

Camp before York 8 oClock A.M. 19th October

I have detain'd William untill this moment that I might be the first to communicate good news to the Charmer of my soul. A glorious moment for America! This day Lord Cornwallis & his Army marches out & piles their Arms in the face of our victorious Army. The day before Yesterday he desir'd commissioners might be named to treat of the surrender of his troops, their ships and every thing they possess. He at first requested that the Britons might be sent to Britain & the Germans to Germany. But this the General refused, and they have now agreed to surrender prisoners of War to be kept in America untill exchanged or released. They will have the same honors as the Garrison of Charlestown, that is they will not be permitted to unfurl their Colours or play Yankee doodle. We know not yet how many they are.

The General has just requested me to be at head quarters instantly. Therefore I cannot be more particular.

I have a note from Biddle,[77] Lucy is well & perfectly contented. I send you the last letter I rec'd of my Brother by which you will see in some degree the state of our affairs which are not bad.

I wish your situation had been such as to have come with Mrs. Washington. Truth is that you might have done it with out the least particle of injury. I shall see you if possible by the 12th, 15 or 20th of next month. How much I long for the happy moment!

I forgot one circumstance Billy wrote us in a letter which I can't find, that the Miss Cummings[?] from Halifax send their love to you by one of your Cousin Waldos, that they had just heard from England and that your dear connections were all well. Excuse this hasty scrawl. William will be able to inform you how little time I have had even for sleep.

Adieu the best beloved of my heart, and believe me to be your ever affectionate

Love

HKnox

———————

LUCY FLUCKER KNOX TO HENRY KNOX, MOUNT VERNON, VA, TUESDAY, 23 OCTOBER 1781

Mount Vernon October 23rd 1781

My Only Love,

After ten thousand anxietys we are at length informed by a letter from Colo. Wadsworth,[78] that the capture of Lord Cornwallis had, or shortly would, take place he having offered terms which were rejected, and unconditional submission, without alternative his only hope. If this should prove true and my Harry is Safe how gratful ought I to be to heaven.

I received a line from you by an express dated the 16th inst., wherein you inform me that you shall dispatch Wm in one or at most two days, in consequense of which I am watching for his arrival with impatient eyes.

This will be handed you by Mr. Lund Washington[79] who is going to look at the French fleet. He will inform you what a lovly Boy your Son is and that he eats homine [i.e., hominy] like a Virginian. He is a turbulent fellow, very unlike his dear Sister who I am very unhappy at not hearing from. Surly you must have received a letter from Biddle agreable [i.e., according] to [his] promise. My Letter by Wm will I trust inform me when I may hope to see you, and perhaps give me some idea of your determination, relative to the matter you mentioned in Philadelphia. Mrs. Washington has or will deliver you a very low spirited letter from me.[80] She will be just in time to dance at your Ball where I should like to be present.

Adieu

Compliments to Mr. Blair, Mr. Shaw[81] &c, the latter of whom I had a sad presentiment would not come off well in this matter

LK—

PS

if my bag has not been sent by William, ask Major Shaw to have it put on board Mr. Washingtons boat

---

HENRY KNOX TO LUCY FLUCKER KNOX, YORKTOWN, VA, WEDNESDAY, 31 OCTOBER 1781

Camp near York 31 October 1781

Your favor by Mrs. Washington I received, and it gave me inexpressible pleasure to find that my Lucy, the joy of my heart, was in good Spirits. I hope to have the sweet felicity of embracing you in ten days from today and perhaps sooner. The duty which I have to execute is so extensive and from circumstances so embarras'd that my time is as fully employ'd at present as in the moment of the siege. We are now making the disposition of the numerous cannon, arms, and other trophies, in order to place them in a state of security when we shall depart. The French Army will winter here and in the vicinity. All the troops belonging to the states south of Pennsylvania inclusive will march to join General Greene. All the troops from Jersey inclusive will in a day or two commence their march by land northward except the Artillery who go by Water.

I enclose the last letter from our good friend and Brother William. You will see by it he is just on the point of setting off. God bless him. I shall have a light Waggon and shall bring the bag you have mentioned with me. The British fleet of 26 ships of the line, including 2 of 50 Guns, have at last made their appearance at the Capes in order to releive Lord Cornwallis. They have come too late, and too weak for such an attempt. Count de Grasse has or will attack them with 35 sail of the line the moment the wind shall serve. But the english will be too cautious for him I fear. It would end the campaign gloriously to take five or six ships from the imperious english.

I have receiv'd no other letter from Biddle than the one I mentioned or enclosed to you. Dear little Girl I long to see her as I do her infinitely dearer mother. How is Hal? Cannot you impress his memory so powerfuly with the taking of Lord Cornwallis, as to make the little fellow tell it to his children?

Adieu, my partner,

friend and highest hope

HKnox

I have sent the bag.

1782

HENRY KNOX TO LUCY FLUCKER KNOX, ELIZABETH, NJ, SUNDAY, 31 MARCH 1782

Elizabeth Town 31 March 1782

To my extreme mortification we are here yet and, what is worse, I cannot at present form an opinion when we shall be able to get away & I fly to the arms of my love. Yesterday the British commissioners arrived here, and are Genl. Dalrymple, formerly of the 14th rgt.[82] and Andrew Eliot Esqr.[83] They are accompanied by some other officers among whom is Mr. Loring.[84] We have exchanged our respective powers, and shall begin on business tomorrow morning. If they are disposed to go [to] all lengths which the interest of both sides dictate, we shall not be able to get from hence untill the 10th of April. It is painful beyond bearance to be absent from you, at this season which is not within our calculation of seperation. The more I am with you, the less I can endure to be absent from my love & those essential & rapturous pledges of love our sweet children. Every child I see brings them in full view, and your image dwells with me.

Mr. Loring informs me that he received a letter from Mr. Jon.n Simpson[85] dated in January last, acquainting him of a number of Boston families [in England] and among others yours was particularly mentioned to be in perfect health. Your Cousin, young Isaac Winslow, is here and a charming boy he is, very unlike the small genius at Boston.[86] Kiss my sweet babes a thousand times, and don't forget the man who loves you supremely. I hope to receive a letter by the next opportunity. Colonel Biddle will inform you when the stage sets out. Give my love to him.[87] The stage is now waiting at the door. Heaven bless you and the dear little images.

Adieu

HKnox

LUCY FLUCKER KNOX TO HENRY KNOX, PHILADELPHIA, PA,
WEDNESDAY, 10 APRIL 1782

Philadelphia April 10th

My dearest friend,

I received a letter this morning from my dear Harry, which to my un-speakable mortification informed me that my happiness was delayed for some days longer, or in other words that he, the sole pleasure of my life, was detained beyond his expectations.

My love complains that I have not wrote to him, but he does not con-sider how very very uncertain his stay has been. For the first fortnight his return was daily expected, and since that time I have been prevented by events or rather causes which I will relate by mouth and trust they will be satisfactory.

I have received a long letter from our brother Wm and one from Mr. Williams,[88] both of which I should have forwarded could I have immag-ined you would have staid so long. William was well and in good Spirits. I am now at Colo. Biddles with our little Treasures. Lucy has grown robust, Harry needed no improvement and Marcus is dearer to me than ever.[89]

The justice which your country has done you would have reached you sooner. Could I have immagined your friends (your political friends) would have neglected to inform you of it by express, but they like me perhaps daily expected your return Sunday evening.[90] I promise myself that happiness in the mean time.

Adieu
My all in life
L Knox

———

HENRY KNOX TO LUCY FLUCKER KNOX, ELIZABETH, NJ,
MONDAY, 15 APRIL 1782

Elizabeth Town 15th April 1782

I received your letter my best beloved, dated the 10th which gave me great pleasure, although some expressions seem to imply that my charmer had been in some difficulty. This implication I hope however is the consequence of an ardent affection. I am mortified that I have been so long absent from you, but I now think that we shall be able to get away from here tomorrow. We shall be obliged to stop one day at Morris[town] perhaps to make our report to the General and in two days afterwards be in Philadelphia, which will bring it to Friday or Saturday. Untill then adieu my best hope. Kiss the sweet babes, and give my love to our friend Biddle & his amiable family. Shaw joined me yesterday.

HKnox

1783

HENRY KNOX TO HANNAH WALDO FLUCKER, HARLEM, NY,
MONDAY, 24 NOVEMBER 1783

Harlem, 7 miles from New York, 24 Novr. 1783

My dear Madam,

The kindness of Mr. Watson presents an opportunity [in] which I cannot omit to inform you of the health of part of your family whose happiness I assure myself is still dear to you. My Lucy is at West point with her three sweet children in perfect health. They will be in New York as soon as the british forces evacuate it which is intended tomorrow. She will spend this winter in Boston and perhaps the greatest part of next year. I shall write you particularly from thence. We are extremely anxious to hear from you in answer to our several letters. I wrote in May last and Lucy has written twice since once in June & the other in July or August.

I beg my sincere ardent affections may be presented to Mrs. Waldo, Mrs. Urquhart, Capt. Flucker and Lady, & Mrs. & Mr. Jepson. Mrs. Flucker, and Mr. Jepson I hope I shall in some future day have the pleasure of being acquainted with.

I am my very dear Madam
Your truly affectionate
Son
HKnox

Afterwards (1784–1824)

Although peace returned to America, the Knoxes' lives continued to change in the decades that followed the Revolutionary War. Henry remained in the military in the months immediately after the British evacuation, during which time he commanded the several hundred men remaining in the Continental army. He resigned his commission in early 1784 and, the following year, accepted a congressional appointment as the new nation's secretary of war, where he officially oversaw America's tiny postwar military establishment. George Washington asked Knox to continue in this post four years later, at the start of the former commander's presidency. While a member of Washington's cabinet, Henry's duties grew significantly. Not only did he become responsible for managing the federal government's policies toward the American Indians, but he also organized three military expeditions against warring tribes in the Ohio Valley. The ultimate success of these operations opened up vast tracts of land for white settlement north of the Ohio River. A staunch Federalist, Knox involved himself in the emerging party politics of the 1790s. Believing that the nation needed an energetic central government with adequate authority to lead, he strongly supported both the ratification of the Constitution and Washington's later efforts to expand federal power.

Although busy with public affairs throughout these years, Henry and Lucy remained deeply devoted to each other and always avoided being physically apart whenever possible. Continuing to have children well into the 1790s, the couple spent much of their time together rearing their sons and daughters. Tragically, though, most of their offspring died at young ages, with only 3 of the Knoxes' 13 children surviving to adulthood. Lucy, however, remained an assertive spouse after the war. No evidence exists to indicate that she ever directly challenged Henry's patriarchal authority, but she did insist that post-war family decisions be joint ones, and Henry always acquiesced in this. Lucy also reestablished communication with her family in England following the American Revolution, but her contacts with them were few and largely without any real emotion. The Fluckers wanted the Knoxes to use their political connections to help settle the former colonial royal secretary's remaining estate in Massachusetts and secure at least some portion of the great Waldo Patent for his survivors. None of Lucy's immediate family ever returned to America.[1]

For the rest of their lives, Lucy and Henry remained ambitious and were determined to achieve security and wealth for their own family. Toward this end, Henry eventually gained legal control of a significant portion of the Waldo Patent, as well as engaged in other large-scale land speculations. After he left Washington's cabinet in 1795, he and Lucy relocated to the Maine frontier, where they built a grand 23-room mansion near Penobscot Bay. From this imposing seat, Knox became recognized as one of New England's "Great Proprietors." Given his own Federalist leanings, he expected deference and respect from newly arrived small farmers who had migrated from southern New England after the War of Independence. Knox, however, became financially overextended and was caught up in the shifting social climate and economic changes of the 1790s. Many settlers vocally (and sometimes violently) opposed him, both for his increasingly outdated social values and from the perception that he had merely inherited the privileges he enjoyed. In a post-revolutionary world, where equality had become the watchword, such benefits seemed wrong, as well as illegitimate. As a result, in later life, Henry found himself embroiled in money difficulties and frontier protests. He died in 1806, at the age of 56. Heartbroken at the loss of her "only friend," as well as by the deaths of so many children, Lucy gradually sold off the family's lands and lived largely alone inside the couple's enormous mansion until her own death in 1824, at the age of 68.

Introduction

1. Many editions of the Adamses' correspondence been published over the generations. The latest is Margaret A. Hogan and C. James Taylor, eds., *My Dearest Friend: Letters of Abigail and John Adams* (Cambridge, MA, 2007). See also Edith Gelles, ed., *Abigail Adams: Letters* (New York, 2016). The couple has also been the subject of a number of joint biographies, including, most recently, Edith Gelles, *Abigail and John: Portrait of a Marriage* (New York, 2009); Joseph Ellis, *First Family: Abigail and John Adams* (New York, 2010); G. J. Barker-Benfield, *Abigail and John Adams: The Americanization of Sensibility* (Chicago, 2010). These books are part of an important trend in joint biographies of historical couples. For instance, the following award-winning books have recently appeared: Deborah Heiligman, *Charles and Emma: The Darwins' Leap of Faith* (New York, 2009); Mary Gabriel, *Love and Capital: Karl and Jenny Marx and the Birth of a Revolution* (New York, 2011); Flora Fraser, *The Washingtons: George and Martha, "Join'd by Friendship, Crown'd by Love"* (New York, 2015).

2. John and Abigail Adams, by contrast, were 39 and 31 years old, respectively, when the war began.

3. Francis S. Drake, *Life and Correspondence of Henry Knox* (Boston, 1873), 8–9; North Callahan, *Henry Knox: General Washington's General* (New York, 1958), 16–17. For a recent biography of Henry Knox, see Mark Puls, *Henry Knox: Visionary General of the American Revolution* (New York, 2008). The best scholarly biography of Knox, though, remains Callahan's *Henry Knox*.

4. Noah Brooks, *Henry Knox: A Soldier of the Revolution* (New York, 1900), 19–23; Callahan, 17–19; Zachariah G. Whitman, *The History of the Ancient and Honorable Artillery Company* (Boston, 1842), 301–2; Drake, 8–10; "Henry Knox and the London Book-Store in Boston, 1771–1774," *Proceedings of the Massachusetts Historical Society*, 61 (June 1928), 227–28.

5. "Knox and the London Book-Store," *Proceedings*, 227–28; Callahan, 20.

6. Henry Knox to Henry Jackson, 29 Aug 1774, Gilder Lehrman Collection, New York City [hereafter GLC].

7. "Knox and the London Book-Store," *Proceedings*, 228–29; Benjamin L. Carp, *Defiance of the Patriots: The Boston Tea Party and the Making of America* (New York, 2010), 33. For information about Knox's Boston competitors in the bookselling business in the early 1770s, see "Knox and the London Book-Store," *Proceedings*, 229–30.

8. Callahan, 23–24. Otis's recollections about Knox's bookstore are from Drake, 12. Knox's wastebook is in the collections of the Massachusetts Historical Society, Boston. Knox's correspondence with many of his bookstore customers is reprinted in "Knox and the London Book-Store"; the originals are in the GLC. On Boston's economic stagnation, see Carp, 32–33.

9. Drake, 12.

10. Lorenzo Sabine, *The American Loyalists, or Biographical Sketches of Adherents to the British Crown in the War of the Revolution: Alphabetically Arranged; with a Preliminary Historical Essay*, 2 vols. (Boston, 1847), 1:290; Alan Taylor, *Liberty Men and Great Proprietors: The Revolutionary Settlement on the Maine Frontier, 1760–1820* (Chapel Hill, NC, 1990), 39. Beyond her parents' loyalty to the Crown, Lucy's uncle and her siblings were all Tories. Her uncle, Francis Waldo, had to leave Boston in 1778, after being proscribed and banished by the Massachusetts state government; her brother, Thomas Flucker Jr., was an officer in the British Army and was stationed in Antigua when the American Revolution began; her sister Hannah married a British officer named James Urquhart in 1774; and, in 1776, Lucy's youngest sister Sally married an army chaplain named Mr. Jephson, who belonged to an Irish regiment and later became a member of the Irish Parliament. For more information about Francis Waldo and the Fluckers, see Sabine, 1:668–69; James Henry Stark, *Loyalists of Massachusetts and the Other Side of the American Revolution* (Boston, 1907), 403–4.

11. On the assertiveness of Boston's women during the crisis, see Carol Berkin, *Revolutionary Mothers: Women in the Struggle for America's Independence* (New York, 2005), 15.

12. Stark, 403. Lucy shared Knox's rather large physique. Probably the most famous line about her appearance comes from Abigail Adams, who wrote, during the Revolutionary War, that "her size is enormous; I am frightened when I look at her," quoted in Ron Chernow, *Washington: A Life* (New York, 2010), 204. For a recent popular history about Lucy Flucker Knox, see Nancy Rubin Stuart, *Defiant Brides: The Untold Story of Two Revolutionary-Era Women and the Radical Men They Married* (Boston, 2013).

13. Most of these letters are available digitally at the Gilder Lehrman Institute's website, https://www.gilderlehrman.org/collections/.

14. A particularly useful source in tracking down information was one by Mark M. Boatner III, *Encyclopedia of the American Revolution*, 3rd ed. (Mechanicsburg, PA, 1994).

Chapter 1 · Courtship and Marriage (1773–1775)

1. *Winslow Family Memorial* [transcript], 1:190, Massachusetts Historical Society.

2. On the growing role that love and physical attraction played in mid-eighteenth-century courtships and marriages, see especially Nicole Eustace, *Passion Is the Gale: Emotion, Power, and the Coming of the Revolution* (Chapel Hill, NC, 2008); Mary Beth Norton, *Liberty's Daughters: The Revolutionary Experience of American Women, 1750–1800* (Ithaca, NY, 1996); Carol Berkin, *First Generations: Women in Colonial America* (New York, 1996); Carol Berkin, *Revolutionary Mothers: Women in the Struggle for America's Independence* (New York, 2005).

3. See Henry Knox to Lucy Waldo Flucker, 7 Mar 1774, GLC.

4. Henry Knox to Henry Jackson, 29 Aug 1774, GLC. Sarah Erving Waldo (1737–1817) was the wife Samuel Waldo (1723–1770). On the intervention of Isaac Winslow (1709–1777) on behalf of the couple, see *Winslow Family Memorial* [transcript], 1:190.

5. Henry Knox to Henry Jackson, 29 Aug 1774, GLC. The two statutes Knox referred

to were probably two of Parliament's "Coercive Acts." The Administration of Justice Act and the Quartering Act were passed by Parliament in May and June 1774, and news of them arrived in Boston around the time Knox wrote this letter.

6. David Hackett Fischer, *Paul Revere's Ride* (New York, 1995), 44–45, 58–64. In terms of evidence pointing to Knox as a Patriot informant, Fischer cites a letter Paul Revere wrote to Jeremy Belknap in 1798, discussing the Salem raid and stating that he learned of the British action from a Whig with connections to those working in the Town House. Fischer speculates that Thomas Flucker Sr. may have privately mentioned the planned raid to his son-in-law, who, in turn, informed Paul Revere.

7. James Rivington to Henry Knox, 1 Dec 1774, GLC; *Boston Gazette*, 20 March 1775; "Knox and the London Book-Store," *Proceedings of the Massachusetts Historical Society*, 61 (Jun 1928), 234.

8. The originals of the first and second letters have not survived. The transcriptions are from copies made in 1855.

9. Knox probably forwarded Lucy a copy of Allen Ramsey's *The Gentle Shepherd: A Scots Romantic Comedy*, originally published in Edinburgh in 1755.

10. In this letter, Knox refers to Lucy as "Speria" and himself as "Fidelio." "Speria" may be short for Hesperia, one of the Hesperides in Greek mythology. According to tradition, the Hesperides were thought of as the "nymphs of the evening" or "nymphs of the West." On the pattern of many eighteenth-century Americans using classical pseudonyms in their private correspondence and public writings, see Eran Shalev, *Rome Reborn on Western Shores: Historical Imagination and the Creation of the American Republic* (Charlottesville, VA, 2009), 151–87.

Chapter 2 · *The Excitement of War (April 1775–June 1776)*

1. There is debate among historians about when and how the Knoxes left Boston in the spring of 1775. Noah Brooks, in *Henry Knox: A Soldier of the Revolution* (New York, 1900), wrote that the couple left on the evening of 19 April 1775, but he offers no citation to confirm this assertion. Samuel Drake, in *Life and Correspondence of Henry Knox* (Boston, 1873), says that they left on 16 June 1775, though again, no citation is provided. North Callahan, in *Henry Knox: General Washington's General* (New York, 1958), simply asserts that the Knoxes left after the Lexington and Concord battles. The question is most fully explored on J. L. Bell's blog site, *Boston 1775*. In a posting on 17 May 2011, entitled "When Did Knox Leave Boston?," Bell speculates that the Knoxes had left that city prior to mid-May 1775. To support this assertion, he quotes a diary kept by the Reverend Dr. Samuel Cooper, who claimed to have dined with "Mr. Knox and Wife of Boston" at the Reverend William Emerson's home in Concord, Massachusetts, on 13 May 1775. See http://boston1775.blogspot.com/2011/05/when-did-henry-knox-leave-boston.html (accessed 13 March 2012). Although Henry left his younger brother William in charge of the bookstore after his departure, business had all but ceased by April 1775.

2. Brooks, 19–23; Callahan, 19; Zachariah G. Whitman, *The History of the Ancient and Honorable Artillery Company* (Boston, 1842), 301–2.

3. Washington Irving would later write about Henry's military emergence in 1775: "Knox was one of those providential characters which spring up in emergencies, as if they were formed by and for the occasion," quoted in Joseph W. Porter, ed., *Memoir of Gen. Henry Knox, of Thomaston, Maine* (Bangor, ME, 1890), 3.

4. On the possibility that Knox took part in the preparations for this battle, see Paul Lockhart, *The Whites of Their Eyes: Bunker Hill, the First American Army, and the Emergence of George Washington* (New York, 2011), 321–23.

5. See Henry Knox to Lucy Knox, 6 Jul 1775, GLC.

6. See, for instance, Henry Knox to William Knox, 25 Sept 1775, GLC.

7. The story of Knox's Fort Ticonderoga expedition has been told many times; the best account remains that of Callahan, 33–60. Knox's claim to have suffered considerably from the cold is contained in his letter to Lucy of 5 Jan 1776, GLC.

8. Henry Knox to Lucy Knox, 17 Dec 1775, GLC.

9. Colonial Royal Secretary Flucker had left Boston with General Thomas Gage in October 1775. For more information about the Fluckers after their departure from Massachusetts, see Callahan, 58–59; Lorenzo Sabine, *The American Loyalists, or Biographical Sketches of Adherents to the British Crown in the War of the Revolution: Alphabetically Arranged; with a Preliminary Historical Essay*, 2 vols. (Boston, 1847), 1:499 and 2:450; James Henry Stark, *Loyalists of Massachusetts and the Other Side of the American Revolution* (Boston, 1907), 402–4. When Henry Knox reentered the city, he found that his bookstore had been vandalized by British troops. See Callahan, 59–60.

10. Henry Knox to Lucy Knox, ca. 5–17 Mar 1776, GLC.

11. Lucy Knox to Henry Knox, ca. late Apr 1776, GLC; Callahan, 62–63. On the issue of women in the Continental army's encampments, see Caroline Cox, *A Proper Sense of Honor* (Chapel Hill, NC, 2004), 140.

12. Henry Knox to Lucy Knox, 2 May 1776; Henry Knox to William Knox, 23 May 1776, GLC.

13. Henry Knox to William Knox, 23 May 1776 and 3 Jun 1776, GLC.

14. General George Washington (1732–1799). Washington had arrived in Cambridge to assume command of the Continental army on Sunday, 2 July 1775. This letter describes Knox's first meeting with the new commander-in-chief.

15. General Charles Lee (1731–1782) was born in England and joined the British army at the age of 15. He fought in the French and Indian War, including service both in America and Portugal. Settling in Virginia in 1773, Lee supported the American cause and offered his services to the Continental Congress as soon as the war started. Appointed a major general, he had traveled with Washington from Philadelphia to Cambridge, Massachusetts. For more information about Lee's background and Revolutionary War career, see Phillip Papas, *Renegade Revolutionary: The Life of General Charles Lee* (New York, 2014).

16. Dr. Benjamin Church (1734–1778?) of Boston. Church was a member of the Massachusetts Provincial Congress. In July 1775, the Continental Congress appointed him director general of the Continental army hospital in Cambridge, Massachusetts. In September 1775, however, Washington learned that Church might have passed on secret information to the British. A military council of war, presided over by the commander, investigated and determined that Church had indeed carried on a "criminal correspondence" with the enemy. Thus the congress ordered his immediate imprisonment. Church, who was named in the Massachusetts Banishment Act of 1778, sailed from Boston that year, bound for the Caribbean, but his ship disappeared en route and he was presumably lost at sea. The most recent examination of Church's betrayal of the American cause is

John A. Nagy, *Dr. Benjamin Church, Spy: A Case of Espionage on the Eve of the American Revolution* (Yardley, PA, 2013).

17. Major General John Burgoyne (1722–1792). A veteran of the Seven Years' War, Burgoyne possessed considerable military experience, as well as many political connections in London. He arrived in America in May 1775, along with Generals William Howe (1729–1814) and Henry Clinton (1730–1795).

18. Perhaps Samuel Blachley Webb (1753–1807) of Connecticut, stepson of Silas Deane (1738–1789), a member of the Continental Congress and America's first diplomatic minister to France. Several weeks later, in late July 1775, Webb would be made an aide-de-camp to General Israel Putnam.

19. Major Andrew Bruce of the 38th Regiment. Bruce would be promoted to lieutenant colonel in 1777 and, late in the war, served in the 54th Regiment.

20. In these three sentences, Knox is apparently repeating Major Bruce's words to Webb verbatim.

21. Major General Thomas Gage (1721–1787), commander-in-chief of British forces in North America from 1763 to 1775, as well as provincial governor of Massachusetts Bay. Recalled by the British ministry in London in September 1775, he left Boston in October and did not take part in the remainder of the American Revolution.

22. Major General William Howe. Howe, a veteran of the French and Indian War and an officer of considerable military experience, had been openly sympathetic to the colonies throughout the imperial crisis. He arrived in Boston in May 1775, along with Generals Burgoyne and Clinton. Howe led the British assault at the Battle of Bunker Hill on 17 June 1775 and assumed overall command of the British army in Boston in October 1775. His brother was Admiral Richard Howe (1726–1799).

23. Lieutenant Colonel James Abercromby (1732–1775), commander of the grenadier battalion during the Battle of Bunker Hill. Abercromby was the highest ranking British officer killed that day.

24. Knox misdated this letter as Monday, 11 July 1775, but 11 July fell on a Tuesday that year. He probably penned it on 10 July.

25. These letters have not survived.

26. Possibly Captain Michael Jackson (1734–1801), who later commanded the 8th Massachusetts Regiment.

27. The house Knox referred to belonged to Enoch Brown, a Boston retailer and tavernkeeper. Militiamen destroyed the house, because British pickets had been using the structure to observe and fire on American soldiers. See Lockhart, 286.

28. August 9th was a Wednesday. This letter, therefore, was most likely written on Thursday, August 10th.

29. The seven prisoners Knox discusses here were probably from among the 17 British seamen captured on 12 June 1775 at Machias, Maine. With assistance from a Loyalist merchant named Ichabod Jones, the British sailors had attempted to obtain lumber for the British army in Boston when they were attacked and seized by a company of Machias Patriots. There were also 30 other British seamen from the sloop HMS *Falcon* held in captivity in Watertown, Massachusetts, that day. They had been captured on 8 August 1775, when they attempted to seize an American merchant ship anchored near Gloucester, Massachusetts. For more information about Jones and the British prisoners,

see "James Warren to John Adams, 9 August 1775," *Founders Online*, National Archives, https://founders.archives.gov/documents/Adams/06-03-02-0065/, last modified 28 December 2016. [Original source: Robert J. Taylor, ed., *The Adams Papers: Papers of John Adams*, vol. 3, *May 1775–January 1776* (Cambridge, MA, 1979), 114–16, n2].

30. On 6 August, a British squadron of eight ships raided Fishers Island, off the Connecticut coast, and seized its sheep and cattle. The ships then transported the animals back to Boston to help feed the besieged British garrison.

31. Probably Gilbert Warner Speakman. He later enlisted in the Continental army and served in the 14th Continental Regiment, as well as commissary of military stores in Springfield, Massachusetts.

32. For Washington's specific orders to Knox, see "Instructions to Colonel Henry Knox, 16 November 1775," *Founders Online*, National Archives, https://founders.archives .gov/documents/Washington/03-02-02-0351/, last modified 28 December 2016. [Original source: Philander D. Chase, ed., *The Papers of George Washington: Revolutionary War Series*, vol. 2, *16 September 1775-31 December 1775* (Charlottesville, VA, 1987, 384–85.]

33. Knox's close lifelong friend, Henry Jackson (1747–1809) of Boston. Jackson, however, did not accompany Knox to Fort Ticonderoga. Later in the war, Jackson would command a regiment of Continental troops, and he served as Knox's business partner in land-speculation ventures in northern New England in the 1780s and 1790s.

34. William Knox (1756–1795), Henry's younger brother, who accompanied him on the Fort Ticonderoga mission.

35. Henry Jackson.

36. General Philip Schuyler (1733–1804) of New York commanded American forces in the Northern Department.

37. Knox probably felt great anxiety regarding Lucy's physical health during his absence, because she was seven months pregnant with her first child at that time.

38. The success of Knox's expedition depended on sufficient snowfall and cold weather, in order to transport the 59 cannon and howitzers on the large, ox-pulled sleds that he and his men had constructed at Fort Ticonderoga.

39. General Richard Prescott (1725–1788) was captured by the Americans on 17 November 1775. He was singled out, due to his harsh treatment of Ethan Allen (1738–1789) when the latter had fallen into British hands in September. The capture of Fort Ticonderoga, in May of that year, was led by Allen and his Green Mountain Boys, along with Colonel Benedict Arnold (1741–1801). The British exchanged Prescott for American general John Sullivan in 1776, but the unlucky Briton was caught once more in 1777, making him the only such high-ranking officer to have been seized twice by the rebels. The British again exchanged him in 1778, this time for another American general, Charles Lee. For more information about Prescott's experiences in the hands of Americans, see "Philip Schuyler to George Washington, 28 November 1775," *Founders Online*, National Archives, https://founders.archives.gov/documents/Washington/03-02-02-0409/, last modified 28 December 2016. [Original source: Chase, vol. 2, 453–55, n2.]

40. Knox wrote this final passage on the upper right corner of page 1 of this letter.

41. During the period when Knox wrote this letter, the British were preparing to evacuate Boston. On the evening of 5 March, Washington positioned several thousand soldiers, as well as the guns Knox had brought from Fort Ticonderoga, atop Dorchester Heights, directly overlooking the city. General Howe initially planned a frontal attack on

the American position, but a late-winter snowstorm prevented the operation. The British commander then decided to leave Boston altogether. Howe informed Washington that he would leave the city intact if his forces and fleet could depart unmolested. On 17 March, the last British soldiers left Boston and sailed for Halifax, Nova Scotia. Several hundred Loyalists also evacuated the city, including Lucy's mother and two sisters. Colonial Royal Secretary Thomas Flucker had already left Boston with General Gage in October 1775. On the Dorchester operation and the British evacuation, see John Ferling, *Almost a Miracle: The American Victory in the War of Independence* (New York, 2007), 104–7.

42. A reference to the couple's infant daughter, Lucy Knox (1776–1854), born on 26 February.

43. Admiral Esek Hopkins (1718–1802) of Rhode Island. Hopkins, a prominent mariner and merchant before the war, was appointed commander-in-chief of the Continental navy by the Second Continental Congress in October 1775. Although he competed for supplies and men with American privateers, Hopkins's services failed to meet congressional expectations. Therefore, he was censured by the congress in 1776 and dismissed from the service the following year. Hopkins's brother, Stephen (1707–1785), was a member of the congress and a signer of the Declaration of Independence.

44. Admiral Hopkins's son was Captain John Burroughs Hopkins (1742–1796). He was probably wounded in the battle of Block Island on the night of 6 April 1776. Seven ships, under Admiral Hopkins, attempted to capture the HMS *Glasgow*, a 20–gun ship, off the coast of Newport, Rhode Island. Although the British vessel sustained heavy damage, it escaped.

45. Admiral Maarten Tromp (1598–1653).

46. "Aunt Waldo" is probably Sarah Erving Waldo, widow of Samuel Waldo, who was a brother of Lucy's mother. Sarah Waldo did not remarry and died a widow. See *Genealogy of the Waldo Family: A Record of Descendants of Cornelius Waldo*, vol. 1 (Worcester, MA, 1903), 185–87.

47. Catharine Littlefield Greene (1755–1814), wife of General Nathanael Greene (1742–1786), Henry's close friend throughout the American Revolution.

48. Probably Mary Hopkinson Morgan (ca. 1742–1785), wife of Dr. John Morgan (1735–1789), who was the director general of the Continental army's general hospital from 1775 to 1777. Mary Morgan's brother was Francis Hopkinson (1737–1791), one of the signers of the Declaration of Independence.

49. Lucy Knox had her daughter baptized on Sunday, 28 April 1776. The baby's sponsors are also listed in Trinity Church's baptismal records. See Andrew Oliver and James Bishop Peabody, eds., *The Records of Trinity Church, Boston, 1728–1830*, vol. 55–56 (Boston, 1982), 56:569.

50. Lucy probably was referring to some remaining British ships and forces on Georges Island, southeast of Boston. The bulk of the enemy's troops had departed for Halifax, Nova Scotia, the previous month.

51. Most likely Lucy's servant.

52. Romeo was one of the Knoxes' horses.

Chapter 3 · The Perils of War I

1. Henry Knox to William Knox, 11 Jul 1776, GLC.

2. Henry Knox to Lucy Knox, 11 Jul 1776, GLC.

3. Henry Knox to Lucy Knox, 28 Aug 1776, GLC.

4. Henry Knox to Lucy Knox, 10 Nov 1776, GLC.

5. Lucy Knox to William Knox, 20 Sept 1776, GLC.

6. See Henry Knox to William Knox, 10 Oct 1776, GLC, where Henry mentions the stress Lucy was experiencing, due to their ever-lengthening separation.

7. Henry Knox to Lucy Knox, 22 Nov 1776, GLC.

8. Henry Knox to Lucy Knox, 15 Dec 1776, GLC.

9. Henry Knox to Lucy Knox, 28 Dec 1776, GLC.

10. Henry Knox to Lucy Knox, 7 Jan 1777, GLC.

11. Lucy Knox to Henry Knox, ca. early Jan 1777, GLC.

12. Henry Knox to Lucy Knox, 10 Jan 1777, GLC.

13. Henry Knox to Lucy Knox, 6 Mar 1777; Lucy Knox to Henry Knox, 18 Mar 1777, GLC.

14. Lucy Knox to Henry Knox, 3 Apr 1777, GLC. On 9 April 1777, the Massachusetts General Court voted to authorize the judge of probate to formally appoint agents for the estates of absentee Crown supporters. This initial move to seize control of Loyalist property was later followed by the more draconian confiscation law of 1779. See John T. Hassam, *The Confiscated Estates of Boston Loyalists* (Cambridge, MA, 1927), 5. On the location of Thomas Flucker Sr.'s house on Boston's Summer Street, see John Kneeland's deed to Thomas Flucker, 22 Aug 1763, GLC, and James Henry Stark, *Loyalists of Massachusetts and the Other Side of the American Revolution* (Boston, 1907), 403.

15. Lucy Knox to Hannah Flucker Urquhart, ca. Apr 1777, GLC. Hannah Flucker had married James Urquhart in November 1774. Urquhart was a captain in the British 14th Foot (renamed the 14th Regiment in 1782). They divorced after the war.

16. Lucy Knox to Hannah Flucker Urquhart, ca. Apr 1777, GLC. On the outbreak of smallpox epidemics in New England during the American Revolution, see Elizabeth A. Fenn, *Pox Americana: The Great Smallpox Epidemic of 1775–1782* (New York, 2001).

17. Lucy Knox to Henry Knox, 1[?] May 1777, 8 May 1777 [morning], and 8 May 1777 [evening], GLC.

18. Knox is describing the arrival on Monday, 1 July, of a significant portion of the British fleet in New York waters, the event that precipitated Lucy's hasty departure from the city.

19. This line was written vertically down the left margin of the letter.

20. That would have been 6 July. This letter is not extant.

21. Knox and Putnam probably were referring to the title character in Eliza Haywood's novel, *The History of Betsy Thoughtless* (1751). "General Putnam" was Israel Putnam of Connecticut (1718–1790), a veteran of the French and Indian War and a major general in the Continental army, known more for his reckless bravery than his military intelligence.

22. Probably Colonel William Palfrey (1741–1780) of Massachusetts, then paymaster general of the Continental army. In 1780, the Continental Congress appointed Palfrey consul general to France, but his ship disappeared during its transatlantic crossing.

23. A reference to the wife of Captain Jonathan Pollard (1749–1802), then quartermaster of Knox's artillery regiment. Mrs. Pollard fled New York City on 1 July with Lucy, and the pair traveled and lived together in Connecticut throughout the remainder of the year. Before the war, Jonathan Pollard had a shop located next to Knox's London Bookstore.

24. "Mrs. A." is probably a Mrs. Airey, who was perhaps Henry's landlady at No. 1 Broadway in New York City; "Packard" was either a city grocer or a local merchant.

25. Probably Thaddeus Burr (1735–1801), the sheriff of Fairfield County and a member of several statewide Patriot committees. In 1779, the British raided Fairfield and burned much of the town, including Burr's house.

26. Perhaps David Sears Sr., originally a Boston merchant.

27. Probably John Broome (1738–1810), a lieutenant colonel in a New York militia regiment. A merchant before the war, Broome later became lieutenant governor of the state.

28. On the afternoon of 12 July, two British warships, the HMS *Phoenix* and the HMS *Rose*, sailed from Staten Island, passed the mouth of the Hudson River, and exchanged fire with Knox's shore batteries. The American fire was largely ineffective, and during the exchange, six artillerymen died when their cannon exploded, due to the crew's inexperience in handling and firing their guns. For more information on this exchange and the American reaction to it, see George C. Daughan, *Revolution on the Hudson: New York City and the Hudson River Valley in the American War of Independence* (New York, 2016), 44–53. Knox also mentions this exchange to Lucy in his letter of 13 Jul 1776, which is in GLC but not reproduced in this volume.

29. Richard Howe, 4th Viscount Howe, commander of the North American fleet. The British ministry, under Lord North, had also appointed Howe, as well as his younger brother William, to be peace commissioners to the colonists; hence the brothers' offer to parley with Washington.

30. Colonel Benjamin Tupper (1738–1792) commanded several American gunboats on the Hudson River in the New York campaign.

31. Colonel Joseph Reed (1741–1785), Washington's one-time aide-de-camp, then serving as the Continental army's adjutant general.

32. Perhaps British colonel Archibald Campbell (1739–1791), captured in 1776 and exchanged in 1778 for Ethan Allen.

33. Captain James Urquhart of the 14th Foot, who married Lucy's sister in November 1774. The couple would later divorce.

34. This postscript is written along the left-hand margin of the letter's first page.

35. William Knox, Henry's younger and only surviving brother. William had accompanied Henry on the Fort Ticonderoga expedition and, after the British evacuation from Boston, he remained in the city. He wrote this letter to Lucy on 11 July 1776; it is in the GLC.

36. Probably a reference to Henry's wastebooks and ledger books, which he inquired about in his letter of 4 Jul 1776, GLC.

37. Captain Jonathan Pollard, quartermaster of the artillery regiment.

38. "Mrs. Jarvis," the wife of Samuel Jarvis of Boston, was a close friend of Lucy's before and during the war.

39. A reference to the family of Captain Sebastian Bauman (1739–1803). Born in Germany, he came to America before the war and gained a captain's commission in the army in 1776. He eventually rose to the rank of major and served in the Continental artillery until the end of the war.

40. Romeo was one of Lucy's two carriage horses.

41. Elbridge Gerry (1744–1814) of Massachusetts, who was a signer of the Declaration of Independence.

42. Knox's lodgings (and the house from which Lucy had fled three weeks before) were located at No. 1 Broadway in New York City.

43. Lieutenant Colonel James Paterson, adjutant general of the British army in North America from April 1776 to July 1777.

44. HMS *Active*, a sixth-rate, 28–gun frigate. Although the ship suffered damage and casualties off of Charleston, it remained in British service until 1778, when it was captured by the French in the Caribbean.

45. This action, usually known as the battle of Sullivan's Island, occurred on 28 June 1776 and, as Knox conveys, was considered to be an overwhelming American victory.

46. Knox means that the strain of the smallpox virus that year was mild.

47. Knox is probably referring to a servant, Thomas Eliot, he had recently purchased on a three-year indenture earlier, in the month of July. See Knox's letter to Lucy, 22 Jul 1776, GLC.

48. This letter is not extant.

49. Knox is discussing the possibility of Lucy traveling to Boston under Mr. Tracy's protection, so she and little Lucy could receive smallpox inoculations. Lucy ultimately decided against such a move and was not immunized until the spring of 1777.

50. Dr. William Eustis (1753–1825) of Massachusetts, who served in the Continental army from 1776 to 1777. He also served as President James Madison's secretary of war from 1809 to 1813.

51. William Knox. Henry typically used the nickname "Billey" for his brother.

52. Knox, probably rushing to complete this letter, neglected to include the name of the person with whom Howe was conversing.

53. Probably a reference to the arrival of Hessian troops from Germany.

54. Knox is referring to Sir Peter Parker (1721–1811) and the HMS *Bristol*, a fourth-rate ship with 50 guns. Parker led the naval attack against Charleston, and the *Bristol* was badly damaged.

55. "Peter" is Knox's younger brother, William Knox. The couple occasionally used this name when referring to him.

56. Knox is referring to himself here in the third person, as Lucy's "friend."

57. William Heath (1737–1814) of Roxbury, Massachusetts, was appointed a major general by the Continental Congress in August 1776, hence the expansion of his military staff. Before the war, he had been a member of Boston's Ancient and Honorable Artillery Company, serving at the same time as Henry Knox. "Mr. Henley" is Thomas Henley, who served as Knox's regimental adjutant during the New York campaign, until his appointment as Heath's aide-de-camp. Henley would be killed in skirmishes with British troops at Montresor's Island in September 1776.

58. Knox is describing the preliminary maneuvers before the battle of Long Island. General William Howe landed 15,000 troops at Gravesend Bay on Long Island on 22 August, with another 5,000 men arriving two days later. Approximately 8,000 Continental army troops occupied nearby Brooklyn Heights. Commanded by General Israel Putnam, these men engaged in a number of minor skirmishes as British and Hessian forces probed the American positions.

59. This is a reference to the financial compensation German princes received from Great Britain for soldiers lost or injured while serving in America.

60. The battle of Long Island, on 27 August 1776, was a terrible defeat for the Continental army. Beginning at dawn, British forces in front of Brooklyn Heights launched

a series of diversionary attacks, while the main body, under General Howe, conducted a flanking maneuver through the largely unguarded Jamaica Pass. At 9 a.m., these troops launched a flank attack that turned and then routed the American left. The battle ended in midafternoon, with the surviving Continental forces gathered inside prepared fortifications around Brooklyn village. Instead of following up on his success, however, Howe halted his assaults and prepared to besiege the seemingly trapped American force. The Continental army suffered approximately 1,400 casualties in the battle, while the British lost only 400 men. Knox remained on Manhattan Island throughout the day and did not participate in the battle. For a recent account of the British operation, the battle, and Washington's subsequent retreat off the island, see Daughan, 63–82.

61. Major General James Grant (1720–1806). Knox's intelligence regarding Grant's death was incorrect.

62. Major General John Sullivan (1740–1795) and Brigadier General William Alexander (1726–1783), often referred to as "Lord Stirling" because of a disputed claim to the earldom of Stirling. Here, Knox's intelligence was correct, as both men were captured by the British and later exchanged.

63. Brigadier General Samuel Holden Parsons (1747–1789).

64. The 52nd Regiment was stationed in Boston before the war, as well as having fought at the Battles of Lexington and Concord and the Battle of Bunker Hill in 1775. Therefore, Henry and Lucy undoubtedly knew several of its officers.

65. Lucy's letter of 22 Aug 1776 is not extant.

66. This letter has not survived. All of Lucy's correspondence to her husband from late summer to December 1776 has been lost.

67. Probably Robert Temple (d. ca. 1780–1783) of Charlestown, Massachusetts. Temple was a Tory who, in 1776, wished to return to his home in New England. Howe asked Washington if he objected to Temple's landing in New York and proceeding overland to Massachusetts. Temple was later made a prisoner by Massachusetts authorities but managed to leave for England in 1780. He died in the mother country before the war's end. See Lorenzo Sabine, *Biographical Sketches of Loyalists in the American Revolution*, 3 vols. (Boston, 1864), 3:349–50.

68. Knox is quoting Alexander Pope, "An Essay on Man: Epistle I," published in 1733–1734.

69. Henry Jackson of Boston, Knox's close friend.

70. Perhaps Colonel Rufus Putnam (1738–1824) of Massachusetts. Putnam knew Knox and was then serving as a chief of engineers in the Continental army. He was a cousin of General Israel Putnam of Connecticut.

71. Lucy is referring to the battle of Harlem Heights, which took place on Monday, 16 September 1776, and was an American victory. Henry Knox discusses this battle with his brother in his letter of 23 Sept 1776, which is in the GLC.

72. Knox is describing the battle of White Plains, which occurred on Monday, 28 October 1776, and was another defeat for the Continental army. The "Hill" Knox mentions was Chatterton's Hill, defended by an American brigade that was commanded by Brigadier General Alexander McDougall (1732–1786). After McDougall's 2,000 men were driven from this eminence, the remainder of Washington's forces had to withdraw from the field. For more information about this battle, see John Ferling, *Almost a Miracle: The American Victory in the War of Independence* (New York, 2007), 146–47.

73. General Guy Carleton, 1st Baron Dorchester (1724–1808). In the fall of 1776, Carleton led British forces out of Canada and into the Lake Champlain region. Several American delaying actions led by Benedict Arnold and the lateness of the season prevented Carleton from advancing farther than Lake Champlain. After Yorktown, Carleton would command the main British army in America, stationed in New York.

74. James Lovell of Massachusetts (1737–1814). Lovell, a teacher at the Boston Latin School, was taken prisoner by the British in Boston in the summer of 1775, due to his suspected Whig sympathies, and sent to Halifax, Nova Scotia. In late 1776, he was exchanged for a British officer, Colonel Philip Skene. Lovell later became a member of the Continental Congress, serving from 1777 to 1782. See Henry Knox to William Knox, 5 Aug 1776, GLC, for a previous discussion of Lovell's situation.

75. Ralph Isaacs of Wallingford, Connecticut. He and his wife seem to have befriended Lucy Knox during the latter months of 1776, when she lived in New Haven. See Ralph Isaac to Lucy Knox, 30 Apr 1777, GLC.

76. Colonel Robert Magaw (1738–1790) of Pennsylvania. He was held by the British in New York City until October 1780, at which time he was exchanged.

77. The battle at Fort Washington occurred on 16 November 1776 and ended with the loss of its entire garrison of slightly over 3,000 men. The disaster marked the Continental army's lowest point in the 1776 campaign. Washington badly misjudged the fort's strength, hesitated on deciding whether to evacuate, and relied too heavily on the advice of subordinates (in this case, the usually reliable Nathanael Greene). For an excellent account of Fort Washington's fall, see Ferling, 148–55.

78. Perhaps the wife of Lieutenant Colonel David Rhea of the 2nd New Jersey Regiment.

79. Fort Lee was located opposite Fort Washington, on the New Jersey side of the Hudson River. Washington considered holding it after Fort Washington's fall but ordered its evacuation on the evening of 19 November 1776. British troops under Lord Cornwallis seized the fortification and a great deal of equipment and stores the following morning. Knox clearly had not yet been informed of these events.

80. The bracketed text is inferred language. This page of Knox's letter suffered damage at some point and part of the text was lost.

81. Probably Mrs. Jonathan Pollard, wife of Knox's quartermaster.

82. This postscript is written on the letter's address leaf.

83. General Charles Lee was captured by the British on 13 December 1776 in Basking Ridge, New Jersey. He remained a prisoner for 16 months, until he was exchanged.

84. In December 1776, General Henry Clinton, leading a British expedition of 83 ships and 6,000 British and Hessian soldiers, captured Newport, Rhode Island. The British occupied the city for three years.

85. Probably Major Samuel Shaw (1754–1794), Knox's aide-de-camp during the Revolutionary War.

86. Colonel Johann Rall (ca. 1726–1776), a German officer of considerable military experience, both in European wars and in the American Revolution. At Trenton, he commanded a Hessian brigade consisting of three regiments: the Rall Regiment, the Knyphausen Regiment, and the von Lossberg Regiment. The garrison's approximate strength was 1,500 men.

87. Knox is referring to the movement of American troops back to New Jersey, which

soon led to the second battle of Trenton on 2 January 1777 and the battle of Princeton on 3 January 1777.

88. Probably William Knox.

89. This letter only survives as an undated draft. Lucy penned it on the back of a separate letter written by Jotham Horton, an officer in the Continental army's artillery regiment, to Henry Knox and dated 3 January 1777. Horton was quarantined somewhere in New York State, along with several other officers and enlisted men, due to either their illness from smallpox or recovery from smallpox inoculations. Horton requested "hard money" from his commander, in order to obtain "the Common Necessaries." Somehow this note ended up in Lucy's hands, and she wrote her draft on its reverse side.

90. See Henry Knox to Lucy Flucker Knox, 2 Jan 1777, GLC. With regard to Knox's reference to "another tussle" with the enemy, he specifically wrote on the afternoon of 2 January 1777: "We are collecting our force at this place [Trenton] & shall give Battle to the enemy very soon. Our people have exerted great fortitude & staid beyond the time of their inlistment in high Spirits but want Rum & cloathing." Knox described the second battle of Trenton in this letter.

91. Probably Captain John Fleming (d. 1777), acting commander of the 1st Virginia Regiment during the battle. See "The Ancestors and Descendants of John Rolfe, with Notes on Some Connected Families: The Fleming Family (Concluded)," *Virginia Magazine of History and Biography*, 24:4 (October 1916), 440–41.

92. Captain Daniel Neil, a battery commander who had fought with General John Sullivan's column. For more information regarding his death, see William Stryker, *The Battles of Trenton and Princeton* (Boston, 1898), 282.

93. General Hugh Mercer (1729–1777) of Pennsylvania and Virginia actually died of his wounds on 12 January 1777.

94. Captain William Leslie (1751–1777) was a company commander of the 17th Regiment. In addition to Knox, George Washington, Dr. Benjamin Rush, and those British officers captured at the battle attended Leslie's funeral.

95. Knox is describing a clash that occurred near Elizabethtown, New Jersey, on 5 January 1777, with a German regiment of troops from the principality of Waldeck.

96. At approximately the same time as Knox wrote this letter, Washington ordered Major General William Heath, then in upstate New York, to attack a British outpost garrisoned in Fort Independence, at King's Bridge. The attack later that month failed, and Heath's forces were scattered.

97. Knox is paraphrasing two lines from William Shakespeare's *Julius Caesar*, act 4, scene 3. The original dialogue reads: "There is a tide in the affairs of men / Which, taken at the flood, leads on to fortune."

98. On 8 January 1777, Knox wrote Lucy another letter, in which he explained why, the previous day, he had avoided his typical expressions of love and affection when writing to her: "as the subject [i.e., the American victory at the battle of Princeton] is important to the public & I suppos'd you would have importunities [i.e., opportunities] to communicate [it], I've forwarded it that you may shew without the danger of [others] discovering the tender connexion of souls, not but that our Love is known & ought to be so, but then the tender expression in consequence, altho highly proper between Lovers, yet it's of too delicate nature to be entrusted to the curious eye of the common uninterested Heart." See Henry Knox to Lucy Flucker Knox, 8 Jan 1777, GLC.

99. Knox misdated the year in this letter.

100. This letter is not extant.

101. Lieutenant Colonel Walter Stewart (ca. 1756–1796) of Pennsylvania was born in Ireland. He was known throughout the army for his unusually good looks. His nickname was the "Irish Beauty."

102. A portion of this page of the original letter is damaged, with considerable loss of text. The bracketed text is inferred. Knox is referring here to papers relating to the reorganization and expansion the Continental army's artillery branch. On the reorganization of the artillery, as well as Washington's army in general in early 1777, see Robert K. Wright Jr., *The Continental Army* (Washington, DC, 1983), 98–99.

103. Knox is referring to his close friend Henry Jackson. In January 1777, the Massachusetts militia unit that Jackson commanded, the Boston Independent Company, was taken into the ranks of the Continental army. The unit was then named "Jackson's Additional Continental Regiment," later designated as the 16th Massachusetts Regiment. It saw combat in nearly all of the army's major campaigns between 1777 and 1781. Knox apparently had a hand in securing the transfer, as well as in obtaining a commission in the Continental army for his friend.

104. Knox left the army in Morristown, New Jersey, in mid-January 1777. He first visited Springfield, Massachusetts, and then proceeded to Boston. He had arrived in the city by 1 February 1777, as he wrote to Washington that same day, dating his letter from the town. Knox left Boston on 3 March 1777 and was heading back to New Jersey.

105. Knox visited Springfield, Massachusetts, in order to inspect the preparations for the establishment of an armory. Washington had approved the location for the armory during the siege of Boston, after Knox had suggested the site, which overlooked the Connecticut River. During the Revolutionary War, the armory stored weapons, manufactured musket cartridges, and gun carriages. It remained in operation, serving the US military, until 1968.

106. This action took place on 23 February 1777, near modern-day Rahway, New Jersey, when 2,000 British troops under Colonel Charles Mawhood encountered an American force under Brigadier General William Maxwell (1733–1796). In the engagement, the Americans outmaneuvered the enemy and drove the British from the field. British losses were approximately 75–100 men killed and wounded, not the 500 Knox had heard in the initial reports. On this action and on the Forge War in the winter of 1777, see David Hackett Fischer, *George Washington's Crossing* (New York, 2004), 346–62.

107. Dr. Isaac Rand (1743–1822) of Boston. Rand managed the smallpox hospital for the authorities in Boston after the evacuation of the British in 1776.

108. Possibly Henry Jackson.

109. Probably Colonel Nicholas Eveleigh (ca. 1748–1791) of South Carolina. He later served in the Continental Congress and as the first comptroller of the United States during George Washington's first term.

110. The Peacock was a tavern on North Street in Boston. See Samuel Adams Drake, *Old Boston Taverns and Tavern Clubs* (Boston, 1917), 117.

111. William Knox.

112. This may be a reference to Nathaniel Austin (1734–1818), a pewterer and goldsmith. Austin is listed in the Boston Directory of 1789 as a goldsmith, and a number of his pewter items, stamped with his distinctive mark, are extant.

113. Probably Lewis Gray (1743?–?), a Boston merchant, whose father, Harrison Gray, was the last royal treasurer of Massachusetts. Lewis Gray's sister, Elizabeth, was married to Samuel Otis, brother of pamphleteer James Otis Jr., who is associated with the phrase "taxation without representation is tyranny."

114. Colonel John Crane (1744–1805) of Massachusetts commanded "Crane's Continental Artillery Regiment," later designated the 3rd Continental Artillery Regiment. He was in Boston that spring, recruiting for the army's upcoming campaign.

115. *Caspipina's Letters; Containing Observations on a Variety of Subjects* was written by Jacob Duches (1737–1798) of Philadelphia in 1777. Duches, an initial supporter of the American Revolution and chaplain to the First Continental Congress, turned against the cause of independence after the fall of Philadelphia to the British in the autumn of 1777. He eventually fled to Great Britain.

116. This letter seems to have been a first draft of one Lucy Knox composed and sent to her sister. Therefore, some of her strikeouts are included to illustrate changes she most likely made in the copy she sent to her sister.

117. Joseph Gardner was a surgeon's mate in the 12th Continental Regiment.

118. Benjamin Hichborn (1746–1817) of Massachusetts was a prominent Boston lawyer who did a great deal of legal work for Knox throughout his lifetime.

119. Probably James Bowdoin (1726–1790) of Massachusetts. Bowdoin served as president of the Massachusetts Provincial Congress's executive council from 1775 to 1777. Bowdoin College was later named in his honor. The Knoxes were anxious in the spring of 1777, believing that the state's revolutionary government was preparing to seize the properties of absentee Loyalists, including Lucy's father.

120. Lucy might have meant to write "Halifax" instead of "New York."

121. Captain Gilbert Warner Speakman of Massachusetts. He served as commissary of military stores at Springfield in 1777–1778.

122. Captain Lieutenant Samuel Treat (d. 1777) of New York. He was an officer in the 2nd Continental Artillery Regiment.

123. The Knoxes were apparently attempting to purchase Thomas Flucker Sr.'s home in Boston, to avoid its possible confiscation by state authorities. Six days after Lucy wrote this letter, on 9 April 1777, the Massachusetts General Court authorized the judge of probate to formally appoint agents for the estates of absentee Crown supporters. This initial move to seize control of Loyalist property was later followed by the more draconian confiscation law of 1779. Lucy and Henry probably were aware that this legislation was about to be passed. For more information about the actions of the Massachusetts legislature that spring, see Hassam, 5.

124. Samuel Austin operated a dry goods store on Boston's Union Street during this period.

125. Lucy is referring to Elizabeth Deblois's rejection of General Benedict Arnold's courtship. Deblois (1761–1843) belonged to a prominent Loyalist family from Boston.

126. Perhaps Robert Treat Paine (1731–1814), Massachusetts' attorney general from 1777 to 1790 and one of the signers of the Declaration of Independence.

127. Lucy was probably referring to an article in the Loyalist newspaper, the *New York Gazette*, dated 17 March 1777 and headed "Paris, December 20," that falsely claimed Benjamin Franklin had both abandoned his diplomatic mission at Versailles and denounced the American cause, thus resuming his loyalty to the British Crown.

128. Colonel Nicholas Eveleigh.

129. Lucy is referring to George Washington and an illness that afflicted him in the spring of 1777.

130. Lucy's letter to Henry, dated 18 Mar 1777, GLC.

131. Knox is referring to Colonel John Crane's recruitment efforts in Boston that spring, which Lucy mentioned in her letter of 18 Mar 1777, GC.

132. Springfield, Massachusetts, the location of the American armory.

133. This letter was written on 10 Apr 1777 and is not extant.

134. This may be a reference to Sarah Erving Waldo, the widow of Samuel Waldo. She never remarried.

135. William Knox, who was to join his brother Henry.

136. Lucy's only brother, Thomas Flucker Jr. (d. 1783), was a captain in the British army and stationed on the island of Antigua during the American Revolution.

137. Samuel Jarvis of Boston.

138. Probably the Duchess of Brandenburg.

139. Knox's brother, William, who was then preparing to join the Continental army.

140. Henry Jackson.

141. Colonel John Crane of the Continental Artillery Regiment, then in Boston on a recruiting trip. See Lucy's letter of 18 Mar 1777, GLC.

142. Probably the Passaic River.

143. Perhaps a Freudian slip on Knox's part in omitting "not" in this sentence.

144. Gabriel Johonnot (1748–1820) was a Huguenot merchant from Boston who, along with Knox, was a member of the Boston Grenadier Corps. He served as a lieutenant colonel in Colonel John Glover's Massachusetts regiment from May 1775 until December 1776. He left the army at the end of 1776, when he failed to receive a promotion to full colonel, and returned to Boston.

145. British general William Howe.

146. Sandy Hook, New Jersey.

147. Knox is referring to Lucy's brother, Captain Thomas Flucker Jr.

148. Silas Deane, America's first diplomatic minister to France.

149. This postscript was written on the letter's address leaf.

150. Lucy Knox dated this letter 31 Apr 1777, but it was probably written on 1 May.

151. Lucy is referring to pox marks. She and her daughter had their smallpox inoculations on 14 April.

152. William Knox was about to set off to join Henry and the Continental army in Morristown, New Jersey.

153. Possibly Thomas Eliot. In July 1776, Knox purchased a three-year indenture on his service. See Henry's letter to Lucy on 22 Jul 1776, GLC.

154. Lucy's attending doctor for the inoculation was Joseph Gardner, a surgeon's mate in the 12th Continental Regiment.

155. Lucy refers to this misunderstanding in her letter of 1[?] May 1777, GLC. Her letter of 19 April 1777, mentioned at the outset, has not survived.

156. Knox was probably referring to the Massachusetts General Court's action of 9 April 1777 to authorize the judge of probate to formally appoint agents for the estates of absentee Crown supporters.

157. Knox is describing the British raid on coastal Connecticut and Danbury from 25 to 28 April 1777.

158. General Guy Carleton was the commander of the British forces in Quebec in 1777 but was passed over for command of the expedition to invade the Hudson River Valley. The British and Hessian force was instead given to General John Burgoyne.

159. Like most Americans in the spring of 1777, Knox knew that General John Burgoyne and the British were preparing to invade from Quebec, but no one yet knew what the British army commander's ultimate objective would be. As Knox explains, many expected the British to invade New England. Lucy expresses these same fears in her letters written during this month.

160. The final page of this letter is missing.

161. Henry also mentioned the British raid on the Connecticut coast in his previous letter to Lucy.

162. Lucy is referring to Isaac Winslow (1709–1777) of Roxbury. Winslow had been very close to the Knoxes before the war. Not only was Lucy named after Winslow's first wife, but he had intervened with Thomas Flucker Sr. in 1774, in order to convince him to accept Lucy's marriage to Henry. While Flucker grudgingly accepted the match, he and his wife refused to attend the wedding; therefore, Winslow gave his niece away at the ceremony. A Loyalist in his political sentiments, Winslow evacuated Boston with the British in March 1776. He emigrated to London and died there early the following year.

163. Colonel David Mason (1731–1792) of Virginia, commander of the armory at Springfield, Massachusetts.

164. Sarah Learnard Heath (1735–1814), wife of General William Heath.

165. Henry Joseph Gardner, Massachusetts' treasurer and receiver general during the American Revolution.

Chapter 4 · The Perils of War II

1. Henry Knox to Lucy Knox, 30 Jul 1777, GLC.

2. Henry Knox to Lucy Knox, 25 Aug 1777, GLC.

3. Henry Knox to Lucy Knox, 13 Sept 1777, GLC. For more information on Knox's participation in the campaign, see North Callahan, *Henry Knox: General Washington's General* (New York, 1958), 106–26.

4. Knox referred to the spirits of the troops in a letter from Henry Knox to Lucy Knox, 6 Oct 1777, GLC. For a recent comprehensive study of the Philadelphia campaign of 1777, see Thomas J. McGuire, *The Philadelphia Campaign*, 2 vols. (Mechanicsburg, PA, 2006–2007).

5. Henry Knox to Lucy Knox, 15 Oct 1777, GLC.

6. Henry Knox to Lucy Knox, 6 Oct 1777, GLC.

7. Lucy Knox to Henry Knox, 26 May 1777, GLC.

8. Lucy Knox to Henry Knox, 3–5 Jun 1777, GLC. Because William Knox decided to join Henry in the Continental army in the summer of 1777, the store in Boston did not open that year. Repairs and other work to restart the business operation were not completed until 1778.

9. Lucy Knox to Henry Knox, 3–5 Jun 1777, GLC.

10. Lucy Knox to Henry Knox, 23 Aug 1777, GLC.

11. These charges seem to have been made in a letter Lucy wrote to Henry on either 13 Nov or 20 Nov 1777. Neither letter is extant.

12. Henry Knox to Lucy Knox, 2 Dec 1777, GLC.

13. Henry Knox to Lucy Knox, 3 Dec 1777, GLC.

14. Lucy is referring to Philippe du Coudray (1738–1777), a French officer who had been promised command of the Continental army's artillery by the American diplomatic minister to France, Silas Deane.

15. Probably Dr. Thomas Bullfinch, listed in the Boston Directory of 1789 as living in Boston's Bowdoin's Square.

16. William Knox might have had a case of *Sarcoptes scabiei*, or itch mites.

17. Probably Colonel David Henley (1749–1823) of Massachusetts, commander of the Additional Continental Regiment.

18. Colonel Thomas Crafts (1740–1799) of Boston, who commanded the Massachusetts Regiment of Artillery; Paul Revere (1734–1818), who commanded Castle Island in Boston Harbor at that time; and probably David Sears, who was listed as a merchant in the Boston Directory of 1789.

19. Henry Knox to Lucy Flucker Knox, 17 May 1777, GLC.

20. General William Howe.

21. See Henry's letter of 4 May and Lucy's letter of 8 May [morning], GLC, on American uncertainty regarding Burgoyne's ultimate invasion objectives.

22. Knox perhaps feared that he and William would have to permanently close Henry's Boston store, with them both in the Continental army.

23. Probably a reference to the couple's attempt to purchase Thomas Flucker Sr.'s home, to avoid its confiscation by Massachusetts' state authorities.

24. This may be a reference to the wife of Knox's quartermaster, Mrs. Jonathan Pollard, who fled New York City with Lucy in the summer of 1776. The two women also traveled and lived together in Connecticut throughout much of the remainder of that year. Knox did not like his comrade's spouse, writing to his brother William in July, "Mrs. Pollard, . . . from her Melancholy dumpish disposition, is a very unfit Companion for [Lucy]." See Henry Knox to William Knox, 11 Jul 1776, GLC.

25. Camp Middlebrook was located approximately 15 miles south of Morristown, New Jersey, near the Raritan River. Washington moved his headquarters to Camp Middlebrook from Morristown on 29 May 1777.

26. Captain Lieutenant John Lillie (1753–1801) of Boston. Before the war, Lillie had been a cooper and a member of the city's Ancient and Honorable Artillery Company. In 1777, he belonged to the 3rd Continental Artillery Regiment. Later in the war, he became an aide-de-camp to Knox. In the spring of 1777, Lillie was in Boston, and Knox had probably allowed him to leave the army's encampment for the city without any letters for Lucy. Lillie might be the "young man" Lucy refers to in her letter to Henry of 26 May 1777, GLC. On Lillie's background, see "General William Heath to George Washington, 19 May 1777," *Founders Online*, National Archives, https://founders.archives.gov/documents/Washington/03-09-02-0466/, last modified 28 December 2016. [Original source: Philander D. Chase, ed., *The Papers of George Washington: Revolutionary War Series*, vol. 9, *28 March 1777–10 June 1777* (Charlottesville, VA, 1999), 472–75, n5].

27. Major Lemuel Trescott (1751–1826) of Massachusetts, who served in Colonel David

Henley's Additional Continental Regiment in 1777. The other letter Knox wrote to Lucy on 1 Jun 1777 has not survived.

28. Knox is referring to a skirmish that occurred on the evening of 31 May 1777, near Bound Brook. First Lieutenant William Martin was leading a scouting party of ten men when they were attacked by a Hessian jäger patrol. In the melee, the Germans bayoneted Martin 17 times while he supposedly cried out for quarter. Afterwards, his corpse was decapitated. Six of Martin's men were also killed in the encounter. The Americans recovered Martin's body the following day and brought it into Camp Middlebrook. When Washington saw the corpse, he ordered it displayed to his troops, in order to demonstrate the enemy's barbaric method of warfare. On 2 June, the American commander attempted to send Martin's mangled remains to Lord Cornwallis, along with a letter demanding an explanation regarding the behavior of his troops. The British refused to accept Martin's remains but did forward Washington's letter to their general. For more information regarding this encounter, see McGuire, 1:28–31. For Washington's letter to Cornwallis, see "George Washington to Lieutenant General Cornwallis, 2 June 1777," *Founders Online*, National Archives, https://founders.archives.gov/documents/Washington/03-09-02-0588/, last modified 28 December 2016. [Original source: Chase, 9:591–92].

29. Perhaps the Knoxes' daughter had just started to walk on her own.

30. Thomas Russell, a Boston merchant who was active throughout the American Revolution, smuggling goods past British warships and into New England. According to a letter William Knox wrote to his brother on 3 June 1777, Russell had just returned to Boston from a visit to the Continental army.

31. Knox's letter of 24 May 1777 has not survived, but apparently he wrote to his wife that someone he had trusted made off with part of his wardrobe. "John" was perhaps Knox's servant in the field, who attended to his clothes.

32. William Turner owned a grocery shop in Boston's Cornhill section, where Lucy lived. On 5 June 1777, he ran an advertisement in the *Independent Chronicle* stating that he had for sale "Wines, by Wholesale and Retail; best Scotch Snuff; Syrup of Sugar; Durham Mustard, per Bottle or Pound; Cyder, per dozen; Spices, Olives, Capers and Ketchup."

33. Elizabeth Deblois. General Benedict Arnold apparently wished to give some articles of clothing as gifts to Elizabeth Deblois during their courtship. The courtship ended, however, before the gifts could be presented to her; hence they were still in Lucy's possession.

34. Probably Major William Blodget (1754–1809), aide-de-camp to General Nathanael Greene.

35. Lucy's carriage horse.

36. Written along the right margin of the letter's final page.

37. Lucy is again referring to the French officer, Philippe du Coudray, to whom Silas Deane had promised command of the army's artillery. See her letter of 18–24 May 1777, GLC. Phaethon was a Greek mythological figure. The son of Helios, he supposedly plunged toward earth when he lost control of his father's "chariot of the sun," thus forcing Zeus to kill him, in order to prevent the world's destruction.

38. Colonel David Mason.

39. See Henry Knox to Henry Jackson, 21 Jun 1777, GLC. Knox explained that Howe

had been preparing to cross the Delaware River into Pennsylvania, probably for an attempt on Philadelphia, but on 9 June, the British commander began withdrawing his army from western New Jersey. Knox believed that this movement was in preparation for a move up the Hudson River, to support Burgoyne's army. On these early stages of what would soon be the Philadelphia campaign, see McGuire, 1:5–62.

40. Hudson River.

41. This letter is not extant.

42. Brigadier Generals William Maxwell and Thomas Conway (1735–ca. 1800).

43. The action Knox describes in detail in this letter is often known as the battle of Short Hills. In mid-June, General Howe began slowly withdrawing from his positions in western New Jersey. As his men moved eastward, he sought to lure Washington's forces out of the Watchung Mountains and into open terrain, where the British commander confidently expected he could annihilate the Americans. Washington followed Howe with caution. But on 24 June, the American commander sent Lord Stirling's division forward, in order to harass what seemed to be a retreating enemy. This gave Howe the opening he had been looking for, and he struck at dawn on 26 June. After heavy fighting, Stirling successfully extracted his vulnerable division and retreated back to the Continental army's strong position in the mountains. For more information about this action, see McGuire, 1:52–59.

44. Lucy is probably referring to members of the Continental Congress in this sentence. She seems to have feared that, after the present campaign, they would remove Henry from command of the Continental army's artillery and replace him with a French officer, Philippe du Coudray. As Knox's letter of 21 Jun 1777 reveals, however, her fears were unfounded.

45. Henry's name was written in a young child's handwriting and, given Lucy's own closing words, was probably penned by the couple's 16–month-old daughter, probably with her mother's help.

46. Camp Pompton Plains was located approximately 40 miles northeast of Camp Middlebrook, in present-day Pequannock Township, New Jersey.

47. Neither letter has survived.

48. Knox is discussing the opening stages of the Saratoga campaign. General Arthur St. Clair (1737–1818) commanded a small American garrison stationed at Fort Ticonderoga. Although St. Clair believed he had no choice but to retreat, he was roundly criticized for not putting up a fight before his withdrawal. In 1778, he faced a court-martial but was exonerated and restored to the rank of major general.

49. General Philip Schuyler of New York commanded American forces in the Northern Department. In July, however, the Continental Congress removed him from this post, largely because of the Fort Ticonderoga debacle.

50. Theodorick Bland Jr. (1741–1790) of Virginia. Bland commanded the 1st Continental Light Dragoons in the Philadelphia campaign but left the army in 1779, due to poor health. His wife was Martha Daingerfield Bland (d. 1803) of Virginia.

51. The letter to the Continental Congress to which Knox refers was written on 1 July 1777. Addressed to John Hancock, then the congress's president, the artillery commander specifically sought to learn if "Congress has appointed a Mr. du Coudray a French Gentleman to the Command of the Artillery"; if so, "I beg the favor of a permission to Retire." See Henry Knox to John Hancock, 1 Jul 1777, GLC. Knox's fellow

generals, Nathanael Greene and John Sullivan, also wrote letters threatening to resign. On 7 July, the congress unanimously resolved that it considered the letters "an Invasion of the Liberties of the People," for the officers had used threats of resignation in order to influence the decisions of the people's representatives. On 8 July, Hancock wrote to Washington, demanding that his generals acknowledge "the Impropriety of the[ir] Conduct." See "John Hancock to George Washington, 8 July 1777," *Founders Online*, National Archives, https://founders.archives.gov/documents/Washington/03-10-02-0216/, last modified 28 December 2016. [Original source: Frank E. Grizzard Jr., ed., *The Papers of George Washington, Revolutionary War Series*, vol. 10, *11 June 1777-18 August 1777* (Charlottesville, VA, 2000), 227–28.] Because Washington staunchly supported Knox, the congress refused to give du Coudray the artillery command. The French officer then joined the American army as a volunteer. He drowned, however, in a ferry accident in September 1777.

52. Probably Henry Jackson.

53. Perhaps the wife of the Loyalist William Tyng (1737–1807). Tyng was the sheriff of Cumberland County, Maine, and a member of the Massachusetts General Court, representing Falmouth, before the war. This couple left America shortly after the Battles of Lexington and Concord but returned to the United States following the war. Mrs. Tyng died in 1831 in Gorham, Maine. See Lorenzo Sabine, *Biographical Sketches of Loyalists of the American Revolution*, 3 vols. (Boston, 1864), 3:369–72.

54. The 28–gun HMS *Fox* was captured by two American frigates, the USS *Hancock* and the USS *Boston*, on 7 June 1777 but it was then retaken by the British in July. Fourteen months after Lucy's letter, the French captured the *Fox*, and it remained in their hands until the vessel ran aground in 1779 and could not be refloated. For more information regarding the ship, see "HMS *Fox*, 28 guns, engaged by USS *Hancock*, 32 guns, and USS *Boston*, 30 guns," Royal Navy History, www.royal-navy.org/HMS%20Fox%2C%2028%20guns %2C%20engaged%20by%20USS%20Hancock%2C%2032%20guns%2C%20and%20 USS%20Boston%2C%2030%20guns./ (accessed 23 January 2017).

55. Probably Camp Hill, Pennsylvania.

56. This letter has not survived.

57. Sinepuxet was a village in Worcester County in eastern Maryland, on the Atlantic Ocean.

58. During the American Revolution, Knox (together with Henry Jackson and Samuel Jarvis) purchased financial interests in several American privateer vessels, which sought to capture British resupply ships crossing the Atlantic Ocean. He is clearly referring to such investments here. The one in the *Tartar*, commanded by Captain John Grimes, seems to have paid off. Boston's *Continental Journal* wrote on 11 September 1777 that on "Tuesday arrived safe at port, a prize brig laden with oil, taken by the Tartar privateer, John Grimes, Esq. commander."

59. The *Hero* was one of the privateers in which Knox had a financial interest, and this ship is mentioned in his 12 Aug 1777 letter to Lucy. Perhaps the vessel was sailing to various harbors in search of another American privateer with which to jointly cross the Atlantic Ocean.

60. Lucy is discussing the Saratoga campaign.

61. Ebenezer Oliver owned a general store located across the street from Boston's Old South Meeting House. In May 1777, he advertised for sale a "Fresh Assortment of Garden Seeds, taken in a Prize Ship last Fall." See *Boston Gazette*, 5 May 1777.

62. Lucy is referring to Philippe du Coudray.

63. Captain Thomas Randall (d. 1811) of the 2nd Continental Artillery Regiment. He was later wounded and captured by the British at the battle of Germantown on 4 October 1777.

64. Christiana River, a tributary of the Delaware River, located south of Philadelphia.

65. Knox is referring General John Stark's decisive victory over Burgoyne's forces on 16 August 1777, at the battle of Bennington, in Vermont.

66. The bracketed text in this sentence is inferred language, due to text loss.

67. Captain Thomas Theodore Bliss (1745–1802), of the 2nd Continental Artillery Regiment. He had been captured by the British in May 1776 and was not yet exchanged.

68. Bostonians were celebrating General Stark's victory at Bennington on 16 August.

69. Lucy is referring to a letter William Knox apparently wrote to Colonel Henry Jackson, who was then in Boston, which was delivered by the same post as a letter William had written to Lucy.

70. Knox is discussing the battle of Brandywine on 11 September 1777. The American forces fought well, but Howe successfully turned Washington's right flank and inflicted over 1,000 casualties on the Continental army. Although it was a clear British victory, the Americans withdrew from the field in good order and were eager to fight the enemy again. In fact, Knox also wrote to his friend Henry Jackson on 13 September, confidently explaining that "one more such a victory would in my opinion ruin Mr. Howe—the fire of the Musquetry was infinite—one universal clatter—our men are in good Spirits and wish for nothing more than to engage them again." See Henry Knox's "Letter to Col. Henry Jackson about Battle of Brandywine," 13 Sept 1777, American Revolutionary War manuscript in the Boston Public Library, *Internet Archive*, https://archive.org/details /lettertocolhenry00knox_13/ (accessed 20 December 2014).

71. See Henry Knox to Lucy Flucker Knox, 1 Sept 1777, GLC.

72. Knox is discussing the British crossing at Flatland Ford on the night of 22–23 September, which is where the Continental army had originally been positioned. Howe's army actually marched into Philadelphia on 26 September, two days after Henry penned this letter.

73. Knox is referring to the battle of Paoli (sometimes called the Paoli massacre) on 20 September 1777. On the evening of the 20th, Major General Charles Grey (1729–1807) conducted a surprise British attack on General Anthony Wayne's (1745–1796) division, encamped near the Paoli Tavern. In the course of the engagement, Wayne's men were driven from their bivouac and fled the field in panic. During the pursuit by the British, General William Smallwood (1732–1792) brought up his American militia troops, but they, too, were driven from the battlefield. During the engagement, the British inflicted nearly 250 casualties (including over 50 dead), while they suffering less than a dozen. Anxious not to let his reputation suffer, Wayne demanded and received a court of inquiry, after which a board of officers unanimously declared him not guilty of misconduct. For more information regarding this battle, see McGuire, 1:313–18.

74. Knox's letter ends here. Its last page(s) is missing.

75. The place in a military encampment where the artillery is posted, not only to allow for general repairs and training exercises, but also to ensure its combat readiness in case of an enemy attack.

76. This letter has not survived.

77. Knox is describing the battle of Germantown, nine miles north of Philadelphia,

on 4 October 1777. Washington hoped to surprise the 9,000 British forces positioned there with a dawn assault simultaneously launched by four separate columns. Although two American columns got lost, due to the night march and the early morning fog, the Continental army succeeded in surprising the enemy and initially forced them to retreat. The battle changed course, however, when a determined British detachment of 100 men doggedly defended a large stone structure known as Cliveden (better known today as the Chew House), located at the center of the American line. Instead of bypassing the building, Washington (acting in part on Knox's advice) halted a number of his troops and launched an assault on Cliveden. The attempt not only failed, but also greatly disrupted the momentum of the main American attack. This delay provided Howe with time to rally his men and bring up reinforcements from Philadelphia. When British resistance across the battlefield stiffened and American casualties mounted, Washington ordered a withdrawal. As at Brandywine, Continental forces fought well and retreated from the field in good order. For a recent account of the battle of Germantown, see McGuire, 2:3–124.

78. Brigadier General Francis Nash (1742–1777) of North Carolina. He died of his wounds three days after the battle.

79. Captain Thomas Randall. Although wounded and captured at Germantown, Randall apparently was free on parole.

80. Knox is discussing General Howe's initial efforts to open the Delaware River to British naval and transport ships. Two American forts guarded the lower Delaware River: Fort Mifflin, on the Pennsylvania side, and Fort Mercer, on the New Jersey side. Washington and the American high command recognized the strategic importance of these fortifications, ordering them to be garrisoned with hundreds of Continentals and fiercely defended.

81. A reference to General Henry Clinton's capture of Forts Montgomery and Clinton, located on the Hudson River approximately 50 miles north of New York City, on 6 October 1777. Clinton commanded British troops in the city during Howe's absence throughout the Philadelphia campaign. He was attempting to assist General Burgoyne's increasingly imperiled army to the north with his capture of the American fortifications. Clinton's force, however, did not proceed any farther northward. Burgoyne surrendered his army to the Americans on 17 October 1777.

82. Colonel Carl Emil Kurt von Donop (1740–1777). A well-connected military officer from the German principality of Hesse-Kassel, von Donop came to America in 1776 and fought in the New York campaign. As Knox describes in this letter, von Donop led the Hessian attack on Fort Mercer on 22 October 1777, during which he was fatally wounded. He died on 25 October. This battle is generally known as the battle of Red Bank.

83. Colonel Christopher Greene (1737–1781) of Rhode Island. A distant cousin to General Nathanael Greene, he commanded the American troops at Fort Mercer and later commanded the 1st Rhode Island Regiment, a unit that was composed of many African Americans. In the spring of 1781, Colonel Greene was killed by New York Loyalists.

84. A reference to the British actor David Garrick (1717–1779), who performed in many plays on the London stage.

85. Knox dates this letter simply from "Camp." After the battles of Brandywine and Germantown, the Continental army had its main encampment at Whitemarsh, approximately ten miles northwest of Philadelphia. Knox dated several other letters written in early November 1777 from this locale.

86. Perhaps Richard Cary (ca. 1746–1806) of Charlestown, Massachusetts. In 1776, Cary briefly served in the Continental army as an aide-de-camp to Washington but resigned at some point early in the war to pursue his mercantile career.

87. This letter is not extant.

88. The British launched another assault on Fort Mifflin on 10 November, which continued into the 11th. After nightfall, the surviving members of the garrison escaped from the fort. For more information about the American defense of Fort Mifflin, see McGuire, 2:181–222.

89. Samuel Treat of the 2nd Continental Artillery was killed by British cannon fire on 11 November 1777.

90. Colonel John Crane, commander of Crane's Continental Artillery Regiment.

91. Neither letter has survived.

92. Probably Abraham Lott (1726–1794) of New York. A wealthy merchant, Lott supported the American cause and fled the city when the British captured it in 1776. He moved his family eight miles east of Morristown, New Jersey, into a house that he named "Beverwyck." The house served as Washington's headquarters in July 1777.

93. Knox was probably referring to Frederika Charlotte Louise von Massow, the Baroness von Riedesel (1746–1808) of Prussia. Married to General Friedrich Adolph Riedesel, she travelled across the Atlantic Ocean in 1777 to join her husband in Canada. When Burgoyne surrendered his command in October 1777, the Americans took both General and Mrs. Riedesel prisoner, and they remained in American hands for nearly four years. For more information about this couple's experiences, see Carol Berkin, *Revolutionary Mothers: Women in the Struggle for America's Independence* (New York, 2005), 79–91.

94. Written vertically along the left margin of the letter's last page.

95. Knox is referring to Henry Jackson, who was then heading south with his regiment to join the Continental army in Pennsylvania.

96. This letter is not extant.

97. Knox left the army at Valley Forge and headed for Boston in early or mid-January, arriving in the city during February 1778.

Chapter 5 · Enduring the War (1778–1783)

1. Henry Knox to William Knox, 27 May 1778, GLC.

2. Henry Knox to Lucy Knox, 29 Jun 1778, GLC.

3. Henry Knox to William Knox, 5 Jul 1778, GLC. In late July, the Knoxes traveled north to the Hudson Valley Highlands, where they spent the remainder of the summer and autumn. With the onset of winter in 1778/79, the family relocated to Middlebrook, New Jersey, where Washington had established the Continental army's main winter encampment.

4. North Callahan, *Henry Knox: General Washington's General* (New York, 1958), 155–56.

5. Henry Knox to William Knox, 28 Feb 1779, GLC. The quote concerning the Knoxes' "splendid entertainment" and Washington leading the first dance are from James Thatcher, *Military Journal during the American Revolution, 1775–1783* (Boston, 1823), 156.

6. Henry Knox to Lucy Knox, 29 Jun and 8 Aug 1779; Lucy Knox to Henry Knox, 29 Sept 1781, GLC.

7. Henry Knox to William Knox, 3 Apr 1779, GLC.

8. Henry Knox to Lucy Knox, 29 Jun 1779, GLC.

9. Henry Knox to Lucy Knox, 8 Aug 1779, GLC.

10. Henry Knox to Lucy Knox, 26 Jul 1781, GLC.

11. Lucy Knox to Henry Knox, 26 Jul 1781, GLC.

12. Henry Knox to Lucy Knox, 3 Aug 1781, GLC.

13. Henry Knox to William Knox, 5 Aug 1781, GLC. Thomas Flucker Sr. was, in fact, not fatally ill during the summer of 1781. He lived for almost two more years, dying in London on 16 February 1783. On Flucker joining the "Brompton Row Tory Club" and collecting his salary after his migration to the mother country, see *Genealogy of the Waldo Family: A Record of Descendants of Cornelius Waldo*, vol. 1 (Worcester, MA, 1903), 194.

14. Henry Knox to William Knox, 4 Sept 1781, GLC.

15. George Washington to Henry Knox, 5 Sept 1781, GLC.

16. Henry Knox to William Knox, 4 Sept 1781, GLC.

17. Lucy Knox to Henry Knox, 29 Sept 1781, GLC.

18. Henry Knox to Lucy Knox, 1 Oct and 16 Oct 1781, GLC.

19. Henry Knox to Lucy Knox, 19 Oct 1781, GLC.

20. Henry Knox to William Knox, 3 Jan 1782, GLC.

21. Lucy Knox to Henry Knox, 10 Apr 1782; Henry Knox to Lucy Knox, 31 Mar 1782, GLC.

22. Henry Knox to George Washington, 10 Sept 1782, GLC.

23. Henry Knox to George Washington, 11 Mar 1783; George Washington to Henry Knox, 12 Mar 1783, GLC. See also Henry Knox, letterbook related to the Newburgh conspiracy, ca. Mar 1783, GLC; Richard H. Kohn, "The Inside History of the Newburgh Conspiracy: America and the Coup d'Etat," *William and Mary Quarterly*, 3rd ser., 27 (April 1970), 187–220. For a recent assessment of the Society of the Cincinnati and Knox's role in its creation, see William Doyle, *Aristocracy and Its Enemies in the Age of Revolution* (New York, 2009), 86–137.

24. Henry Knox to Hannah Waldo Flucker, 24 Nov 1783, GLC.

25. Henry Knox to the Marquis de Lafayette, 14 Dec 1783, GLC.

26. This letter is not extant.

27. Nathaniel Ramsey (1741–1817), commander of the 3rd Maryland Regiment. Ramsey was wounded and his regiment suffered heavy casualties in the battle of Monmouth.

28. Lieutenant Colonel Henry Monckton (1740–1778), commander of the 2nd Grenadiers Battalion. A younger son of John Monckton, 1st Viscount Galway, Colonel Monckton had fought in America since 1776 and was wounded at the battle of Long Island, where he commanded the 1st Grenadiers Battalion.

29. Henry Jackson commanded Jackson's Additional Continental Regiment (later the 16th Massachusetts Regiment) in the battle.

30. The battle of Monmouth took place on 28 June 1778 and is generally considered by historians to have been a draw. Having been ordered by the ministry in London to give up Philadelphia after Howe's recall, General Henry Clinton left what was then the American capital on 18 June and marched overland through New Jersey, toward Sandy Hook. Washington pursued and ordered General Charles Lee to strike at Clinton's rear guard at dawn on the 28th. The British commander, however, initially drove Lee's forces back in confusion and aggressively pursued the retreating Continentals. Washington then arrived on the field with the army's main body. He rallied Lee's men and, in fighting that lasted throughout much of an extraordinarily hot day, repulsed all subsequent

British attacks. Clinton withdrew toward Sandy Hook during the night. Each side lost approximately 350 men in the engagement. During this battle, Mary Ludwig Hays supposedly manned one of Knox's artillery pieces when her husband, William Hays, was either wounded or suffered from heatstroke. Mary Hays is better known today as "Molly Pitcher." For more information about the battle of Monmouth, see Mark Edward Lender and Garry Wheeler Stone, *Fatal Sunday: George Washington, the Monmouth Campaign, and the Politics of Battle* (Norman, OK, 2016).

31. Julia Knox was the Knoxes' second child, born on 28 March 1779. She died of her illness three days after Henry wrote this letter, on 2 July 1779.

32. A reference to his three-year-old daughter Lucy.

33. Knox obviously wrote "ploughshares," although there is text loss immediately following "ploughs" in the manuscript of the letter. Knox was paraphrasing Isaiah 2:4 (King James version) here: "They shall beat their swords into plowshares, and their spears into pruninghooks."

34. General Henry Clinton.

35. Elizabeth Winslow and Sally Tyng Winslow were daughters of Lucy's uncle, the Loyalist Isaac Winslow, who had died in England in 1777. See *Winslow Family Memorial* [transcript], 1:185, Massachusetts Historical Society.

36. Although his brother William planned to sail for Holland in 1779, he would not leave Boston for several more months. Young Knox traveled to Europe in order to purchase items to sell in the Knoxes' store, which, late in the war, was located on State Street. He remained on the continent for several years.

37. Probably army surgeon Dr. James Craik (1730–1814). Born in Scotland, Craik immigrated to Virginia on the eve of the French and Indian War, where he soon met and became friends with George Washington. The doctor served in the Continental army throughout the American Revolution and, following the conflict, reopened his medical practice in Alexandria, Virginia. Craik was one of the physicians attending Washington when he died at Mount Vernon in 1799.

38. This letter is not extant.

39. Major Sebastian Bauman.

40. Knox is referring to the ill-fated Penobscot expedition, in which an American naval flotilla of 19 warships and approximately 1,000 Massachusetts militia attempted to drive the British out of coastal Maine. The attempt proved to be disastrous. The British warships Knox referred to his letter were part of a British armada that eventually destroyed the small American fleet. For information about the Penobscot expedition, see Michael M. Greenburg, *The Court-Martial of Paul Revere: A Son of Liberty and America's Forgotten Military Disaster* (Lebanon, NH, 2014).

41. Knox is referring to the marriage between William Duer (1747–1799) and Catherine Alexander, daughter of General William Alexander (better known as Lord Stirling). Born in Britain, Duer settled permanently in upstate New York in 1773 and supported the Patriot cause when the American Revolution began. He served in the Continental Congress from 1777 to 1778 and, after the war, worked as assistant secretary for the Department of the Treasury, under Alexander Hamilton. During his tenure in that department, Duer not only speculated heavily in bank bonds, but he also purchased (with a syndicate of investors, one of whom was Henry Knox) millions of acres of land in frontier Maine. Duer's finances collapsed in 1792, and he spent the rest of his life in debtors' prison.

42. "Colonel Hay" is Lieutenant Colonel Udny Hay of New York, who served then as the Continental army's deputy quartermaster general.

43. Probably Colonel Samuel Ogden (1746–1810) of the New Jersey militia. He also operated an iron foundry near Morristown, New Jersey. In 1775, he married Euphemia Morris, sister of Gouverneur Morris.

44. Knox's greeting to the "Beverwyck Family" is a reference to Abraham Lott's family. Lott lived near Morristown, New Jersey, and his home was named "Beverwyck."

45. Livingston Manor is located on the east bank of the Hudson River, approximately 50 miles south of Albany. It was later renamed "Clermont." In October 1777, a British raiding party led by Major General John Vaughan (ca. 1731–1795) burned the mansion down, in retaliation for the family's support for the American cause. Philip Livingston (1716–1778), for instance, had signed the Declaration of Independence. The family rebuilt the house and its outbuildings during the latter years of the American Revolution. The mansion still stands today.

46. Peter Robert Livingston (1737–1794), son of Robert Livingston (1708–1790). Peter was the fourth lord of Livingston Manor and a colonel in the New York militia. He also served in New York's Provincial Congress and convention.

47. Perhaps Colonel Morgan Lewis (1754–1844) of New York. He served as deputy quartermaster general of the Northern Department from 1776 until the end of the war. He later became governor of New York, serving from 1804 to 1807.

48. Manhattan Island.

49. Knox's paragraph reflects the general uncertainty regarding American and French plans for the summer campaign of 1781. Washington and the Comte de Rochambeau, commander of the French troops in North America, had both chosen to cooperate in the coming operation but remained undecided about where to strike. Key to their thinking was the status of the French West Indian fleet under the Comte de Grasse, which was available for service in North American waters that summer. At a conference at Dobb's Ferry on 19 July, Washington told Rochambeau that, if this fleet could sail as far north as New York, he favored an operation against Clinton's forces there, but he also admitted that he was open to an effort to trap Lord Cornwallis's army in Virginia. The French believed that the British fortifications in New York were too strong to be carried. Thus Rochambeau separately (and without Washington's knowledge) wrote de Grasse, urging him to sail only as far north as the Chesapeake Bay. For more information on the strategic situation confronting Washington and the allied high command in the spring and summer of 1781, see John Ferling, *Almost a Miracle: The American Victory in the War of Independence* (New York, 2007), 501–5.

50. Knox is describing the battle of Green Spring, in James County, Virginia, on 6 July 1781, which cost the American forces approximately 140 men and 2 field pieces. For more information about this battle, see John R. Maass, *The Road to Yorktown* (Charleston, SC, 2015), 136–44.

51. Knox is referring to General Nathanael Greene's failed siege against the Loyalist garrison in Ninety-Six, South Carolina. After the battle of Guilford Courthouse in March, Greene had marched into the state, where he and other Patriot forces began reducing the number of British outposts there. In May, the only remaining enemy force of any significance was approximately 500 Loyalists in the town of Ninety-Six. Greene besieged the garrison for nearly a month, but he was forced to abandon the effort when a British

relief column of 2,000 men, under Lord Rawdon (1754–1826), approached. On the war in the interior of the Carolinas, see John C. Pancake, *This Destructive War: The British Campaign in the Carolinas, 1780–1782* (Tuscaloosa, AL, 1985).

52. Colonel Samuel Blachley Webb of Connecticut, commander of Webb's Additional Continental Regiment.

53. Colonel Hugh Hughes (1727–1802), deputy quartermaster general for the Continental army.

54. The letter ends here. Its last page(s) has not survived.

55. Only Lucy's letter of 26 Jul 1781 has survived.

56. Knox is referring to John Ellison's house in New Windsor, New York. Henry often made it his headquarters during the latter years of the war.

57. Lucy was in the early stages of her fourth pregnancy at this time, which probably accounts for Knox's anxiousness.

58. Knox is encouraging Lucy to write letters to her family in England.

59. Reverend Samuel Blair (1741–1818). Before the war, Blair held a pastorate in Boston prior to settling in Germantown, Pennsylvania. He served as a Continental army chaplain from 1780 to 1781 but then retired from the military, due to ill health.

60. Major General Benjamin Lincoln (1733–1810) of Massachusetts. Lincoln served in the Continental army throughout the Revolutionary War. In 1780, he commanded American forces during the British siege of Charleston, South Carolina. Although forced to surrender his army, Lincoln was soon paroled and exchanged, whereupon he rejoined the Continental army. In August 1781, he commanded one of Washington's divisions, and he would lead the allied army's American wing during the Yorktown campaign.

61. Lucy's letter to Henry of 9 Aug 1781 has not survived.

62. Washington reiterated this offer the following day. See George Washington to Henry Knox, 5 Sept 1781, GLC.

63. Launched in 1779, the *Amsterdam* was a 170–ton Massachusetts privateer. On 19 October 1781, while on its way to Boston from Sweden, laden with dry goods, iron, steel, copper, and tea, the brig was captured by the HMS *Amphitrite* off Cape Ann, Massachusetts. Knox, along with his mercantile friends in the city, probably had invested in the ship. On the ship's capture, see *Connecticut Gazette*, 16 November 1781.

64. Most likely Samuel Hodgdon (1745–1824) of Philadelphia. In September 1781, the Continental Congress appointed Hodgdon to the post of commissary general of military stores. He would later serve as quartermaster general of the US Army when Knox was secretary of war.

65. John Parke Custis (1754–1781), Martha Custis Washington's son and George Washington's stepson. Custis traveled from Mount Vernon to Yorktown in order to serve as a civilian aide-de-camp to Washington during the siege.

66. Colonel Clement Biddle (1740–1814) and Rebekah Cornell Biddle of Philadelphia. A member of the Society of Friends before the Revolutionary War, Clement Biddle nevertheless raised a company of volunteers in 1775, which was soon called the "Quaker Blues." Two years later, Washington appointed him as commissary general of forage for the Continental army. Although Biddle resigned in 1780 to return to his mercantile business, he agreed to serve as quartermaster general of the Pennsylvania militia during the Yorktown campaign. Rebekah Cornell Biddle was the daughter of Gideon Cornell (1710–1766), who had served as lieutenant governor of Rhode Island before the war.

67. Knox is referring to Lord Cornwallis's withdrawal of his forces from their outermost works at Yorktown. The British commander did this because he remained confident that reinforcements and a rescue fleet from New York would soon arrive and save his army.

68. Perhaps Reverend Samuel Blair.

69. This letter is not extant.

70. "William" was probably one of the Knox family's servants. Knox mentions a servant named William in his letter of 26 Jul 1781, GLC.

71. Knox's aide-de-camp, Samuel Shaw.

72. Knox's letter to Lucy of 6 Oct 1781 has not survived. Lucy is probably referring to Alexandria, Virginia.

73. Probably William Pierce (1740–1789) of Virginia. Earlier in the war, Pierce had been an officer in the 1st Continental Artillery, but in 1781 he was serving as an aide-de-camp to General Nathanael Greene. That autumn, he was travelling northward to inform the Continental Congress of the American victory over the British at the Battle of Eutaw Springs, South Carolina. For more information about Pierce, see "George Washington from Patrick Henry, 8 September 1777," *Founders Online*, National Archives, last modified 28 December 2016, https://founders.archives.gov/documents/Washington/03-11-02-0173/. [Original source: Philander D. Chase and Edward G. Lengel, eds., *The Papers of George Washington: Revolutionary War Series*, vol. 11, *19 August 1777– 25 October 1777* (Charlottesville, VA, 2001), 173, n1].

74. This final sentence was written in the margin, probably as a postscript.

75. Colonel David Humphreys (1752–1818) of Connecticut, one of George Washington's aides-de-camp in the latter years of the American Revolution. Afterwards, Humphreys served as personal secretary to the former commander.

76. Knox is referring to the successful Franco-American attacks on British redoubts numbers 9 and 10 on the evening of 14 October. Knox's future cabinet colleague, Alexander Hamilton, led the American troops in this assault.

77. Clement Biddle of Philadelphia.

78. Colonel Jeremiah Wadsworth (1743–1804) of Connecticut. Wadsworth had been commissary general for the Continental army but served in that position for the French forces during the Yorktown campaign.

79. Lund Washington (1737–1796), a distant cousin of the commander. He managed Mount Vernon's daily operations throughout the general's absence during the Revolutionary War.

80. Lucy's letter of 16 Oct 1781, GLC.

81. Probably Reverend Samuel Blair and Major Samuel Shaw.

82. Major General William Dalrymple (1736–1807) was quartermaster general of the British army in New York. In 1768, he commanded the 14th Regiment of Foot, one of the two regiments of troops sent to Boston that year.

83. Andrew Elliot (1728–1797) was a native of Scotland who came to America in 1746 and eventually settled in New York. When the war began, he remained loyal to the Crown and returned to New York City when British troops captured it in 1776. In 1782, he served as the royal lieutenant governor of the province and left America the following year, when the British evacuated the city.

84. Joshua Loring Jr. (1744–1789), a Loyalist from Massachusetts. Before the Amer-

ican Revolution, Loring has been a subaltern in the 15th Regiment of Foot and, later, a member of Boston's Ancient and Honorable Artillery Company. Siding with the Crown after the Battles of Lexington and Concord, he eventually became a commissary of prisoners for the British army, a lucrative position from which he supposedly made a great deal of money. Moreover, Loring's wife, Elizabeth Lloyd Loring, apparently had a notorious romantic affair with British army commander General William Howe. Mrs. Loring returned to England in 1778, the same year as General Howe's recall, but Joshua Loring remained in America until the war's end.

85. Possibly Jonathan Simpson (d. 1834), a Loyalist from Boston, who left when the British evacuated the city in March 1776. He later became a commissary of provisions for the British army.

86. Perhaps Knox is referring to young Isaac Winslow (1774–1856), a cousin by marriage to Lucy.

87. Clement Biddle of Philadelphia. Lucy was living in the city with the Knoxes' children at this point.

88. Probably Jonathan Williams (1750–1815). Williams grew up in Boston and was related to Benjamin Franklin. In 1770, Williams travelled to England to serve as Franklin's secretary. During Revolutionary War, Williams served in France as an American diplomat. Knox had written to Williams announcing the Continental army's victory at Yorktown. See Henry Knox to Jonathan Williams, 21 Oct 1781, GLC.

89. Marcus Camillus Knox (10 December 1781–ca. September 1782). Henry discusses his second son's death in a 10 Sept 1782 letter to George Washington, GLC.

90. Lucy is referring to the Continental Congress's promotion of Knox to the rank of major general. The congress approved the promotion, based on Washington's recommendation, on 22 March 1782.

Afterwards (1784–1824)

1. Soon after Captain Thomas Flucker Jr.'s death in 1783, his widow, Sarah Lyons Flucker, along with their two children, came to America, whereupon they established a warm and close friendship with the Knoxes.